BARMY
DERBY

ANDREW BEARDMORE

Thanks:

My sincerest thanks to Andy Ellis of The Derby County Collection, Louisa Fuller and Angela Leeson of W.W. Winter Ltd, and Colin Panter of PA Images, for supplying and allowing me use of their images in this book. I would particularly like to thank Andy Ellis also for his patience, as we had an awful lot of toing and froing on the lion's share of the images in this book, before drawing up the final list. Thanks also to David Hitchcock for allowing me to use his brilliant sketch of a scene from *Up The Ramblings*, and which first appeared in the *Derby Evening Telegraph* in January 2009.

Dedication:

As promised, I would like to dedicate this book to my dear friend and big Rams fan, Mick Hindle, who passed away tragically young on 1 March 1999. It took a bit longer than planned old friend, so I look forward to a suitable put-down when we next meet!

First printed in 2018

Copyright © Andrew Beardmore 2018

British Library Cataloguing-in-Publication Data
A CIP record for this title is available from the British Library

ISBN 978 0 85710 120 4

PiXZ Books
Halsgrove House, Ryelands Business Park, Bagley Road, Wellington, Somerset TA21 9PZ
Tel: 01823 653777
Fax: 01823 216796
email: sales@halsgrove.com

An imprint of Halstar Ltd, part of the Halsgrove group of companies
Information on all Halsgrove titles is available at: www.halsgrove.com

Printed and bound by Parksons Graphics, India

Contents

Introduction

Welcome to *Barmy Derby*, a light-hearted and somewhat lateral view of Derby County F.C., one of the founding members of the Football League, way back in 1888. The aim of the book is to have fans of the club chortling away, while frequently exclaiming: "well, I never knew that!" A blend of fact and fun, the book provides fans with a multitude of conventional football-related statistics and stories, presented side-by-side with the quirky and the downright whacky – with a couple of aspects presented in ways that you won't have seen before. Guaranteed!

The main core of the book, though, is a chronology of Derby County's 134-year history, starting in 1884 and finishing with the 2017/18 Championship season. Each year and each of Derby's 119 football league seasons are built up, step-by-step, via succinct, one-sentence facts alongside exact dates. This helps to portray the ebb and flow of each season, leading the reader to feel the ecstasy and the agony (mainly the agony) of their counterpart fans, back in the day.

However, in keeping with the offbeat nature of the book, each chapter in the Rams Chronology is accompanied by a host of quirky facts, strange events, bizarre coincidences and striking statistics, all relating to the period just covered, and which are presented as either a "Quirk Alert" or a "Stats Blast"; but all the time, preserving the sensation of a journey through time…during which there have been 25 Prime Ministers – and 33 Derby County managers! Finally, also interspersed, are "Perspective" snippets – which demonstrate that football is just a game, but life is a whole lot tougher.

Having said that, if it's plain "barmy" that you want, then check out the Barmy Yarny, a short piece of fiction about Derby County that is sure to have you laughing out loud. Entitled *Up The Ramblings*, the tale is all about a hen-pecked husband, who takes his love for the Rams so far that he weaves current and ex-players' names into his everyday speech – leading to an inevitable but hilarious confrontation with his long-suffering wife!

Each featured footballer from the Barmy Yarny is then covered in terms of conventional club statistics – i.e. years at the club, number of appearances, goals scored, etc., as well as some left-field stats relating to members of the Barmy 154!

The book is then rounded off with yet another offbeat chapter, this one entitled *Surname Synergy* – where namesake comparisons are made between some of the club's footballers and former England rugby union internationals! Don't knock it until you've checked it out; you *will* be surprised at some remarkable coincidences!

Anyway, that's the introduction completed. As you have probably gathered by now, this book is indeed a little Barmy…so it's time to prime the ramometer and take your seat at Pride Park. Or given the offbeat nature of parts of this book, perhaps you'd prefer an away trip…perhaps to St Flanneldrews, The Guffawthorns or The Stadium of Tripe…

How Football's Barmy Yarnys Started

So this all started way back in 2007, when I entered the *Derby Telegraph's* Short Story competition with a certain quirky tale called *Up The Ramblings* – a tale featuring a hen-pecked husband, who takes his love for Derby County so far that he weaves current and ex-players' names into his everyday speech!

Up The Ramblings came second in the competition which was judged by Stephen Booth, the prolific crime writer and author of the hugely successful Fry and Cooper series of detective novels set in the Peak District. Stephen commented: *"This is an incredibly clever story which must have taken a tremendous amount of work. It showed a huge amount of wit and cleverness on the part of the author."*

Also commenting on the story was Su Parnell of the competition sponsor, Waterstone's. Su said: *"A major strength in this story is its sense of humour, as well as a very clever and topical use of language."*

Meanwhile, the *Derby Telegraph* reporter stated that: *"Andrew's story made judges laugh out loud with its clever use of Derby County football players past and present."*

Having scored local success with *Up The Ramblings*, I then began to wonder how the format could be applied elsewhere. One similar format was applied to books about English counties, weaving county place-names into a quirky poem known as a Shire-Ode, which then became the driver to a unique county almanac. This eventually evolved into the successful *Unusual & Quirky* series of books, also published by Halsgrove Publishing, and currently at county number 8 – see www.halsgrove.com or www.andybeardmore.com for more.

The more obvious direction, though, was to apply the same format used in *Ramblings* to similar tales centred on other English football clubs. This involved seamlessly weaving players' surnames into the flow of all sorts of different football club-related tales – using comedy, fantasy and even suspense…

Anyway, the result was the birth of the Barmy Yarny! There is one key difference, though, between *Up The Ramblings*, and the Barmy Yarnys for other clubs. This is because *Ramblings* is about a man who weaves current and former players' names into his everyday speech, so it made sense to include the *full* player's name. It's genuinely more amusing that way. However, this just doesn't work for the other stories, so they simply use the surname as seamlessly as possible, while full player names are supplied alphabetically in a column on the right-hand side of the appropriate page.

Finally, each club's story includes one imposter – an alleged player who played for the club, but which has been totally made up. Be warned though: anyone who gets them is probably due an even bigger anorak than mine…and that's just not cool!

So, there you have it: some history. Some barmy history, I guess!

DERBY COUNTY: Facts & Figures

TEAM and GROUNDS:	
Founded:	1884
Nickname:	The Rams
Nickname Origin:	Named after the club's links with the First Regiment of Derby Militia, which also had a ram as its mascot, while the song "The Derby Ram" was its regimental song.
Modern Anthem:	Steve Bloomer's Watching
First Ground:	The Racecourse (also known as The County Ground)
Incumbent:	1884 to 1895
Highest Attendance:	c.15,500 vs. Blackburn Rovers on 24/02/1894
First Full International Hosted:	09/03/1885: England 9 Ireland 0
Second Ground:	The Baseball Ground
Incumbent:	1895 to 1997
Highest Attendance:	41,826 vs. Tottenham Hotspur on 20/09/1969
First Full International Hosted:	11/02/1911: England 2 Ireland 1
Current Ground:	Pride Park Stadium
Capacity:	33,597
Incumbent Since:	1997
Highest Attendance:	33,758 vs. Liverpool on 18/03/2000
First Full International Hosted:	25/05/2001: England 4 Mexico 0
Highest Attendance Anywhere:	120,000 vs. Real Madrid, Bernabéu Stadium, 05/11/1975
Highest League Attendance:	75,725 vs. Manchester United, Old Trafford, 08/12/2007
Highest FA Cup Attendance:	98,215 vs. Charlton Athletic, Wembley, 27/04/1946
Highest League Cup Att:	73,374 vs. Manchester United, Old Trafford, 20/01/2009
Lowest League Attendance:	500 vs. Grimsby Town, Baseball Ground, 22/04/1903
Lowest FA Cup Attendance:	1,500 vs. Walsall Town, The Racecourse, 08/11/1884
Lowest League Cup Att:	1,611 vs. Hartlepool United, Baseball Ground, 04/09/1985

The Baseball Ground in September 1967 shown during a 1-0 victory over Plymouth Argyle. The Offilers Ales advert had graced the roof of the Vulcan Street terrace for over twenty years by this stage. PHOTO: Andy Ellis.

Looking towards the Osmaston End at the BBG in August 1969. It is Derby's first match back in Division One (0-0 vs. Burnley), and the scaffolding is still visible around an unfinished Ley Stand. PHOTO: Andy Ellis

PLAYERS (APPEARANCES):		
Most Appearances:	Kevin Hector	**589**, 1966-1978; 1980-1982
	Ron Webster	**535**, 1962-1977
	Roy McFarland	**530**, 1967-1981; 1983-84
Most League Appearances:	Kevin Hector	**486**, 1966-1978; 1980-1982
	Jack Parry	**483**, 1950-1962
	Geoff Barrowcliffe	**475**, 1951-1965
Most FA Cup Appearances:	Jimmy Methven	**52**, 1891-1906
	Steve Bloomer	**50**, 1892-1905; 1910-1914
Most League Cup Appearances:	Kevin Hector	**42**, 1966-1978; 1980-1982
	Roy McFarland	**37**, 1967-1981; 1983-84
Most European Appearances:	Colin Todd	**21**, 1972-1976
	Archie Gemmill	**21**, 1972-1976
Most Consecutive Apps (All):	Archie Goodall	**167**, October 1892 to October 1897
(League):	Archie Goodall	**151**, October 1892 to October 1897
(FA Cup):	Colin Todd	**30**, 1972-1978
(League Cup):	Kevin Hector	**36**, 1966-1978; 1980-1982
Most Games in a Season:	Marco Gabbiadini	**62**, 1992-1993
	Paul Kitson	**61**, 1992-1993
Longest Serving Player:	Sammy Crooks	**19 years, 18 days** (445 apps; 111 goals)

Left: Tommy Powell played 406 games for Derby County between 1948 and 1961. Meanwhile, his son, Steve (Right), played 430 games for Derby between 1971 and 1985; a combined total of 836 games. Remarkably, they are also ranked side-by-side, 10th and 11th in Derby County's all-time list of player appearances.
PHOTOS: Andy Ellis

PLAYERS (SCORED CONSECUTIVE GAMES):			
Jack Bowers	7, 1930-31 – 17 goals	Jack Bowers	6, 1933-34 – 10 goals
Francesco Baiano	6, 1997-98 – 8 goals	John Goodall	6, 1891-02 – 8 goals
Horace Barnes	6, 1913-14 – 7 goals	Jimmy Lyons	6, 1922-23 – 7 goals
Alf Bentley	6, 1909-10 – 8 goals	George Stephenson	6, 1927-28 – 8 goals
Steve Bloomer	6, 1896-97 – 10 goals	Ray Straw	6, 1956-57 – 7 goals
Jack Bowers	6, 1932-33 – 11 goals	Eddie Thomas	6, 1964-64 – 7 goals

PLAYERS (GOALS):		
Most Goals Scored:	Steve Bloomer	332, 1892-1905; 1910-1914
	Kevin Hector	201, 1966-1978; 1980-1982
	Jack Bowers	183, 1929-1936
Most League Goals:	Steve Bloomer	293, 1892-1905; 1910-1914
Most FA Cup Goals:	Steve Bloomer	38, 1892-1905; 1910-1914
Most League Cup Goals:	Kevin Hector	15, 1966-1978; 1980-1982
Most Goals in a Season:	Jack Bowers	43, Division One/FA Cup, 1932/33
Most European Goals:	Kevin Hector	16, 1972-1976
Most Anglo-Italian Cup Goals:	Paul Kitson	9, 1992-1994
Most Play-Off Goals:	Tommy Johnson	4, 1992-1994
Most League Goals in a Season:	Jack Bowers	37, Division One, 1930/31
	Ray Straw	37, Division Three North, 1956/57
Most Goals in a Match:	Steve Bloomer	6, vs. Sheff Wed, 21/01/1899, Div One
	Roger Davies	5, vs Luton T, 29/03/1975, Div One
Most Goals in an FA Cup Match:	Harry Bedford	4, vs. Bradford City, 08/01/1927
	Jackie Stamps	4, vs. Luton Town, 05/01/1946
Most Goals in a League Cup Match:	Alan Hinton	4, vs. Stockport County, 04/09/1968
	Kevin Wilson	4, vs. Hartlepool United, 29/08/1984
Most Goals in a Euro Match:	Kevin Hector	5, vs. Finn Harps, UEFA Cup, 15/09/76
Most Hat-Tricks:	Steve Bloomer	20, including 1 four-goal haul and 1 six-goal haul (1892-1914)
	Jack Bowers	16, inc. 5 four-goal hauls (1929-1936)
	Harry Bedford	13, inc. 3 four-goal hauls (1925-1930)
Most Full Members Cup Goals Scored:	Gary Micklewhite	6, 1986-1991
	Dean Saunders	5, 1988-1991

One of Kevin Hector's 201 goals for Derby, during a 5-2 victory over QPR in Nov-1974. PHOTO: Andy Ellis.

PLAYERS (MISC):

First International:	Ben Spilsbury	For England vs. Ireland, 1885
Most Capped International:	Deon Burton	42 caps for Jamaica between 1997 and 2002; 56 caps in total
Most Capped English International:	Peter Shilton	34 caps for England between 1987 and 1992; 125 caps in total
First Players at the World Cup:	Bruce Rioch & Don Masson	For Scotland vs. Peru, Córdoba, Argentina, 03/06/1978
First English Players at the the World Cup:	Peter Shilton & Mark Wright	For England vs. Republic of Ireland, Cagliari, Italy, 11/06/1990
Record Transfer Fees Paid:	Matěj Vydra	£8m from Watford, 27/08/2016
	Tom Lawrence	£7m from Leicester, 15/08/2017
Record Transfer Fees Received:	Tom Ince	£11.3m to Huddersfield, 04/07/2017
	Jeff Hendrick	£10.5m to Burnley, 31/08/2016
Youngest Player:	Mason Bennett	15 years, 99 days, vs. M'brough, 22/10/2011
Youngest Goalscorer:	Mason Bennett	16 years, 176 days, vs. Tranmere, 05/01/2013
Youngest Debut Goal:	Tony Reid	17 years, 187 days, vs Chelsea, 12/11/1980
Youngest Hat-Trick:	Andy Garner	18 years, 30 days, vs. Crystal Pal, 07/04/1984
Oldest Hat-Trick:	Steve Bloomer	38 years, 261 days, vs. Sheff Utd, 09/11/1912
Oldest Player:	Peter Shilton	42 years, 164 days, vs. Watford, 29/02/1992
Most Substitute Apps:	Steve Cross	41, September 1986 to September 1991

LANDMARK MATCHES:

First Match:	13/09/1884: Great Lever vs. Derby County (L 6-0)
First FA Cup Match:	08/11/1884: Derby County vs. Walsall Town (L 0-7)
First Football League Match:	08/09/1888: Bolton Wanderers vs. Derby County (W 3-6)
First Play-Off Match:	18/04/1895: Derby Co (15th Div1) vs. Notts Co (2nd Div2) (W2-1)
First League Cup Match:	11/10/1960: Derby County vs. Watford (W 5-2)
First European Match:	13/09/1972: Derby County vs. FK Željezničar (W 2-0)
Record League Win (H):	10/01/1891: Derby County vs. Wolverhampton W (W 9-0); 21/01/1899: Derby County vs. Sheffield Wednesday (W 9-0)
Record League Win (A):	29/09/1923: Bristol City vs. Derby County (W 0-8)
Record FA Cup Win:	30/01/1897: Derby County vs. Barnsley St Peter's (W 8-1)
Record League Cup Win:	07/10/1992: Derby County vs. Southend (W 7-0)
Record European Win:	15/09/1976: Derby County vs. Finn Harps (W 12-0)
Highest Score-Draw:	15/10/1898: Derby County vs. Everton (D 5-5), Division One 09/04/1966: Birmingham City vs. Derby Co (D 5-5), Division Two 14/08/2012: Derby Co vs. Scunthorpe Utd (D 5-5), League Cup

CLUB RECORDS:	
Most League Wins in a Season:	**28** in 46 matches, Third Division North, 1955/56
Least League Wins in a Season:	**1** in 38 matches, Premier League, 2007/08
Most League Defeats in a Season:	**29** in 38 matches, Premier League, 2007/08
Least League Defeats in a Season:	**5** in 42 matches, Second Division, 1968/69
Most League Goals in a Season:	**111** in 46 matches, Third Division North, 1956/57
Least League Goals in a Season:	**20** in 38 matches, Premier League, 2007/08
Most Lg Goals Conceded/Season:	**90** in 42 matches, First Division, (1936/37)
Least Lg Goals Conceded/Season:	**28** in 38 matches, Second Division, 1911/12
Most Points in a League Season (2 pts/win):	**63** points from a possible 84/92: - Second Division, 1968/69 (42 matches) - Third Division North, 1955/56 (46 matches) - Third Division North, 1956/57 (46 matches)
Most Points in a League Season (3 pts/win):	**85** points from a possible 138 (46 matches): - Championship, 2013/14 (Rams not promoted!)
Least Points in a League Season (2pts/win):	**23** points from a possible 84 (42 matches): - Second Division, 1954/55 **15** points from a possible 44 (22 matches): - Football League, 1890/91
Least Points in a League Season (3pts/win):	**11** points from a possible 114 (38 matches): - Premier League, 2007-08
Most Years (Seasons) in Top Tier:	**27** (20) from 1926 to 1953
Most Consecutive League Wins:	**9** (15th March 1969 to 19th April 1969)
Most League Games Unbeaten:	**22** (8th March 1969 to 20th September 1969)
Most Home Clean Sheets on Spin:	**8** (15th October 2016 to 31st December 2016)
Season Most Players Used:	**39** during season 2005/06
Season Least Players Used:	**16** during seasons 1895/96, 1971/72 and 1974/75

Heady Days! It is 25 October 1972, and here we see Roy McFarland (partly obscured) heading Derby into the lead against the mighty Benfica in the Second Round of the European Cup. The Rams eventually ran out 3-0 winners.

PHOTO: Andy Ellis

10

Although not renowned as an English force in Europe, check out Derby County's impressive European statistics, which are as follows:

THE RAMS IN EUROPE:							
Competition	Pld	W	D	L	GF	GA	GD
Texaco Cup	8	5	2	1	18	9	+9
European Cup	12	6	2	4	18	12	+6
UEFA Cup	10	5	2	3	32	18	+14
Anglo-Italian Cup	15	9	1	5	38	24	+14
Total	45	25	7	13	106	63	+43

A rare photograph of Steve Bloomer, pictured here in his England kit. Bloomer scored an incredible 28 goals in 23 England appearances – an average of 1.22 goals per game. (PHOTO: W.W. Winter Ltd).

The INCREDIBLE STEVE BLOOMER:

669 career appearances and 414 goals (Derby, Middlesbrough, Football League)

Derby County all-time top goal-scorer with 332 goals (1892-1905; 1910-1914)

Most goals in a match for Derby (6), vs. Sheffield Wednesday, 21-01-1899, Division One

Most hat-tricks for Derby (20), including one 4-goal haul and one 6-goal haul

Derby County's top scorer for 13 consecutive seasons (1893/94 to 1905/06)

Middlesbrough's top scorer for 2 consecutive seasons (1906/07 to 1907/08)

Derby County's top scorer for 2 more consecutive seasons (1910/11 to 1911/12)

Div One top scorer on 6 occasions (1895/96, 1896/97, 1898/99, 1899/1900, 1900/01, 1903/04)

Scored twice on his England debut on 09/03/1895 – England vs. Ireland (W 9-0)

Scored in his first 10 internationals, still a record at international level

In those first 10 international, he scored 19 goals

This included 5 goals vs. Wales (16/03/1896) and 4 vs. Wales (07/03/1901)

First player to score 2 hat-tricks for England

First player to score 4 goals for England twice

Scored 28 goals in 23 England appearances (1.22 goals per game)

RAMS BARMY YARNY: Up the Ramblings!

My missus swears blind I'm Derby County mad. Accuses me of talking about nothing else, whether they win, draw or **Richard Goulooze**. She even says that I use ex-players' names in me **Christian Dailly** speech – which is clearly a load of old **Jimmy Bullions**. But when I deny it, she gets all **Steve Cross** with me. Says if I keep it up, then one day, she'll have **Frank Upton** left, and I'll end up on me **Colin Todd**!

Now, don't get me wrong, I'm very **Ike Keane** on the Rams, I'll **Lee Grant** you that. But my missus – she doesn't know she's **Jeff Bourne**! I've got a mate who's a **Calvin Plummer** who lives up our **Floyd Streete** – and he goes to *all* the matches, home or away. And, what's **Darren Moore**, he's always messing about with other **Dickie Bird's** behind his missus' back; a right **Alf Tinker**, he is. And he's had 'em all, too – from the **Ryan Noble** to the **Kris Commons**. He even had an affair with a **Reg Callender** girl, once. Mind you, she was a bit of a **Paul Trollope** – if I remember **Mark Wright**!

Then there's our neighbour, who's actually a teacher, so most of the time he's a wise old **Mel Sage** who likes to **Tony Reid** a lot; he's always got his head buried in some **Emerson Thome**. He's a bit of an eccentric, too – dresses for work like a 1960s' London businessman, what with his **George Bowler** and his **Mike Brolly**. But on a Saturday, he's completely transformed. And if Derby **Martyn Chalk** up a victory, well, that's just the **Steve Cherry** on the **George Bakewell**, and he ends up going out for a celebratory **Bill Curry**.

And then there's Ian and Chris. Now Ian is a **Taylor** by trade and Chris is a **Porter** on the railways. So, working on their Saturday afternoon's – well, that's pretty much **Jack Parr** for the course. But they don't half hate being **Mick Coop**ed up on their Saturday's. So, if they get out to Pride Park for a Tuesday night game, well, they go all **Jack Wild** and **Robbie Savage**; basically, they turn into a couple of **Dick Pratleys**!

It's a similar story with Tommy and Billy, 'cos **Tommy** is a **Barbour** and **Billy** is a **Baker**. But for midweek night matches, they don't **Tommy Dilly Dally Duncan** about; home or away, they're off in either Tommy's **Lee Morris** minor (which didn't cost much **Richard Money**), or Billy's **Alf Bentley** (which **Candido Costa** packet). Anyway, last Wednesday – away game at **Colin Boulton** – they were there. And *they're* both married, too – although there *are* those rumours that they're a couple of old **Hugh McQueens**. They are a bit **Lee Camp**, I suppose. But the point is, they're lucky **Percy Fellows**, because their wives don't whinge at 'em.

I've also got a mate called **George** – he's a right **Charlie** who lives in some converted **Giles Barnes** – which you can find by turning left at the end of our front **Henry Garden**, down the **Sean Lane**, over the **George Brooks**, past the **Lee Mills**, through the **Alf Wood**, over some open **Vic Moreland**, and then up the **Gordon Hill**…and his **Charlie Place** is there, opposite two sturdy **Andy Oakes** on the **Les Green**. Anyway, George married his missus when they were both still very **Ray Young**; she thought he was **Steve Devine**, and he thought she was a **Brett Angell**; he always used to call her his little **John Poppitt**, too. So it appeared to everyone as though they were the proverbial **Steve Round** pegs in the proverbial Steve Round holes. Unfortunately, though, George likes to **Frank Gamble** on the Rams a lot, so he wove this **David Webb** of deceit for years and his missus didn't **Gary Twigg** until they got into serious debt. Now, they **George Rowe** all the time – in fact, it's pretty much **Gerry Daly!**

And then there's the Docherty brother's – all **James Severn** of 'em. You don't mess with them; seriously **Craig Burley** blokes and each is a **Jack Hardman** in his own **Harry Wright**. In fact, to be honest, the **Jimmy Long** and **Craig Short** of it is…that they're a bunch of old **Sammy Crooks!** And if you go to an away game with them, you need to have nerves of **Eric Steele**. Last week, me and George drew the short **Ray Straw** – which was pretty difficult to **Ray Swallow** – and we ended up going with them to **Ken Oxford**. As ever, they started a little **Bob Waugh** with the locals and then ran off. Me and George, we wuz **Jimmy Dunn** up like kippers – and we both ended up on the same **Jamie Ward!**

Anyway, the other day, my charmed life came to a shuddering **Russell Hoult**. I'd just had me dinner – two **Tom Shanks** of lamb and a fillet of **Conor Sammon**, followed by some **Michael Jacobs** cream crackers and a tube of **Ben Pringle**s. And I was stood in our **Ian Hall**, with these letters, waiting for the missus to give me some **Jackie Stamps**. And she was looking at me **Albert Shiner** – that was still pretty **Albert Soar**, I can tell you – and then she starts to lay down the **Cecil Law** with me. "Do you know what?" she says. "I've had enough of this."

And within seconds, I'm getting the third **Marco Reich**; I'm **Frankie Fielding** all sorts of flack! Worse still, she's holding a **Fred Cleaver**, and to be honest, I was starting to fear for me old **Bert Mann**! So I try and keep things **Martin Kuhl**. "Love," I said. "Keep your **John O'Hare** on. Strewth, you'll be using ex-players names in your speech, next!"

"Don't give me that **Jessie Pye** in the sky!" she hollers. "Like I was saying **Spencer Prior**: I've had enough of this infantile malarkey, and I'm going to **Ted Clamp** down on it."

"All right, love," I say. "There's no need to get your **Steve Bloomer**s in a blather!"

Well, that was it! Any chance of a truce had gone for a **Deon Burton**, and she just rips into me. After five minutes of this, I'm thinking "right, lad: in for a **David Penney**", and so I decide to voice my thoughts. "You aren't half getting on my **Stevie Wicks**, woman!"

"Oh, I am, am I!" she shouts, waving her **Paul Blades** about. "Well let me tell you something, matey: if you don't want our marriage to go **Taribo West**, you need to be a **Tommy Little** bit **Adam Bolder** with your mates and tell 'em where to get off. Cos I'm **Jeff King** fed up with 'em!"

"Now look, love," I begin, attempting to backtrack (but secretly wishing she'd fly away on her **Frank Broome**). "The Docherty's aren't that much of a **Frank Payne**."

"Oh yes they **Tom Ruddy** are," she rants. "There's no **Jack Hope** for 'em, and if you can't see that, then you're more **Thomas Daft** than I thought you were. The police'll always **Bob Brand** you the same as them Docherty brothers, just like they did last month. It's always the same **Kelle Roos**; *they* start it, *they* run off – and *you* and *George* are the two **John Moran**s left **Eddie Holding** their **Ronnie Dix**! So *sort* it, or else I'll be slinging me **Paul Hooks**!"

A potential **Blessing Kaku** in disguise, thinks I, ruefully; a chance to throw off the **Jason Shackell**s; the proverbial **Callum Ball** and chain. (I'm dreaming now). A chance to become a **Kieron Freeman**, no less, and get rid of that perennial **George Thorne** in my side; to no longer be at her **Mikkel Beck** and call…

But given that I was pretty much on the **Darren Wrack**, I decided to save my **Arthur Bacon** and button it instead!

Unfortunately, it all blew up again two weeks later, mainly because over the last few months, our **Jimmy Kidd**, Nicholas, couldn't have **Alf Dunmore** to wind her up. It all started in a **Billy Carr** park, would you believe? My missus drives an old **George Minney**, but she's rubbish at **Geoff Parkin**. Anyway, she's giving Nicholas some serious grief about some aggro that she knows he's got involved in at **Charlie York**, when she backs into this **Bernie Vann**.

Well, Nicholas gets the blame, doesn't he, but not having the greatest amount of **Andre Wisdom**, he decides to whinge back – and then gets the inevitable **Michael Tonge**-lashing.

"You're always **Albert Picken** on me," he moans.

"That's because I can **George Kinsey** where your life's heading, son," she responds. "It's there, sat in front of you!" she moans, jabbing her finger at me. "You should be **Ryan Shotton** sight, the pair of you!"

And so now the **Andreas Buck** passes back to me; suddenly it's **John McAlle** my fault again!

Anyway, we eventually calm her down, although goodness knows **Jack Howe**, and Nicholas promises his **Leon Best** behaviour. I hadn't got the **John Hart** to tell her what he'd been up to three weeks before; he'd only got caught on **Mo Camara** in **Harry Bedford**, knocking seven **Colin Bell**'s out of some **Emanuel Villa** fan!

"Oh, I know all about it!" she says, reading my mind. "**Junior**'s a **Matt Carbon** copy of his stupid dad. The pair of you are a dead **Colin Loss**!"

Quirk Alert: Cumberland Lossage
Over Derby County's 134 seasons in the football league, only three clubs have a positive goal differ-ence from all games played at Derby – i.e. combined Derby County home games at The Racecourse, The Baseball Ground and Pride Park. The first team will come as no surprise – this being Liverpool. Neither will the second – this being Wigan Athletic, who keep winning at Pride Park regardless of their position in the league. But the third team…is Workington Town! Derby played them twice at home in Division Three North seasons 1955/56 and 1956/57, drawing 2-2 in the first season, but losing 2-3 in the second season!

Quirk Alert: Vivaldi's Influence
Between 1915 and 1969, Derby County and Nottingham Forest were only in the same division FOR FOUR SEASONS! Basically, and remarkably, it means that the historic fortunes of both clubs have been largely inverse! Until recently, that is!

RAMS BARMY YARNY: Conventional Stats

KEY:	Goalkeeper	Defender	Midfielder	Forward

#	Surname	Forename	When	App	Gls
1	Angell	Brett	1988-1988	0	0
2	Bacon	Arthur	1925-1927	9	3
3	Baker	Billy	1914-1920	44	7
4	Bakewell	George	1888-1890	64	12
5	Ball	Callum	2009-2014	29	3
6	Barbour	Tommy	1908-1920	294	3
7	Barnes	Giles	2005-2009	84	10
8	Beck	Mikkel	1998-1999	21	3
9	Bedford	Harry	1925-1930	218	152
10	Bell	Colin	1950-1954	79	2
11	Bentley	Alf	1906-1910	168	112
12	Best	Leon	2014-2015	20	0
13	Bird	Dickie	1934-1935	5	2
14	Blades	Paul	1982-1989	200	1
15	Bloomer	Steve	1892-1906 1910-1913	525	332
16	Bolder	Adam	2000-2005	166	11
17	Boulton	Colin	1964-1977	344	0
18	Bourne	Jeff	1970-1976	72	14
19	Bowler	George	1912-1912	1	0
20	Brand	Bob	1890-1890	3	0
21	Brolly	Mike	1982-1983	50	5
22	Brooks	George	1914-1914	34	0
23	Broome	Frank	1945-1949	119	45
24	Buck	Andreas	2002-2002	0	0
25	Bullions	Jimmy	1946-1947	29	0
26	Burley	Craig	1999-2002	80	13
27	Burton	Deon	1997-2002	143	31
28	Callender	Reg	1913-1914	5	0
29	Camara	Mo	2006-2009	29	0
30	Camp	Lee	2002-2007	92	0
31	Carbon	Matt	1995-1997	22	0
32	Carr	Billy	1925-1932	109	0
33	Chalk	Martyn	1991-1992	11	2
34	Cherry	Steve	1979-1984	90	0
35	Clamp	Ted	1948-1949	1	0
36	Cleaver	Fred	1905-1906	12	3
37	Commons	Kris	2008-2011	97	24
38	Coop	Mick	1981-1982	21	0

#	Surname	Forename	When	App	Gls
39	Costa	Candido	2003-2004	35	1
40	Crooks	Sammy	1927-1946	445	111
41	Cross	Steve	1986-1991	94	5
42	Curry	Bill	1960-1964	164	76
43	Daft	Thomas	1890-1891	3	0
44	Dailly	Christian	1996-1998	78	4
45	Daly	Gerry	1976-1980	122	34
46	Devine	Steve	1983-1985	11	0
47	Dilly	Tommy	1907-1908	10	2
48	Dix	Ronnie	1936-1939	96	35
49	Duncan	Dally	1931-1946	289	69
50	Dunmore	Alf	1930-1932	0	0
51	Dunn	Jimmy	1952-1955	58	21
52	Fellows	Percy	1913-1914	2	1
53	Fielding	Frank	2010-2013	80	0
54	Kieron	Freeman	2012-2015	27	0
55	Gamble	Frank	1981-1982	8	2
56	Garden	Henry	1892-1892	1	0
57	George	Charlie	1975-1978 1982-1982	147	56
58	Goulooze	Richard	1992-1993	17	1
59	Grant	Lee	2002-2005 2013-2016	139	0
60	Green	Les	1968-1971	129	0
61	Hall	Ian	1959-1962	51	16
62	Hardman	Jack	1913-1914	15	0
63	Hart	John	1925-1926	4	3
64	Hill	Gordon	1978-1979	27	6
65	Holding	Eddie	1952-1953	0	0
66	Hooks	Paul	1982-1985	59	4
67	Hope	Jack	1926-1930	9	2
68	Hoult	Russell	1994-1994 1995-1999	138	0
69	Howe	Jack	1936-1949	244	2
70	Jacobs	Michael	2012-2014	47	3
71	Junior	José	2003-2005	33	5
72	Kaku	Blessing	2004-2004	4	0
73	Keane	Ike	1930-1938	239	5
74	Kidd	Jimmy	1919-1921	21	0

#	Surname	Forename	When	App	Gls
75	King	Jeff	1975-1977	21	0
76	Kinsey	George	1895-1897	41	0
77	Kuhl	Martin	1992-1994	84	2
78	Lane	Sean	1983-1983	1	0
79	Law	Cecil	1951-1953	33	2
80	Little	Tommy	1892-1894	17	2
81	Long	Jimmy	1906-1907	65	19
82	Loss	Colin	1990-1994	0	0
83	McAlle	John	1981-1984	66	2
84	McQueen	Hugh	1895-1901	168	22
85	Mann	Bert	1926-1929	6	0
86	Mills	Lee	1995-1995	16	7
87	Minney	George	1920-1921	2	0
88	Money	Richard	1981-1982	6	0
89	Moore	Darren	2006-2008	90	5
90	Moran	John	1954-1955	2	0
91	Moreland	Vic	1978-1980	45	1
92	Morris	Lee	1999-2004	100	18
93	Noble	Ryan	2010-2010 2012-2012	3	0
94	Oakes	Andy	1999-2005	46	0
95	O'Hare	John	1967-1974	308	81
96	Oxford	Ken	1957-1964	162	0
97	Parkin	Geoff	1949-1950	9	0
98	Parr	Jack	1945-1953	134	0
99	Payne	Frank	1948-1948	1	0
100	Penney	David	1985-1989	29	3
101	Picken	Albert	1927-1928	0	0
102	Place	Charlie	1954-1956	2	0
103	Plummer	Calvin	1983-1984	33	4
104	Poppitt	John	1946-1950	16	0
105	Porter	Chris	2008-2011	50	9
106	Pratley	Dick	1983-1988	40	1
107	Pringle	Ben	2009-2011	23	0
108	Prior	Spencer	1998-2000	63	1
109	Pye	Jesse	1954-1957	65	27
110	Reich	Marco	2004-2005	55	7
111	Reid	Tony	1980-1983	34	1
112	Roos	Kelle	2014-	2	0
113	Round	Steve	1991-1993	9	0
114	Rowe	George	1926-1926	1	0
115	Ruddy	Tom	1928-1931	22	9

#	Surname	Forename	When	App	Gls
116	Sage	Mel	1986-1992	175	4
117	Sammon	Conor	2012-2015	90	13
118	Savage	Robbie	2007-2011	137	7
119	Severn	James	2010-2012	1	0
120	Shackell	Jason	2011-2012	49	1
			2015-	63	2
121	Shanks	Tom	1898-1901	28	9
122	Shiner	Albert	1920-1920	1	0
123	Short	Craig	1992-1995	143	13
124	Shotton	Ryan	2014-2016	36	2
125	Soar	Albert	1903-1903	2	0
126	Stamps	Jackie	1939-1953	262	126
127	Steele	Eric	1984-1987	53	0
128	Straw	Ray	1951-1957	98	60
129	Streete	Floyd	1984-1985	41	0
130	Swallow	Ray	1958-1964	128	22
131	Taylor	Ian	2003-2005	88	15
132	Thome	Emerson	2005-2005	4	0
133	Thorne	George	2014-	68	5
134	Tinkler	Alf	1910-1910	2	0
135	Todd	Colin	1971-1978	371	9
136	Tonge	Michael	2010-2010	19	2
137	Trollope	Paul	1994-1997	74	6
138	Twigg	Gary	2001-2005	9	0
139	Upton	Frank	1954-1961	233	12
			1965-1966	38	6
140	Vann	Bernie	1907-1907	3	0
141	Villa	Emanuel	2007-2009	53	9
142	Ward	Jamie	2010-2015	149	34
143	Waugh	Bob	1912-1914	29	1
144	Webb	David	1978-1980	29	1
145	West	Taribo	2000-2000	20	0
146	Wicks	Steve	1979-1979	24	0
147	Wild	Jack	1909-1911	7	1
148	Wisdom	Andre	2013-2014	55	0
			2017-	28	0
149	Wood	Alf	1905-1907	66	3
150	Wrack	Darren	1994-1996	31	1
151	Wright	Harry	1937-1939	26	0
152	Wright	Mark	1987-1991	171	10
153	York	Charlie	1902-1904	27	6
154	Young	Ray	1951-1966	269	5

NB: The above statistics are as I believe to be correct on 24/01/2018.

RAMS BARMY YARNY: Quirky Stats

The next set of quirky statistics all relate to players appearing in the Rams Barmy Yarny…

• **Best Strike Rates:** The following table reveals which of our Barmy Yarny outfield players had the best strike rates, per appearances.

#	Surname	When	App	Gls	St Rate	#	Surname	When	App	Gls	St Rate
1	Hart	1925-26	4	3	75%	5	Straw	1951-57	98	60	61%
2	Bedford	1925-30	218	152	70%	6	Fellows	1913-14	2	1	50%
3	Bentley	1906-10	168	112	67%	7	Stamps	1939-53	262	126	48%
4	Bloomer	1892-06 1910-14	525	332	63%	8	Curry	1960-64	164	76	46%

NB: Not in the Barmy Yarny, and therefore not "eligible" for the above table is Jack Bowers (1928-1936), who scored 183 goals for Derby County in 220 games – a strike rate of 83%.

November 1955: Ray Straw scores one of his 60 goals for Derby as part of a hat-trick in the 5-1 win over non-league Crook Town during an FA Cup first round replay. PHOTO: Andy Ellis

• **Alf and Steve:** Interestingly, Alf Bentley (nicknamed "Snobby" by the players, but not recorded why) largely slotted into the vacancy left by Steve Bloomer between 1906 and 1910, when Steve was off playing for Middlesbrough.

• **Snobby:** But the 5ft 5in Bentley was no slouch either and actually had a better strike rate at Derby than the legendary Bloomer, albeit largely at one league lower.

• **Peerless:** However, the last words on this matter must rest with the peerless Steve Bloomer, who actually scored 28 goals in his 23 appearances for England. That's an astonishing strike rate of 122% (1.22 goals per international).

• **Blooming Marvellous:** Steve Bloomer also scored 59 goals in 125 games for Middlesbrough between 1906 and 1910, which means that in 536 First Division games, he scored 317 goals – making him the second highest all-time goalscorer in the English top-flight. Number One is Jimmy Greaves, with 357 goals in 516 games (a strike rate of 69%). Small wonder, therefore, that Bloomer is still a huge Derby folk hero, and hence why the Rams run out to the rousing "Steve Bloomer's Watching" anthem for each home game.

17

• *Harry and John:* Steve Bloomer and Alf Bentley were actually topped in the *Best Strike Rates* table by Harry Bedford and John Hart. Bedford is another club legend who was top scorer in each of his five full seasons with the club between 1925 and 1930, scoring 152 goals in 218 games at a stunning strike rate of 70%. However, even he is topped by John Hart, who bagged 3 in his 4 games for the Rams in the same era – and who only played on the rare occasions when Harry Bedford was out injured! As for Harry, when he retired from football, he worked for the Rolls-Royce Fire Service from 1941 to 1964.

• *Worst Strike Rates:*

#	Surname	When	App	Gls	St Rate
1	Parr	1945-53	134	0	0%
2	Carr	1925-32	109	0	0%
3	Kinsey	1895-97	41	0	0%

#	Surname	When	App	Gls	St Rate
4	Streete	1984-85	41	0	0%
5	Wisdom	2013-	83	0	0%
6	Brooks	1914-14	34	0	0%

• *Parr for the Course:* Full-back Jack Parr played 134 games between 1945 and 1953 without ever scoring. So given they didn't have substitutes in those days, that's 12,060 minutes without a goal!

• *Brookingesque:* Another long-serving defender, Paul Blades, avoids the Worst Strike Rates table on account of the single goal that he scored for Derby in exactly 200 appearances in the 1980s. His goal came against Coventry City on 1 April, 1989. Blades had formed a classy central defensive partnership with Mark Wright in the late 1980s, but rarely ventured over the half-way line. He did so on this occasion, though, unleashing a thirty yarder that got stuck inside one of the stanchions, down at the Normanton End – making it reminiscent of Trevor Brooking's famous strike against Hungary in 1981.

• *"O" keepers:* You might think that with three goalkeepers whose surname starts with the letter "O" (Andy Oakes, Ken Oxford and Ben Olney), that **Derby** would lead the way in this particular league table, but not so. **Darlington** has had an incredible five "O-surnamed goalkeepers", Chesterfield has also had three (Oggy, Oggy, Oggy), and a handful of other clubs have had two – including both **Doncaster** and **Dagenham**. This means that the four D's of the English Football League have had 11 goalkeepers between them whose surname starts with the letter "O". Given there have only ever been 26 "O" keepers in the English Football League, this is a remarkable statistic! And for the record, there are two double counts: Andy Oakes (Derby and Darlington) and Ken Oxford (Derby and Doncaster). As for Ken, he became a Securicor guard on retirement from football, and on one occasion, he foiled an armed robbery in Ilkeston!

Quirke Alert: For the record, Derby also joint-lead the list in goalkeepers whose surname begins with the letter "Q" – this thanks to Andy Quy, who was at Derby between 1994 and 1996. Quy made one substitute appearance for the club in the League Cup, against Portsmouth on 26 October 1994 when he came on for the injured Steve Sutton. Coventry's Michael Quirke is the other "Q" keeper (2009-2011).

RAMS CHRONOLOGY: Fledgling Rams

The 1880s

Year	Event
1884	Derby County are founded as an offshoot of Derbyshire County Cricket Club
1884	Derby County's kit uses the Derbyshire CCC colours of amber, chocolate and blue
1884	Derby Co play home games at the Racecourse – also known as The County Ground
1884	13/09: First match: Great Lever vs. Derby County (L 6-0) – John Goodall scores 5 of them
1884	08/11: First FA Cup match: Derby County vs. Walsall Town (L 0-7)
1885	28/02: Ben Spilsbury becomes Derby's first England (amateur) player vs. Ireland
1885	Derby Co controversially poach star winger, George Bakewell, from Derby Midland
1885	14/11: FA Cup 2nd Rd: Derby Co vs. Aston V (W 2-0) – Evans, Smith – major Cup upset!
1885	12/12: FA Cup 3rd Rd: Small Heath A vs. Derby Co (L 4-2) – Evans 2 – joy short-lived!

Year	Event	Pos
Season 1888/1889 (Division One)		
1888	08/09: First lg match: Bolton vs. Derby (W 3-6) – Plackett 2, Bakewell 2, Cooper 2	2
1888	15/09: First home lg match: Derby County vs. West Bromwich A (L 1-2) – Plackett	5
1889	16/02: FA Cup 2nd Rd: Aston Villa vs. Derby County (L 5-3) – Cooper 2, L Plackett	12
1889	09/03: Derby Co vs. Aston V (W 5-2) – Sandy Higgins first Ram to score 4 in a game	10
1889	Derby finish season 10th (10:12) on 16 points, 24 points behind Champs, Preston	10
1889	Sandy Higgins is Derby's leading scorer with 11 league goals (12 in all competitions)	
Season 1889/1890 (Division One)		
1889	Derby sign England striker John Goodall from Preston NE – a huge coup!	
1889	09/11: West Brom vs. Derby Co (W 2-3) – Rams are 3 pts behind leaders, Everton	5
1889	28/12: Derby Co vs. Aston V (W 5-0) – Sandy Higgins first Ram to score 5 in a game	5

Quirk Alert: Beginnings

In March 1884, the Derbyshire Cup Final (football) took place at the County Ground in Derby, home of Derbyshire County Cricket Club, who had been founded thirteen years earlier in 1871. The football match between Derby Midland and Staveley attracted a crowd of c.7000 spectators. Derbyshire CCC immediately saw the potential for extra revenue, and Derby County FC were born – although the club were almost named Derbyshire County FC – but it was changed at the last minute as the name was deemed to be too long (the name was also objected to by the Derbyshire FA who had been founded the previous year in 1883).

Quirk Alert: The Bishop of Derby

When Derby County played Crewe Alexandra in the 5th Round of the FA Cup on 7th January 1888, their centre-forward was the Reverend Llewellyn Gwynne, curate of Derby St Chad's! Gwynne went on to become an Anglican bishop in Egypt and Sudan from 1920 to 1946, ultimately becoming Archdeacon of The Sudan.

Quirk Alert: Comeback Kings at Pikes Lane

Derby's first ever league match was away at Bolton Wanderers, which they won 6-3. But what you may not know, is that firstly, Derby were actually 3-0 down in this game, and secondly, they conceded the first ever league goal in English football – to Bolton Wanderers' winger, Kenny Davenport, who scored after just two minutes – and at 03:47 p.m., as they kicked off at 03:45 p.m., in those days. And with not a Sky camera in sight!

Stats Blast: Spilsbury vs. Goodall

John Goodall – The Invincible! (PHOTO: W.W. Winter Ltd).

There is some confusion over who Derby's official first England international is. Ben Spilsbury – born in Findern and educated at Repton – played for Derby between 1884 and 1889, and made his England debut against Ireland on 28th February 1885 – scoring 4 goals too! However, as he was also affiliated to Cambridge University between 1884 and 1887, and therefore played for both clubs during the same period, it isn't clear which team had first claim. The game was also still played at an amateur level until 1888. Therefore the first professional Derby County footballer to don the England jersey was John Goodall, when he lined up against Wales on 7th March 1891. He was also nicknamed Johnny Allgood due to his exemplary character (he once saved a man from drowning in the River Derwent), while he also played cricket for Derbyshire and Hertfordshire.

Stats Blast: Eight Aint Great!

Despite starting their football league history with a win, defeat and a draw, Derby County then went on an eight-game losing streak, from 29 September 1888 until 8 December 1888. This made it the worst run in the club's history, although eight straight defeats were later matched during the 1987/88 season in Division One, and across the end of season 1964/65 and the beginning of 1965/66.

Quirk Alert: Derby's Local Derby

Derby County's first FA Cup tie as a football league club was a 1-0 victory against Derby Junction on 2 February, 1889. Derby Junction was an amateur football club who played in the Midland League between 1880 and 1890, and were based at Derby Arboretum. Remarkably, Derby Junction had been FA Cup semi-finalists the year before (1888) when they were beaten by West Bromwich Albion, having previously knocked out the FA Cup holders, Blackburn Rovers, in an earlier round. Up the Junction indeed!

Quirk Alert: Safe Harbour

When Derby County lost 6-2 away to Everton on 27 October, 1888, they only turned up with ten men. Being still the days of chivalry, Everton donated one of their reserve players, Henry Harbour, to make up the Rams' eleven!

Quirk Alert: Superstar
In May 1889, Derby rocked the fledgling football world when they signed striker John Goodall from Preston North End. England striker Goodall was the country's top player, having topped the league goal-scoring charts the previous season with 21 goals – and this for a Preston side known as "The Invincibles", after having won the league and cup double during the inaugural 1988/89 season without losing a single game.

Quirk Alert: Hurricane Higgins
In two games against Aston Villa in 1889, Sandy Higgins scored an incredible 9 goals. His first name was, of course, Alexander! Records don't state, though, whether he was a chain smoker or not, or whether he was prone to the odd facial tic or two!

The 1890s

Year	Event	Pos
1890	04/01: Derby Co vs. Burnley (W 4-1) – Rams now 7 pts behind leaders, Preston	5
1890	11/01: Preston vs. Derby (L 5-0) – 10-man Rams, as Archie Goodall's wife taken ill	6
1890	18/01: FA Cup 1st Rd: Everton vs. Derby Co (L 11-2) – Derby's biggest ever defeat	6
1890	08/02: Derby vs. Blackburn (W 4-0) – Roulstone, Higgins, Milarvie, Holmes	6
1890	08/02: Above is Derby's only victory in last 6 league games; they lose the other five	6
1890	Derby finish season 7th (7:12), on 21 points, 12 points behind Champions, Preston	7
1890	Sandy Higgins is Derby's leading scorer with 14 league goals	
Season 1890/1891 (Division One)		
1890	06/09: Derby vs. Blackburn R (W 8-5) – J Goodall 4, Nelson 2, Chalmers, McLachlan	4
1890	04/10: Everton vs. Derby (L 7-0) – Anfield (yes, Anfield) not a good hunting ground!	10
1890	18/10: Derby Co vs. Aston Villa (W 5-4) – J Goodall 3, Bakewell, Holmes	10
1890	15/11: Burnley vs. Derby (L 6-1) – an 8th defeat in 9 leaves Rams bottom of Div One	12
1890	22/11 & 29:11: Back-to-back wins over West Brom (3-1 and 3-4); Rams off bottom	11
1890	13/12: Derby Co vs. Everton (L 2-6) – J Goodall, Holmes – (W4, D0, L10)	11
1891	03/01: Blackburn R vs. Derby Co (L 8-0) – revenge is sweet for Rovers – GD is -39	11
1891	10/01: Derby vs. Wolverhampton (W 9-0) – Derby's joint-best league win in history	11
1891	10/01: Johnny McMillan scores 5 and becomes second Ram to bag 5 in one game	11
1891	07/03: John Goodall is Derby's first England pro-player & scores vs. Wales (W 4-1)	9
1891	Derby finish season 11th (11:12), on 15 points, 14 points behind Champs, Everton	11
1891	John Goodall is Derby's leading scorer with 13 league goals (14 in all competitions)	
Season 1891/1892 (Division One)		
1891	Derby County absorb Derby Midland, founder members of Midland Football League	
1891	05/09: Jimmy Methven makes the first of 511 appearances for Derby County	9
1891	03/10: Derby Co vs. Aston Villa (W 4-2) – J Goodall, Storer 2, Mills – 4th win on spin	1
1891	03/10: DERBY COUNTY GO TOP OF DIV ONE FOR FIRST TIME IN THEIR HISTORY	1
1891	21/11: Derby vs. Darwen (W 7-0) – McMillan 2, McLachlan 2 – 6th but with 4 GIH	6
1891	19/12: Derby County vs. Burnley (L 0-1) – 4 defeats on spin – (W6, D1, L7)	10

Year	Event	Pos
1892	19/03: Derby County use the Baseball Ground for first time, vs. Sunderland (L 0-1)	11
1892	Derby finish season 10th (10:14), on 24 points, 18 pts behind Champs, Sunderland	10
1892	John Goodall is Derby's leading scorer with 15 league goals	
Season 1892/1893 (Division One)		
1892	03/09: Steve Bloomer makes Derby debut, aged 18, vs. Stoke (W 1-3) – RAMS TOP	1
1892	24/09: Bloomer scores first of 332 goals for Derby vs. West Brom (D 1-1)	9
1892	01/10: Archie Goodall makes first of record 167 consecutive appearances for Derby	10
1892	19/10: Derby Co vs. Notts Co (L 4-5) – Storer 2, McMillan, J Goodall	12
1892	19/10: Walter Roulstone becomes first Derby Co player to reach 100 appearances	12
1892	12/11: Derby use the Baseball Ground for second time, vs. Burnley (W 1-0)	13
1892	24/12: Derby vs. Stoke (W 1-0) – A Goodall – 6 without defeat – (W5, D5, L6)	12
1893	Derby finish season 13th (13:16), on 27 points, 21 pts behind Champs, Sunderland	13
1893	John Goodall is Derby's leading scorer with 13 league goals (14 in all competitions)	
Season 1893/1894 (Division One)		
1893	09/09: Derby vs. Everton (W 7-3) – Bloomer 2, McMillan 2 – the tide is turning!	3
1893	11/11: Everton vs. Derby County (W 1-2) – Bloomer 2 – (W5, D2, L5)	6
1893	23/12: Derby vs. Stoke (W 5-2) – Bloomer 2, J Goodall, Allan, A Goodall	11
1893	26/12: Derby vs. Bolton (W 6-1) – McMillan 3, J Goodall, A Goodall – Rams 5 GIH	10
1894	17/03: Derby Co vs. Newton Heath (W 6-2) – McMillan 3, Francis 2, Abbott	9
1894	23/03: Blackburn R vs. Derby Co (W 0-2) – J Goodall, Francis – (W13, D3, L10)	6
1894	24/03: West Brom vs. Derby Co (W 0-1) – Francis – Rams now 8 points off top	4
1894	31/03: Derby vs. Blackburn (W 5-2) – Bloomer 2, Cox, J Goodall, Francis	3
1894	Derby finish season 3rd (3:16), on 36 points, behind Aston V (44) & Sunderland (38)	3
1894	Steve Bloomer is Derby's top league scorer (19) for first of 13 consecutive seasons	
1894	Johnny McMillan is top scorer in all comps with 21 goals – first Ram to top 20 goals	
1894	J Methven, A Goodall, J Allan, J McMillan, 4 league ever-presents – a club record	
Season 1894/1895 (Division One)		
1894	01/09: Derby Co vs. Sunderland (L 0-8) – Derby's heaviest-ever home league defeat	16
1894	08/09: Derby Co vs. Nottm For (W 4-2) – McMillan 2, Bloomer, Raybould	11
1894	17/11: Preston vs. Derby (L 3-2) – A Goodall, Keay – 8 w/o a win – Rams bottom	16
1894	15/12 & 25/12: Back-to-back wins over Sheffield Utd (4-1 & 1-4) – (W4, D3, L8)	14
1895	09/03: Racecourse hosts first international vs. Ire (W 9-0) – Bloomer 2, J. Goodall 2	15
1895	13/04: Everton vs. Derby (W 2-3) – Bloomer 2, J Goodall – Rams season ends	12
1895	West Brom, Stoke and Small Heath win remaining games to go back above Derby	15
1893	Derby finish season 15th (15:16), on 23 points, 1 point above relegated Liverpool	15
1895	Div Two introduced 1892/93, so Derby have to play a "Test Match" with Notts Co	
1895	27/04: Derby Co (15th Div1) vs. Notts Co (2nd Div2) (W2-1) – Bloomer, McMillan	
1895	Steve Bloomer is Derby's leading scorer with 10 league goals (11 in all comps)	
Season 1895/1896 (Division One)		
1895	Derby Co move to the Baseball Ground permanently for start of 1895/96 season	
1895	Derby also change their strip to black and white from the start of the season	
1895	05/10: Nottingham F vs. Derby Co (W 2-5) – Bloomer 3, McQueen, Stevenson	10
1895	26/10: Derby Co vs. Wolverhampton (W 5-2) – Bloomer 3, Stevenson 2	3
1895	30/11: Derby vs. Small Heath (W 8-0) – Miller 2, Paul 2, Stevenson 2	3

Year	Event	Pos
1895	07/12: Derby County vs. Nottingham F (W 4-0) – Bloomer 3, Miller – (W10, D1, L3)	2
1895	14/12: Derby vs. West Brom (W 4-1) – Rams 2 points behind Everton with 3 GIH	2
1895	28/12: Sheffield Wed vs. Derby Co (W 0-4) – Stevenson 2 – RAMS GO TOP OF DIV 1	1
1896	01/01: Bolton W vs. Derby Co (L 2-1) – Miller – Derby replaced by Everton at top	2
1896	04/01: Small Heath vs. Derby County (W 1-3) – RAMS GO BACK TO TOP OF DIV 1	1
1896	18/01: West Brom vs. Derby (D 0-0) – Rams lose top spot to Villa & never re-gain it	2
1896	01/02: FA Cup 1st Rd: Derby County vs. Aston Villa (W 4-2) – Bloomer 2, Miller 2	2
1896	08/02: Steve Bloomer becomes first Derby player to reach 20 league goals/season	3
1896	19/02: FA Cup 2nd Rd: Derby vs. Newton Heath (W 5-1) – Miller 3, Bloomer, McQ'n	3
1896	29/02: FA Cup 3rd Rd: Derby County vs. West Bromwich Albion (W 1-0) – A Goodall	2
1896	04/03: Derby Co vs. Preston (W 1-0) – Rams 2 points behind Aston Villa with 1 GIH	2
1896	21/03: FA Cup Semi-Final: Derby County vs. Wolverhampton W (L 1-2) – Bloomer	2
1896	Derby only take five points from the last six league games	2
1896	Derby finish season 2nd (2:16), with 41 points, 4 points behind Champs Aston Villa	2
1896	Steve Bloomer finishes as Division One's joint-leading scorer (22 goals)	
1896	Steve Bloomer is also Derby's leading scorer with 22 league goals (27 in all comps)	
1896	Four more ever-presents (A Goodall, G Kinsey, J Miller, J Robinson)	
1896	14/08: Derby County FC becomes a limited company	
Season 1896/1897 (Division One)		
1896	12/09: Archie Goodall becomes first Derby Co player to reach 200 appearances	11
1896	19/09: Derby Co vs. Wolverhampton (W 4-3) – Bloomer scores all four	11
1896	26/09: Derby vs. Bury (W 7-2) – Bloomer 3, McQueen 2, Goodall, Stevenson	9
1896	24/10: Aston V vs. Derby Co (L 2-1) – Bloomer – 5 defeats in first 8	14
1896	07/11: Derby vs. Stoke (W 5-1) – Turner, Cox, Stevenson, J Goodall, Miller	10
1896	14/11: Nottingham F vs. Derby (W 1-2) – Bloomer, Stevenson – 3rd win on spin	7
1896	21/11: Derby vs. Blackburn (W 6-0) – Stevenson 4, A Goodall, Bloomer – 4 on spin	6
1896	25/12: Derby vs. West Brom (W 8-1) – Bloomer 3, A Goodall 2, McQueen 2	4
1897	09/01: Derby vs. Sheff Wed (W 2-1) – Fisher, A Goodall – Rams 1 point off top	3
1897	30/01: FAC 1st Rd: Derby vs. Barnsley (W 8-1) – Bloomer 3; Rams record FA Cup win	3
1897	06/02: West Brom vs. Derby (W 1-4) – A Goodall 2 – Rams still 1 point off top	2
1897	13/02: FA Cup 2nd Rd: Derby Co vs. Bolton Wanderers (W 4-1) – Bloomer 3, Fisher	2
1897	20/02: John Robinson plays for England – Derby's first international goalkeeper	2
1897	27/02: FAC 3rd Rd: Derby County vs. Newton Heath (W 2-0) – Bloomer, McQueen	2
1897	06/03: Bolton vs. Derby (W 1-3) – Bloomer, Paul, Fisher – an astonishing run of 15 wins in 18 (all comps), but FA Cup run sees Rams fall 5 points behind Aston Villa	2
1897	20/03: FA Cup Semi-Final: Derby County vs. Everton (L 2-3) – J Goodall 2	3
1897	05/04: Burnley vs. Derby (W 2-3) – Bloomer 2, Fisher – Rams now 7 pts off Villa	2
1897	19/04: Derby County vs. Everton (L 0-1) – Derby required a point to finish second	3
1897	Derby finish season 3rd (3:16), on 36 points, 11 points behind Champs, Aston Villa	3
1897	Steve Bloomer finishes as Division One's leading scorer again with 24 goals	
1897	Steve Bloomer is also Derby's leading scorer with 24 league goals (31 in all comps)	
1897	Steve Bloomer becomes first Derby player to score more than 30 goals in all comps	
1897	Derby Co win the 1897 English Cup at baseball, with S Bloomer fielding 2nd base!	

Year	Event	Pos
Season 1897/1898 (Division One)		
1897	04/09: Derby vs. Blackburn (W 3-1) – Steve Bloomer scores his 100th Derby goal	6
1897	18/09: Derby vs. West Brom (W 3-2) – Bloomer 2, A Goodall – 3 wins in 4	3
1897	25/09: Notts County vs. Derby County (D 1-1) – McQueen – Rams 1 point off top	3
1897	25/09: A Goodall plays last of 167 consecutive games (151 league) – club records	3
1897	30/10: Nottm F vs. Derby Co (W 3-4) – Maconnachie 2, A Goodall, Bloomer	6
1897	06/11: Derby County vs. Stoke (W 4-1) – J Goodall 3, A Goodall – (W5, D2, L4)	5
1898	29/01: FA Cup 1st Rd: Derby County vs. Aston Villa (W 1-0) – McQueen	9
1898	12/02: FA Cup 2nd Rd: Wolverhampton W vs. Derby County (W 0-1) – Leonard	9
1898	02/03: FA Cup 3rd Rd: Liverpool vs. Derby County (W 1-5) – Boag 3, Bloomer 2	9
1898	19/03: FA Cup Semi-Final: Derby County vs. Everton (W 3-1) – Bloomer 2, J Goodall	9
1898	09/04: Preston NE vs. Derby (L 5-0) – Rams won only 4 of last 17 league games	11
1898	11/04: Derby Co vs. Nottm F (W 5-0) – Bloomer 3, Boag, Turner – peaked too soon!	10
1898	11/04: Steve Bloomer's second goal against Forest is his 100th league goal for Rams	10
1898	16/04: FA CUP FINAL: Derby County vs. Nottingham Forest (L 1-3) – Bloomer	10
1898	Derby finish season 10th (10:16), on 28 points, 14 points behind Champs, Sheff Utd	10
1898	Steve Bloomer is Derby's leading scorer with 15 league goals (20 in all comps)	
Season 1898/1899 (Division One)		
1898	15/10: Derby vs. Everton (D 5-5) – Arkesden 2, Bloomer 2 – Rams equal-highest draw	11
1898	05/11: Aston Villa vs. Derby County (L 7-1) – Arkesden – (W1, D7, L3)	15
1899	07/01: Derby Co vs. West Brom (W 4-1) – Boag 2, Allen MacDonald – (W5, D10, L6)	12
1899	21/01: Derby Co vs. Sheffield Wed (W 9-0) – Bloomer bags 6 – a Rams record; the result is also Derby's joint-record league victory	10
1899	28/01: FAC 1st Rd: Arsenal vs. Derby (W 0-6) – Bloomer 2, Boag 2, MacDon'd, Allen	10
1899	04/02: Derby vs. Wolves (W 6-2) – Boag 2, Oakden, MacDonald, Goodall, Bloomer	9
1899	11/02: FA Cup 2nd Rd: Derby Co vs. Wolverhampton (W 2-1) – Allen, MacDonald	9
1899	18/02: Derby Co vs. Notts County (W 4-2) – Oakden 2, J Goodall, Bull (og)	8
1899	25/02: FA Cup 3rd Rd: Southampton vs. Derby Co (W 1-2) – Bloomer, MacDonald	8
1899	04/03: Archie Goodall becomes first Derby player to represent Ireland (vs. Wales)	6
1899	18/03: FA Cup Semi-Final: Derby County vs. Stoke (W 3-0) – Bloomer 3	11
1898	15/04: FA CUP FINAL: Derby County vs. Sheffield United (L 1-4) – Boag	10
1898	Derby finish season 9th (9:18) on 35 points, 10 points behind Champs Aston Villa	9
1898	Steve Bloomer is Derby's leading scorer with 24 league goals (30 in all comps)	
1899	For third time, Steve Bloomer finishes as the league's leading scorer with 24 goals	
Season 1899/1900 (Division One)		
1899	23/09: Newcastle U vs. Derby Co (L 2-0) – 4 defeats to open season – Rams bottom	18
1899	11/11: Archie Goodall becomes the first Derby player to reach 300 appearances	11
1899	14/10: Derby Co vs. Burnley (W 4-1) – Arkesden 3, Bloomer – 3 straight wins	13
1899	25/11: Derby vs. West Brom (W 4-1) – Bloomer 2, Cooke 2 – 7 without defeat	10
1899	26/12: Derby Co vs. Glossop (W 4-1) – Bloomer 2, Arkesden 2 – (W7, D3, L7)	8
1899	26/12: Derby vs. Glossop is the first of only two all-Derbyshire top flight games	8
1899	30/12: Notts Co vs. Derby Co (D 0-0) – Derby exit 19th century in 8th place in Div 1	8

Quirk Alert: Keeping the Wolves from the Door

When Derby played Wolves away on 25 January, 1890, striker John Goodall was picked to keep goal. Whether this was down to exasperation with Enos Bromage is not known. However, Bromage had conceded 11 goals the previous week in Derby's record 11-2 defeat in an FA Cup tie at Everton – in which Goodall had actually bagged both of Derby's "consolation" goals. Anyway, Derby only lost 2-1 at Molineux, while Bromage never played for Derby again.

Stats Blast: Bad Backs

One of Enos Bromage's successors in the following season (1890/91) was Scottish goalkeeper, David Haddow, who Derby signed from Albion Rovers. However, he let in SIXTY NINE goals in just SIXTEEN appearances before losing his place – to none-other than Charles Bunyan, the former Hyde United goalkeeper who had conceded TWENTY SIX goals in Hyde's famous and all-time record 26-0 defeat to Preston in an October 1887 FA Cup tie! Interestingly, both Enos Bromage and Charles Bunyan were succeeded by sons who also played professional football, and also had exactly the same names as their fathers!

Quirk Alert: Stumper Storer

Also making his debut along with Jimmy Methven, away at Stoke on 5 September 1891, was William Storer – the third of four England Test cricketers to appear for the Rams. Storer was preceded by William Chatterton and Frank Sugg and succeeded by Arnold Warren.

Stats Blast: 334?

Steve Bloomer's first goal for Derby was scored against West Brom at the Racecourse Ground (a penalty, as it happens), on 24/09/1892. However, Bloomer later claimed that he had scored twice during his debut away at Stoke on 03/09/1892, despite contemporary reports crediting two goals of the 3–1 win to Johnny McMillan. Again, no Sky cameras present – so could be!

Stats Blast: Indestructible…and Birthrights

In 1899, Archie Goodall represented Ireland – on account of being born in Belfast. Meanwhile, his brother, John, was playing for England on account of being born in Woolwich – making the pair the first brothers to represent different nations at international level. Ironically, their parents were both Scottish, but their father was a corporal in the Royal Scottish Fusiliers and hence the different postings and birthplaces! Of course, the rule back then was that you played for the country of your birthplace – which must have upset their poor old Dad! As for Archie, he was a controversial character who once refused to play extra time in a United Counties League Cup Final on the basis that that his contract ended after 90 minutes! He later toured Europe and America with a strongman act, which featured him walking around a metal hoop which he had built in a shed at his home in Derby!

Archie Goodall –
The Indestructible.
PHOTO: Andy Ellis

Quirk Alert: The Only Way Is Derby
Here's a fact I bet 99.9% of Derby fans didn't know. During the 1893/94 season, winger Thomas TOWIE appeared eight times for the Rams, scoring one goal!

Quirk Alert: The Game of Three Halves
On the opening day of the 1894/95 season, Derby faced Sunderland away. However, the referee, Mr Kirkham, was late and so another official stood in – but when Kirkham turned up at half-time, he offered Derby the option of starting again – which the Rams instantly took as they were losing 3-0! Thus were played out two further halves, and particularly ironic, was the fact that the "second first half" ended at 3-0 to Sunderland! We'll gloss over the second half!

Quirk Alert: Ambrosia
The above game ended 8-0 – Derby's worst opening game ever – and apparently, goalkeeper Jack Robinson was well-known for stating that he would never concede more than ten goals! Hence as the arguments raged on about whether or not the "first first half" goals were legitimate, Robinson eventually blamed the day's debacle on his lack of rice pudding prior to the game; indeed, this was genuinely the only time in his career that he failed to complete the pre-match rice pudding ritual! Drawn in by this coincidence, Derby players subsequently went to great lengths to ensure that Jack had his Ambrosia prior to each away match!

Quirk Alert: The Gypsy's Curse
When Derby County took over the Baseball Ground in 1895, a party of Gypsies were forced to move, and legend has it that before leaving they put a curse on the ground preventing Derby from winning the FA Cup. If you think that's a load of old rubbish, have another think when you've read the next dozen or so Quirk Alerts and Stats Blasts…

Stats Blast: Top of the Pile
Below is the League Division One table as it stood on 28 December 1895, after Derby County had won 0-4 at Sheffield Wednesday – and so with more than half of the season gone, Derby County sat on top of the pile with a game in hand. Check out Derby's vastly superior Goal Average as well! However, by 11 January, they had lost top spot to Aston Villa and never regained it, finishing second, four points behind eventual Champions, Villa.

| 28th December, 1895 | | | | | | | | | |
#	Team	Pld	W	D	L	GF	GA	GAvg	GD	Pts
1	Derby County	18	13	2	3	53	22	2.409	31	28
2	Everton	19	12	3	4	48	25	1.920	23	27
3	Aston Villa	19	12	3	4	49	29	1.690	20	27

Quirk Alert: Money and Share
When Derby County became a limited company on 14 August 1896, 1508 shares were taken up. However, only four of the 195 shareholders owned a significant number of shares, while Repton plumber, John Wroughton, owned only one share – which presumably wasn't a drain on his finances!

Quirk Alert: Tickets Please

Ten minutes before kick-off at the 1898 FA Cup Final between Derby County and Nottingham Forest, Archie Goodall was nowhere to be seen. It turned out that he was still outside the Crystal Palace ground, frantically trying to sell tickets to avoid being left out of pocket!

Stats Blast: A Bridge Too Far

So, Derby County thrashed Nottingham Forest 5-0, five days before they lost to them in the FA Cup Final of 1898. However, those two stats don't quite paint the full picture. Due to fixture congestion caused by bad weather, the Cup Final was Derby's FIFTH game in EIGHT days, the others being Everton (A) on 8 April (L 3-0), Preston (A) on 9th April (L 5-0), Forest (H) on 11 April (W 5-0), Liverpool (H) on 12th April (W 3-1), and the Cup Final on the 16 April. On top of that, Forest's goalkeeper, Dan Allsop, was an ex-Derby Junction player, and played an absolute blinder! So, was it a game too far…or the first victim of the Gypsy's Curse?

Quirk Alert: Déjà-Vu

Not quite such a hard-luck story one year later, though, as Derby were roundly beaten 4-1 by Sheffield United in the 1899 FA Cup Final. They actually led 1-0 at half-time, though, with Steve Bloomer missing a great chance to make it 2-0. However, Derby lost Johnny May to an ankle injury early in the second half, after which Sheffield United scored three quick goals, with Ernest Needham the main supplier – he who also played for Derbyshire CCC between 1901 and 1912. Derby also weren't helped before the game by the unpredictable Archie Goodall again, who had refused to go for extra training before the semi-final against Stoke, stating that he had private business and was perfectly fit anyway. The directors responded by suspending him and he missed the final.

Stats Blast: The Cream of Derbyshire

When Derby County beat Glossop 4-1 at home on Boxing Day, 1899, this was the first-ever professional meeting between Derbyshire clubs, and the first of only two ever meetings between Derbyshire clubs in the top flight of English football. The second meeting was, of course, the return game at Glossop on 13 April 1900 – which Derby also won (1-3).

The 1900s

Year	Event	Pos
1900	13/04: Glossop vs. Derby County (W 1-3) – May, Bloomer, Wombwell	5
1900	Derby finish season 6th (6:18), on 36 points, 14 points behind Champs, Aston Villa	6
1900	Steve Bloomer is Derby's leading scorer with 19 league goals (19 in all comps)	
1900	For the fourth time, Steve Bloomer is the league's leading scorer with 19 goals	
Season 1900/1901 (Division One)		
1900	Harry Newbould is appointed Derby's first manager, but the board still decide on team selection and new signings!	
1900	08/09: Derby Co vs. Notts Co (W 2-1) – Bloomer 2 – Rams have 5 points from 6	2
1900	22/09: Derby vs. Wolverhampton (L 4-5) – highest scoring Div One game of season	9
1900	13/10: Newcastle United vs. Derby County (L 2-1) – Bloomer – 5th defeat on spin	15

Year	Event	Pos
1900	20/10: Derby County vs. Sheffield United (W 4-0) – Bloomer 3, May	10
1900	20/10: Jimmy Methven reaches 300 appearances for Derby	10
1900	03/11: Derby County vs. Bury (W 5-2) – Boag 2, Bloomer 2, Wombwell	11
1900	24/11: Derby Co vs. West Brom (W 4-0) – Davis, Bloomer, Boag, Wombwell	10
1901	02/03: Charlie Morris becomes Derby's first Welsh international (vs. Scotland)	10
1901	Derby finish season 12th (12:18), on 31 points, 14 points behind Champs, Liverpool	12
1901	Derby finish with a Goal Difference of +13, 5 better than 3rd-placed Notts Co!	
1901	Steve Bloomer is Derby's leading scorer with 24 league goals (24 in all comps)	
Season 1901/1902 (Division One)		
1901	19/10: Derby Co vs. Aston V (W 1-0) – Bloomer – Rams 2nd, 2 points behind S'land	2
1901	30/11: Derby vs. Everton (W 3-1) – Bloomer 2, A Warren – Rams 2 points off top	4
1901	30/11: Steve Bloomer's 2nd goal is his 200th goal for Derby in his 279th appearance	4
1901	26/12: Derby vs. Newcastle (W 1-0) – Bloomer – Rams 3 GIH on leaders Everton	4
1902	01/02: FA Cup 1st Rd: Blackburn Rovers vs. Derby County (W 0-2) – B Warren 2	11
1902	08/02: FA Cup 2nd Rd: Lincoln City vs. Derby County (W 1-3) – B Warren 3	11
1902	27/02: FA Cup 3rd Rd: Derby vs. Portsmouth (W 6-3) – Bloomer 3, B Warren 2, Boag	14
1902	01/03: Nottingham F vs. Derby Co (L 3-1) – Bloomer – 6 games without a win	15
1902	15/03: FA Cup Semi-Final: Sheffield United vs. Derby County (D 1-1) – B Warren	13
1902	20/03: FA Cup Semi Final Replay: Derby Co vs. Sheffield United (D 1-1) – Wombwell	14
1902	27/03: FA Cup Semi-Final 2nd Replay: Sheffield United vs. Derby County (L 1-0)	12
1902	The last 12 league games sees Derby W6, D2, L4 in a compressed league table	
1902	Derby finish season 6th (6:18), on 35 points, 9 points behind Champs, Sunderland	6
1902	Steve Bloomer is Derby's leading scorer with 15 league goals (18 in all comps)	
Season 1902/1903 (Division One)		
1902	13/09: Derby vs. Notts County (W 4-1) – J May, Bloomer, A Goodall, (og)	8
1902	20/09: Nottingham F vs. Derby Co (W 2-3) – Bloomer 2, York – Rams 5th; Forest 1st	5
1902	27/09: Derby vs. Bolton (W 5-0) – Bloomer 3, York, B Warren – Notts Co now 1st	2
1902	01/11: Derby vs. Sunderland (W 5-2) – Goodall, Turner, Bloomer, Warren, Richards	2
1902	08/11: Derby vs. Wolves (W 3-1) – Rams still 2nd, now 1 point behind West Brom	2
1902	15/11: Archie Goodall becomes first Derby Co player to reach 400 appearances	
1902	13/12: Sheffield Wed vs. Derby (W 0-1) – York – Rams still 2 pts behind West Brom	2
1902	27/12: Derby Co vs. West Brom (W 1-0) – Bloomer – 1st to 4th are all on 24 pts	3
1903	07/02: FA Cup 1st Rd: Derby County vs. Small Heath (W 2-1) – Boag, Warrington	4
1903	21/02: FA Cup 2nd Rd: Derby Co vs. Blackburn Rov (W 2-0) – Bloomer, Warrington	4
1903	07/03: FA Cup 3rd Rd: Derby County vs. Stoke (W 3-0) – Warren, Davis, Warrington	4
1903	14/03: Derby vs. Stoke (W 2-0) – Boag, Warrington – Rams 3 pts off top with 2 GIH	4
1903	21/03: FA Cup Semi-F: Derby County vs. Millwall (W 3-0) – Warren, Boag, Richards	4
1903	Derby's league form disintegrates, and they only win one of their last eight games	
1903	11/04: Derby vs. Sheff W (W 1-0) – that only win is against leaders & Champs	6
1903	18/04: FA CUP FINAL: Bury vs. Derby County (L 6-0) – nightmare – see Quirk Alert	8
1903	18/04: Charlie Morris becomes only outfield player to replace a goalkeeper in both an FA Cup Final and an international; Morris was also a Methodist lay preacher!	8
1903	Derby finish season 9th (9:18), on 35 points, 7 points behind Champs, Sheff Wed	9
1903	Steve Bloomer is Derby's leading scorer with 12 league goals (13 in all comps)	

Year	Event	Pos
Season 1903/1904 (Division One)		
1903	01/09: Derby vs. Small Heath (W 4-1) – Richards 2, Bloomer, Warren – RAMS TOP	1
1903	05/09: Derby vs. Wolverhampton (W 2-1) – Davis 2 – Rams slip to 3rd on Goal Avg	3
1903	14/11: Derby vs. Nottm F (L 2-6) – Steve Bloomer scores 200th league goal for Rams	18
1903	21/11: Sheff Wed vs. Derby (L 1-0) – 11th game w/o win (D2, L9) – Rams bottom	18
1903	28/11: Derby vs. Sunderland (W 7-2) – Hodgkinson 3, Bloomer 2, Hall, Richards	17
1903	26/12: Derby vs. Stoke (W 5-0) – Bloomer 3, Hodgkinson, Mercer – 4 wins in 5	14
1904	06/02: FA Cup 1st Rd: Derby County vs. Portsmouth (W 5-2) – Bloomer 2	14
1904	29/02: FA Cup 2nd Rd, 2nd Replay: Derby Co vs. Wolves (W 1-0) – Bloomer	13
1904	03/03: FA Cup 3rd Rd: Derby Co vs. Blackburn R (W 2-1) – Bloomer, Warrington	13
1904	12/03: Nottm F vs. Derby (L 5-1) – Barker – 9 league game w/o win (D6, L3)	14
1904	19/03: FA Cup Semi-Final: Bolton Wanderers vs. Derby County (L 1-0)	16
1904	26/03: Sunderland vs. Derby Co (W 0-3) – May 2, Bloomer	15
1904	02/04: Derby Co vs. West Brom (W 4-2) – May 2, Bloomer, Richards	14
1904	09/04: Small Heath vs. Derby Co (L 1-0) – Rams now 2 points above drop-zone	16
1904	11/04: Derby Co vs. Blackburn R (W 3-0) – Bloomer 2, Richards – back up to 14th	14
1904	Derby finish season 14th (14:18) on 28 points, 2 points above relegated Liverpool	14
1904	Steve Bloomer is Derby's leading scorer with 20 league goals (25 in all comps)	
1904	For sixth and final time, Steve Bloomer finishes as league's leading scorer (20 goals)	
Season 1904/1905 (Division One)		
1904	15/10: Derby Co vs. Aston Villa (W 2-0) – Bloomer 2 – Derby are 6th after 8 games	6
1904	05/11: Derby vs. Sheff Wed (W 1-0) – Richards – Rams now only one point off top	6
1904	26/11: Derby vs. Stoke (W 3-0) – Bloomer, Paton, Hounsfield – Rams 2 pts off top	6
1904	10/12: Derby vs. Small Heath (W 3-0) – Bloomer 2, Fletcher – Rams 2 pts off top	2
1904	17/12: Manchester City vs. Derby County (L 6-0) – Derby fall to 5th place	5
1904	24/12: Derby vs Notts Co (D 1-1) – Bloomer – first of 6 league games in 2 weeks	5
1905	07/01: Newcastle United vs. Derby (L 2-0) – 5th defeat on the spin	11
1905	14/01: Derby vs. Preston NE (W 3-1) – Bloomer 2, Fletcher – rot stopped	9
1905	28/01: Derby vs. Wolves (W 2-1) – Bloomer, Fletcher – only 7 points off top	9
1905	28/02: Derby vs. Nottm F (W 3-2) – G Davis, Hall, Fletcher – now 8 pts off top	9
1905	Derby finish season 11th (11:18), on 32 points, 16 pts behind Champs, Newcastle	11
1905	Steve Bloomer is Derby's leading scorer with 13 league goals (13 in all comps)	
Season 1905/1906 (Division One)		
1905	The First Division is increased to 20 teams for the first time	
1905	16/09: Derby vs. Preston NE (W 3-0) – Bloomer 3 – Rams have won first 3 games	3
1905	23/09: Newcastle vs. Derby (W 0-1) – Richards – 4 wins in 4; 2 GIH on leaders	3
1905	30/09: Derby vs. Aston Villa (W 1-0) – J Davis – 5 wins out of 5, 2 GIH & GAvg 9.000	2
1905	14/10: Derby vs. Sheff Utd (W 1-0) – J Davis – 6 wins out of 7 – Rams still 2 GIH	2
1905	28/10: Derby vs. Stoke (W 1-0) – Paton – 7 wins out of 9 , still with 2 GIH	3
1905	11/11: Derby vs. W Arsenal (W 5-1) – Bloomer 3 – Rams are 1 point off top, 2 GIH	3
1905	25/11: Derby vs. Sunderland (W 1-0) – Richards – Rams are 2 points off top, 2 GIH	4
1905	16/12: Derby vs. Wolves (W 2-0) – Bloomer 2 – Rams 6th, 2 points off top, 1 GIH	6
1905	30/12: Bury vs. Derby (W 0-2) – Bloomer, Warren – Rams 4 points off top, 2 GIH	7

Year	Event	Pos
1906	27/01: Derby vs. Newcastle (W 2-1) – Bloomer, Paton – Rams 6 pts off top, 2 GIH	9
1906	10/02: Derby vs. Liverpool (L 0-3) – first of 9 league games w/o win	10
1906	17/02: Ben Warren makes first of 19 consecutive appearances for England	13
1906	March: In financial difficulty, Derby sell Steve Bloomer to Middlesbrough for £750	
1906	07/04: Derby vs. Birmingham (D 0-0) – Rams 16th but 6 points clear of drop-zone	16
1906	07/04: The club six points below Derby, in 19th position, is Middlesbrough – who beat Stoke 5-0 on this day, including a goal from Steve Bloomer!	16
1906	13/04: Man City vs. Derby (W 1-2) – J Wood, Hardcastle – relief, and still six points clear; M'brough beat Sunderland 2-1; Bloomer scores for third successive game	15
1906	16/04: Aston Villa vs. Derby Co (L 6-0) – Rams still 6 points above M'brough (19th)	16
1906	21/04: Wolves vs. Derby (L 7-0) – Wolves bottom and already relegated; Rams safe	16
1906	28/04: Derby beat 3rd-placed Sheff Wed 2-1; Bloomer's goal for M'brough in a 1-1 draw at Blackburn saves 'Boro from drop and relegates Nottm Forest instead	15
1906	Derby finish season 15th (15:20), on 35 points, 4 points above the drop-zone (19th)	15
1906	Steve Bloomer is Derby's leading scorer with 12 league goals (12 in all comps); his six goals in nine league games also help save Middlesbrough from relegation	
Season 1906/1907 (Division One)		
1906	August: Jimmy Methven becomes Derby County player/manager	
1906	03/09: Derby vs. Man Utd (D 2-2) – Morris, Warren – first league game vs. Man U	14
1906	29/09: Manchester Utd vs. Derby Co (D 1-1) – Long – Rams are 12th after 6 games	12
1906	20/10: Derby vs. Preston (W 3-0) – J Wood, Warren, Ransford – Rams season-high	8
1906	December: Derby sign centre-forward Alf Bentley for £50 from Alfreton Town	
1906	22/12: Derby vs. Woolwich Arsenal (D 0-0) – 6 w/o win (D1, L5) – Rams drop to 16th	16
1906	24/12: Derby vs. Notts County (W 3-0) – Warren, Long, G Davis	14
1906	29/12: Derby vs. Sheff United (W 3-0) – Bentley 2, J Wood – Rams 5 pts above drop	14
1907	26/01: Jimmy Methven plays the last of his 511 games for Derby	18
1907	09/02: Middlesbrough vs. Derby (L 4-1) – G Davis – Bloomer scores for 'Boro	18
1907	16/02: Derby vs. Stoke (W 2-1) – G Davis 2 – Rams are 5 pts clear of Notts Co (19th)	17
1907	16/03: Derby vs. Sunderland (D 1-1) – Hall – Rams are 4 points clear of 19th	18
1907	29/03: Notts Co vs. Derby (L 4-0) – Notts close to 2 points behind Derby with 3 GIH	18
1907	06/04: Liverpool vs. Derby (L 2-0) – Derby drop into the relegation zone	19
1907	13/04: Derby vs. Everton (W 5-2) – Bentley 2, Long 2, J Davis – but still in trouble	19
1907	20/04: Derby vs. Bristol C (L 1-3) – RAMS RELEGATED FOR FIRST TIME	19
1907	Derby finish season 19th (19:20), on 27 points, 4 points from safety/18th/Notts Co	19
1907	Jimmy Long is Derby's top scorer with 8 league goals (9 in all competitions)	
Season 1907/1908 (Division Two)		
1907	02/09: Derby vs. Lincoln (W 4-0) – Ted Garry only Rams debutant to score hat-trick	3
1907	14/09: Barnsley vs. Derby Co (W 2-4) – Bentley 4 – Rams have W2, D0, L1	6
1907	19/10: Derby vs. Leeds City (W 6-1): Bentley 4, Dilly, Garry – (W4, D1, L2)	8
1907	02/11: Derby vs. Gainsborough Trinity (W 5-2) – Bentley 2, Bevan 2, Garry	10
1907	14/12: Derby vs. West Brom (W 2-0) – Bentley, Richards – five straight wins	2
1907	25/12: Derby vs. Grimsby (W 4-0) – Bevan, Bentley, Davis, Garry – RAMS GO TOP	1
1907	28/12: Derby vs. Hull C (W 4-1) – Bentley 2, Dilly, Bevan – Rams Goal Diff is +30	1
1907	18/01: Chesterfield vs Derby (W 0-2) – Riddell, Wheatcroft – Rams GAvg is 2.684	1

Year	Event	Pos
1908	08/02: Derby vs. Clapton Orient (W 4-0) – Bentley 2, G Davis, Long – top & 1 GIH	1
1908	15/02: Leeds City vs. Derby (L 5-1) – Bevan – Rams drop to second, with 1 GIH	2
1908	29/02: Gainsborough T vs. Derby (W 1-4) – Bentley 2, Long, G Davis – 3 pts off top	2
1908	14/03: Glossop vs. Derby (W 2-3) – Bevan 2, Garry – RAMS GO BACK TO TOP	1
1908	14/03: Rams 4 points clear of 3rd-placed West Brom and have 1 GIH on 2nd and 3rd	1
1908	28/03: Blackpool vs. Derby (L 1-0) – Rams passed by Bradford City, but have 2 GIH	2
1908	30/03: Oldham Ath vs. Derby (L 3-1) – Bentley – Oldham go 2nd; Derby drop to 3rd	3
1908	08/04: Derby vs. Wolves (W 3-2) – Bentley 2, Long – RAMS BACK TO TOP (GD +40)	1
1908	But then Derby lose ALL of their remaining five games, including, crucially...	
1908	18/04: Derby (2nd) vs. Bradford C (1st) (L 2-3) – Bradford 4 pts clear of Derby	3
1908	Derby finish season 6th (6:20), on 46 points, 8 points behind Champs, Bradford City	6
1908	Alf Bentley is top scorer with 27 league goals – a new Rams record (28 all comps)	
Season 1908/1909 (Division Two)		
1908	19/09: Leeds City vs. Derby (W 2-5) – Bentley bags 4 against Leeds again	3
1908	03/10: Tottenham H vs. Derby (D 0-0) – Rams first-ever league game vs. Spurs	2
1908	31/10: Derby vs. Chesterfield (D 1-1) – Bentley – Rams have drawn 6 of last 7	3
1908	07/11: Glossop vs. Derby (L 3-1) – Glossop leap-frog Derby into 4th	5
1908	14/11: Derby vs. Stockport County (W 5-0) – Bentley 3, Barnes, Hall	4
1908	19/12: Fulham vs. Derby (W 1-2) – Thompson 2 – Rams 3 pts off 2nd-placed Spurs	5
1909	20/01: FA Cup 1st Rd Replay: Derby vs. Northampton Town (W 4-2) – Bentley 2	4
1909	23/01: Derby vs. Leeds City (W 5-1) – Bentley 2, Barnes 2, Richards	4
1909	06/02: FA Cup 2nd Rd: Leicester Fosse vs. Derby (W 0-2) – Bentley, Trueman	4
1909	20/02: FA Cup 3rd Rd: Derby vs. Plymouth Argyle (W 1-0) – Bentley	6
1909	06/03: FA Cup Quarter Final: Derby County vs. Nottingham F (W 3-0) – Bentley 3	5
1909	17/03: Chesterfield vs. Derby (W 2-4) – Bevan 2 – Rams are 7 points off 2nd	5
1909	27/03: FA Cup Semi-Final: Derby vs. Bristol City (D 1-1) – Garry	5
1909	31/03: FA Cup Semi-Final Replay: Bristol City vs. Derby (L 2-1) – Davis	7
1909	10/04: Derby vs. Gainsborough T (W 5-0) – Bentley 2, Hall, Bevan, Barnes	6
1909	21/04: Derby vs. Glossop NE (W 4-0) – Garry 2 – Rams are now 10 pts behind 2nd	6
1909	Derby finish season 5th (5:20), on 43 points, 8 points behind 2nd-placed Tottenham	5
1909	Alf Bentley is top scorer with 24 league goals – (32 in all comps – new Rams record)	
1909	Alf Bentley is also Division Two's leading scorer	
Season 1909/1910 (Division Two)		
1909	04/09: Derby vs. Burnley (W 5-2) – Bauchop 3, Barnes, Richards	4
1909	18/09: Derby vs. Wolves (W 5-0) – Bauchop 2, Bentley 2, Garry	5
1909	25/09: Gainsborough T vs. Derby (W 2-4) – Bentley 3, Garry – Rams up to 4th	4
1909	02/10: Derby vs. Grimsby (W 6-0) – Bentley 3, Bauchop 2 – now 3 pts off top, 2 GIH	3
1909	13/11: Derby vs. Hull (W 4-0) – Bauchop 2, Bentley, Thompson – 4 pts off top	5
1909	04/12: Derby (3rd) vs. Glossop (1st) (W 2-1) – Bentley 2 – Rams 2 pts behind Glossop	2
1909	11/12: Derby vs. Birmingham C (W 3-1) – Barnes 2, Bentley – still 2 pts off top	2
1909	25/12: Derby vs. Barnsley (W 2-1) – Hall, Bentley – Rams still 2nd (GLO 28, DER 27)	2
1909	31/12: Derby exit the 1900's in 2nd place in Div Two, now 3 points behind Glossop	2

Quirk Alert: Latham's Labours

Before Derby County lost 3-1 at Blackburn Rovers on 19th April 1902, goalkeeper Tom Harrison missed his train – and hence Derby trainer, Arthur Latham, had to keep goal!

Quirk Alert: It's That Curse Again…

So Derby got hammered 6-0 by Bury in the 1903 FA Cup Final. But again, the scoreline doesn't tell the full story. For starters, Steve Bloomer missed the final through injury, but it was goalkeeping which did for Derby. The Rams rued the decision to play goalkeeper Jack "String" Fryer (aka the Cromford Giant) who, despite a strained groin, was passed fit to play. Inevitably he was incapacitated and had to go off (twice), with outfield players Charlie Morris and later Jimmy Methven replacing him. Of course, in those days there were no substitutes, so the Rams played most of the game with ten men and without a recognised goalkeeper! Interestingly, when Methven went in goal, he failed to inform the referee – who informed Methven after the game that he really ought to have awarded a penalty each time he handled the ball in the penalty area! Although to be fair, that would only have been once!

Quirk Alert: An Eggy Sob-Story

Particularly galling for Derby was the fact that they'd absolutely sailed through the previous four rounds of the 1903 FA Cup. And just to complete the sob-story for season 1902/03, Derby only finished 7 points behind Champions, Sheffield Wednesday – having lost SIX of their last eight games! Ironically, the only game they won in that spell was against Sheffield Wednesday! Clearly Derby had put all of their eggs into the Cup basket (egg-cup?) only to be undone by a Fryer!

Stats Blast: Blitzed by Bloomer

On a brighter note, Steve Bloomer scored his 200th league goal in the following November (1903), the only player in the club's history to achieve this. He also went on to bag another 93 league goals after that, leaving him a cool 126 goals clear of second-placed Jack Bowers (167), in the all-time list of Derby County goal-scorers.

Stats Blast: Cup of Woe

Between seasons 1895/96 and 1903/04 (the first 9 seasons after the Gypsy's Curse), Derby were FA Cup semi-finalists SEVEN times… but didn't win the cup once! Still think it's a load of old rubbish?

Perspective: Fred Barker

On the evening of 29 October 1904, Fred Barker must have been one of the happiest men in the world, having scored the only goal of a local derby between Nottingham Forest and Derby County at the City Ground. Alas, it was his last game for Derby; much more tragically, within a month he had died.

Quirk Alert: Public Outrage

Reginald Hounsfield played 21 games for Derby County and scored 4 goals during the 1904/05 season. He was one of the fastest wingers in the country – but he was also an amateur, on account of belonging to Repton School – and the Old Reptonians had first claim on his services, so if matches clashed, Derby had to make do without him!

Quirk Alert: Derbyshire Derby Mark II

The first all-Derbyshire football league match occurred during the 1899/1900 season when Derby County played Glossop North End in Division One. Derby didn't play Chesterfield until they drew them in the first round of the FA Cup and played out a 1-1 draw at the Baseball Ground on 12 January 1907. However, the replay at Saltergate was abandoned due to bad light, seven minutes from the end of extra-time, with Derby leading 2-1 through Jimmy Long and James Ransford – and in front of a then-record Chesterfield crowd of 14,000, too. The second replay took place at Trent Bridge in Nottingham, where Derby ran out 4-0 winners with goals from Long, Wood, Bentley and Morris.

Quirk Alert: Back-to-Back Derbyshire Derby's

Derby County played Chesterfield on 31 October 1908 (D 1-1) and then Glossop North End seven days later on 7th November (L 1-3). Glossop's victory took them above Derby into 4th position, which meant that for the first time ever, there were three Derbyshire clubs in the top half of England's second tier (Glossop 4th, Derby 5th and Chesterfield 9th).

Stats Blast: Derbyshire Dynamics

The following table extract must represent the closest that Derbyshire's three football league clubs have ever been in over 130 years of football league history.

Division Two - 28th November, 1908

Pos	Team	Pld	W	D	L	GF	GA	GAvg	GD	Pts
9	Glossop North End	14	6	5	3	20	14	1.429	6	17
10	**Derby County**	**16**	**5**	**7**	**4**	**20**	**16**	**1.250**	**4**	**17**
11	Oldham Athletic	12	6	1	5	22	12	1.833	10	13
12	Chesterfield Town	15	5	3	7	14	22	0.636	-8	13

Division Two - 4th December 1909

Pos	Team	Pld	W	D	L	GF	GA	GAvg	GD	Pts
1	Glossop North End	15	10	3	2	30	15	2.000	15	23
2	**Derby County**	**15**	**9**	**3**	**3**	**38**	**17**	**2.235**	**21**	**21**
3	Fulham	16	8	4	4	25	14	1.786	11	20
4	Manchester City	15	8	4	3	33	20	1.650	13	20

Division Two - 29th January 1910

Pos	Team	Pld	W	D	L	GF	GA	GAvg	GD	Pts
1	**Derby County**	**23**	**16**	**3**	**4**	**55**	**29**	**1.897**	**26**	**35**
2	Manchester City	22	14	4	4	51	24	2.125	27	32
3	Glossop North End	22	13	4	5	44	26	1.692	18	30
4	Leicester Fosse	23	15	0	8	56	34	1.647	22	30

For those who don't know their geography, you might assume that two Derbyshire teams playing each other would be a quick trip up the road. In which case, check out your Road Atlas (yes there are still some around). At opposite ends of an elongated county, the distance is around 50 miles – but takes well over an hour and a half by road, with two thirds of it through the Peak District.

Perspective: Ben Warren

Ben Warren played for Derby County between 1900 and 1908, and at that time was probably the finest wing-back in the Football League. In 1902, he scored 8 FA Cup goals for Derby; he also made 13 appearances for England whilst with the Rams. In 1908, he moved to Chelsea, and it was with the Londoners that he suffered a knee injury in 1912 which ended his career, and which sparked a dramatic decline in his mental health. Now struggling to support his young family, he became plagued by hallucinations along with delusions that he was being poisoned. This led to him being committed to a lunatic asylum where his condition deteriorated to the extent that he was placed on suicide watch. He died of tuberculosis in 1917 whilst still an inmate, aged only 37.

The 1910s

Year	Event	Pos
1910	01/01: Derby vs. Fulham (W 3-1) – Barnes, Bauchop, Bentley – Rams 1 pt off top	2
1910	08/01: Burnley vs. Derby (W 1-2) – Bentley, Bauchop – RAMS GO TOP OF DIV TWO	1
1910	29/01: Wolves vs. Derby (W 2-3) – Bentley 2, Bauchop – Rams 3 points clear at top	1
1910	26/02: Leicester Fosse vs. Derby (L 6-0) – Rams lose top spot to Manchester City	2
1910	05/03: Derby vs. Lincoln City (W 2-0) – Bagshaw, Bauchop – RAMS BACK ON TOP	1
1910	12/03: Clapton Orient vs. Derby (W 0-2) – Bentley 2 – Rams remain top	1
1910	16/03: Derby (1st) vs. Man City (2nd) (W 3-1) – Bentley 3 – Rams 3 points clear	1
1910	19/03: Derby vs. Blackpool (W 2-1) – Bagshaw, Halligan – Rams 4 points clear	1
1910	Once again, Derby capitulate, winning only 2 of their last 9 games, but...	
1910	26/03: Hull City vs. Derby (D 0-0) – Rams still 4 points clear of 2nd-placed Man City	1
1910	06/04: Manchester City win game in hand to go top on same points as Derby (47)	2
1910	09/04: Derby vs. Stockport Co (W 1-0) – Halligan – Man C/Rams 4 pts clear of Hull	2
1910	16/04: Hull City win two games in a week to go 2nd on Goal Average from Derby	3
1910	23/04: Derby vs. Birmingham City (W 3-1) – Bauchop, Bentley, Halligan – Rams are 3rd on 51 pts, but have 2 games in hand on Hull (53 pts) and Man City (54 pts)	3
1910	26/04: Oldham Ath (4th) vs. Derby (3rd) (L 4-0) – Oldham leap-frog Derby into 3rd	4
1910	28/04: Glossop vs. Derby (D 1-1) – Bentley – Rams back to 3rd, 1 point behind Hull	3
1910	30/04: Day starts with Man City on 54 points, Hull 53, Derby 52 and Oldham 51	3
1910	30/04: Man City (1st) lose, but still finish 1st on 54 pts; Oldham (4th) beat Hull (2nd) 3-0 and go above Hull on Goal Avg on 53 pts; a win for Derby at mid-table West Brom would see Rams promoted, but they draw 0-0 and finish 4th on Goal Avg	4
1910	Alf Bentley is Derby's top scorer with 30 league goals (31 in all competitions)	
1910	Alf Bentley is Derby's first player to score 30 league goals in a season	
Season 1910/1911 (Division Two)		
1910	03/09: Derby vs. Chelsea (L 1-4) – Bentley – and a rude awakening	18

Year	Event	Pos
1910	24/09: Glossop vs. Derby (D 2-2) – Halligan 2 – Rams are 14th in Division Two	14
1910	Derby re-sign Steve Bloomer, now aged 36, from Middlesbrough	14
1910	01/10: Derby vs. Lincoln (W 5-0) – Bloomer scores twice on second debut	11
1910	15/10: Derby vs. Birmingham (W 1-0) – Barnes – Rams only 2 pts off top spot	6
1910	12/11: Derby vs. Bradford PA (W 4-2) – Bloomer 2, Bauchop, Bentley; 1st win in 4	10
1910	10/12: Derby vs. Stockport (W 4-1) – Bloomer 2, Bauchop 2 – Rams 7 points off top	8
1910	26/12: Derby vs. Leicester Fosse (W 3-0) – Bloomer 2, Hall – Rams 5 points off top	9
1910	27/12: Derby vs. Wolves (W 2-0) – Bauchop, Halligan – Rams 4 points off top	7
1911	28/01: Derby vs. Glossop (W 2-1) – Bloomer, Bauchop – Rams 4 points off top	5
1911	04/02: FA Cup 4th Rd: Derby Co vs. West Brom (W 2-0) – Bauchop, Bloomer	5
1911	08/02: Lincoln C vs. Derby (W 0-2) – Bentley, Halligan – Rams now 2 points off top	3
1911	11/02: The Baseball Ground hosts England vs. Ireland in Home Champs (W 2-1)	3
1911	11/02: Huddersfield vs. Derby (W 0-3) – Bentley 2, Bloomer – now 1 point off top	3
1911	25/02: FA Cup 5th Rd: Derby vs Everton (W 5-0) – Bloomer 2, Bentley, Barnes, Beauchap	3
1911	13/03: FA Cup 6th Rd: Newcastle vs. Derby (L 4-0) – Cup a dangerous distraction	6
1911	18/03: Bradford PA vs. Derby (L 2-1) – 5 w/o league win; now 8 points off top	8
1911	25/03: Derby vs. Burnley (W 3-0) – Bloomer 2, Bauchop – Rams 4 points off 2nd	6
1911	29/04: Derby vs. Barnsley (W 5-1) – Bauchop 3, Bloomer, Bentley – but too late	6
1911	Derby finish season 6th (6:20), on 42 points, 9 points shy of 2nd/promotion/Bolton	6
1911	Steve Bloomer is Derby's leading scorer with 20 league goals (24 in all comps)	
Season 1911/1912 (Division Two)		
1911	11/09: Chelsea vs. Derby (L 1-0) – Rams have lost 2 of first 3 and lie 14th	14
1911	16/09: Birmingham City vs. Derby (W 0-4) – Barnes 2, Bauchop, Bloomer	9
1911	23/09: Derby vs. Huddersfield Town (W 4-2) – Bloomer 2, Grimes, Walker	7
1911	23/09: Steve Bloomer's second goal is his 300th for the Rams	7
1911	07/10: Derby vs. Glossop (W 5-0) – Bauchop 3, Bloomer, Barnes	6
1911	04/11: Derby vs. Fulham (W 6-1) – Leonard 4, Bauchop, Bloomer	4
1911	25/11: Derby vs. Leeds C (W 5-2) – Sharpe 2, Bauchop, Bloomer, Grimes	6
1911	02/12: Wolves vs. Derby (W 0-1) – Leonard – Rams 4 points off top/Burnley; 2 GIH	4
1911	06/12: Derby vs. Burnley (W 2-0) – Bloomer, Leonard – Rams 2 points off top	3
1911	09/12: Derby vs. Leicester Fosse (W 5-0) – Bloomer 2, Leonard 2, Wright	3
1911	23/12: Grimsby Town vs. Derby (W 0-3) – Bloomer 2, Bauchop – Rams 2 points off top	2
1911	25/12: Derby vs. Grimsby T (W 2-1) – Bloomer, Bauchop – Burnley 1 point ahead	2
1911	26/12: Nottm F vs. Derby (W 1-3) – Bloomer, Bauchop, Leonard – RAMS GO TOP	1
1911	30/12: Derby vs. Clapton Orient (W 5-1) – Bauchop 3, Bloomer, Leonard	1
1912	13/01: FA Cup 1st Rd: Derby vs. Newcastle (W 3-0) – Bauchop, Richards, Leonard	1
1912	03/02: FA Cup 2nd Rd: Derby vs. Blackburn R (L 1-2) – Bloomer – they've learned!	1
1912	10/02: Glossop vs. Derby (L 3-1) – Bloomer – 4 without a win – déjà-vu?	3
1912	17/02: Derby vs. Hull (L 2-3) – Bloomer 2; 21/02: Derby vs. Birmingham (L 0-1)	3
1912	With 12 games to go, Derby win 9 and draw 3 – but were they too far behind...	3
1912	24/02: Derby vs. Blackpool (W 5-1) – Barnes 3, Sharpe 2 – 2 points behind Chelsea	3
1912	30/03: Leeds C vs. Derby (W 0-1) – Sharpe – Rams 2/7 pts behind Chelsea/Burnley	3
1912	08/04: Derby vs. Chelsea (W 2-0) – Leonard 2 – Rams close to 1 pt behind Chelsea	3
1912	09/04: Derby vs. Nottm F (W 1-0) – Leonard – Rams 2nd, now 3 pts behind Burnley	2

Year	Event	Pos
1912	13/04: Leicester Fosse vs. Derby (W 0-1) – Bloomer – Rams 1 point behind Burnley	2
1912	15/04: Fulham vs. Derby (D 0-0) – RAMS GO TOP OF DIV TWO ON GOAL AVG	1
1912	20/04: Derby vs. Gainsborough T (W 4-0) – Leonard 3 – Derby still top on GAvg	1
1912	22/04: Barnsley vs. Derby (W 0-2) – Buckley, Bauchop – Rams finish on 54 pts	1
1912	25/04: Chelsea win and draw level with Burnley on 52 points; both have 1 to play	1
1912	27/04: Chelsea beat Bradford PA and move into 2nd place behind Derby on GAvg	1
1912	27/04: Burnley have a better Goal Avg than Chelsea but lose to Wolves and blow it	1
1912	Derby finish season 1st (1:20) on 54 points – DERBY PROMOTED TO DIVISION ONE	1
1912	Steve Bloomer is Derby's leading scorer with 18 league goals (19 in all comps)	

Season 1912/1913 (Division One)

Year	Event	Pos
1912	14/09: Sunderland vs. Derby (W 0-2) – Barnes, Leonard sink Champs-in-waiting	10
1912	18/09: Derby vs. Everton (L 1-4) – Leonard – back down to earth with a bump!	12
1912	21/09: Tottenham H vs. Derby (W 1-2) – Bloomer, Leonard – W2, D1, L1; 2 GIH	12
1912	12/10: Derby vs. Man Utd (W 2-1) – Bloomer, Leonard – W4, D1, L2; 2 GIH	10
1912	26/10: Derby vs. Liverpool (W 4-2) – Bloomer 3 – 38 yr-old's 19th hat-trick for Rams	8
1912	09/11: Derby vs. Sheff Utd (W 5-1) – Bloomer 3 – Steve's 20th and final hat-trick	9
1912	16/11: Newcastle vs. Derby (W 2-4) – Bauchop 2, Bagshaw, Sharpe	7
1912	07/12: Derby vs. W Arsenal (W 4-1) – Buckley, Grimes, Bloomer, Leonard	9
1912	21/12: Derby vs. Man City (W 2-0) – Bauchop, Barnes – Rams only 1 point off top!	7
1912	28/12: Derby vs. Blackburn (W 1-0) – Walker – Rams 2 points off top (WBA)	4
1913	18/01: Derby vs. Tottenham H (W 5-0) – Bauchop 3, Bloomer 2 – 4 pts off top, GIH	6
1913	08/02: Derby vs. Notts Co (W 1-0) – Barnes – Rams 3 points off top with 1 GIH	8
1913	21/03: Everton vs. Derby (D 2-2) – Leonard, Barnes – 7 w/o win; Rams drop to 7th	7
1913	19/04: Derby vs. Bradford C (W 4-0) – Leonard 2, Sharpe, Barbour (W17, D7, L13)	9
1913	Derby finish season 7th (7:20), on 42 points, 12 points behind Champs, Sunderland	7
1913	Harry Leonard is Derby's leading scorer with 15 league goals (15 in all comps)	

Season 1913/1914 (Division One)

Year	Event	Pos
1913	06/09: Derby vs. Sheff Utd (L 3-5) – Bloomer 2 – last of Steve's 332 goals for Rams	14
1913	27/09: Derby vs. Bradford City (W 3-1) – Barnes, Scattergood (W2, D3, L1)	6
1913	25/10: Derby vs. West Brom (L 1-2) – Walker – 5 without a win – Rams drop to 12th	12
1913	01/11: Sheffield Wed vs. Derby (W 1-3) – Leonard, Barnes, Moore (W3, D4, L4)	11
1913	29/11: Man Utd vs. Derby (D 3-3) – Moore 2, Leonard – 4 without win	15
1913	20/12: Derby vs. Newcastle (W 2-0) – Moore, Leonard – (W5, D6, L7)	11
1914	01/01: Middlesbrough vs. Derby – (L 2-3) – Barnes 2 – three without a win	18
1914	03/01: Derby vs. Tottenham H (W 4-0) – Barbour, Barnes, Moore, (og)	15
1914	07/02: Derby vs. Blackburn (L 2-3) – Moore, Barnes – 4 w/o win – into drop-zone	19
1914	21/02: Derby vs. Everton (W 1-0) – Fordham – Rams climb out of bottom two	18
1914	28/02: West Brom vs. Derby (L 2-1) – Fellows – Rams slip back to 19th	19
1914	04/04: Derby vs. Man Utd (W 4-2) – Barnes 2, Leonard, Scattergood – 3 pts adrift	19
1914	18/04: Derby vs. Preston (L 0-1) – 4th defeat in 8 days; RAMS ALREADY RELEGATED	20
1914	Derby finish season 20th (20:20), on 27 points, 7 points from safety	20
1914	Horace Barnes is Derby's leading scorer with 24 league goals (25 in all comps)	

Season 1914/1915 (Division Two)

Year	Event	Pos
1914	02/09: Derby vs. Barnsley (W 7-0) – Fordham 3, Moore 2, Baker, Bethune (og)	2

Year	Event	Pos
1914	10/10: Derby vs. Leeds City (L 1-2) – Baker – 3 defeats in 4, Rams 5 points off top	11
1914	24/10: Derby vs. Arsenal (W 4-0) – Benfield 2, Moore, Leonard – (W5, D1, L3)	6
1914	31/10: Derby vs. Blackpool (W 5-0) – Leonard 2, Moore 2, Devonshire	3
1914	21/11: Grimsby vs. Derby (W 1-2) – Leonard, Benfield – Rams 4 pts behind H'field	2
1914	28/11: Derby (2nd) vs. Huddersfield (1st) (W 1-0) – Leonard – gap closed to 2 points	2
1914	05/12: Bristol C vs. Derby (W 2-3) – Leonard, Moore, Benfield – RAMS GO TOP	1
1914	26/12: Derby vs. Nottingham F (W 1-0) – Leonard – Rams now 3 points clear at top	1
1914	28/12: Leicester F vs. Derby (W 0-6) – Leonard 2, Moore 2, Benfield 2 – 5 pts clear	1
1915	02/01: Derby vs. Glossop (D 1-1) – Leonard – Stuart McMillan's one game for Rams	1
1915	16/01: Wolverhampton W vs. Derby (W 0-1) – Baker – Rams are now 6 points clear	1
1915	06/02: Derby vs. Hull C (W 4-1) – Moore 3, Leonard – Rams 5 pts clear of Arsenal	1
1915	13/02: Leeds City vs. Derby (W 3-5) – Leonard 2, Moore 2, Baker – Rams 7 pts clear	1
1915	27/02: Arsenal vs. Derby (W 1-2) – Benfield, Moore – Rams lead reverts to 7 points	1
1915	13/03: Derby vs. Lincoln City (W 3-0) – Moore 2, Baker – 5 points clear of Preston	1
1915	05/04: Derby vs. Leicester F (W 1-0) – Baker – RAMS PROMOTED TO DIV ONE	1
1915	24/04: Derby (1st) vs. Preston (2nd) (W 2-0) – Grimes, Leonard – RAMS CHAMPS	1
1915	Derby finish season 1st (1:20), on 53 points, 3 points ahead of Preston North End	1
1915	Jimmy Moore is Derby's leading scorer with 22 league goals (22 in all comps)	

Stats Blast: Derby's Busy Bees

During season 1909/1910, Alf Bentley (30), Jimmy Bauchop (21) and Horace Barnes (8) scored 59 of Derby County's 72 league goals – a remarkable statistic! No wonder they were nicknamed Derby's Busy B's! They must have been B awesome!

As an aside, Horace Barnes was Derby's leading scorer with 24 goals during season 1913/14, when Derby were relegated to Division Two. However, Barnes then left Derby to join Division One's Manchester City for what was then a record fee of £2500. It was a deal which prompted Arsenal manager, Leslie Knighton, to state: "Men argued with each other in pubs up and down England, not about the menace of the Kaiser's steel-helmeted hordes, but about the price paid for Horace Barnes!"

Quirk Alert: The Fourth Bee

The greatest "B" of all returned the following season (1910/11) and, quite naturally, went on to become top scorer with 20 league goals (we're talking Steve Bloomer, of course). Add in the other "B haul" of Bauchop (19), Bentley (14) and Barnes (10), and this time, the Four Bs had bagged an extraordinary SIXTY THREE of SEVENTY THREE league goals.

It doesn't end there though, as in four FA Cup ties, the Four B's scored ALL of the Rams' nine goals, with all four of them getting on the score sheet in the 5-0 3rd round victory over First Division Everton. This meant that the quartet netted SEVENTY TWO of Derby's 82 goals scored that season – which is 88% of all goals scored. I challenge anyone else to find a better strike rate for four same-initialled players, in one team, in one season! Surely not possible?

This team photo for the 1910/11 seasonincludes Derby's Busy Bees. Bottom row, 3rd, 4th and 5th left are Steve Bloomer, Alf Bentley and Jimmy Bauchop. Horace Barnes is seated, far right. Photo: Andy Ellis

Stats Blast: Hair's-Breadth

When Derby beat Manchester City 2-0 on 21st December 1912, this third win on the bounce moved them up to 7th place in Division One. Remarkably, though, they were only one point off top spot, as the following table reveals:

Pos	Team	Pld	W	D	L	GF	GA	GAvg	GD	Pts
League Division One, 21st December, 1912										
1	Manchester City	17	11	1	5	23	12	1.917	11	23
2	Aston Villa	19	9	5	5	49	28	1.750	21	23
3	Oldham Athletic	17	8	7	2	27	18	1.500	9	23
4	Sheffield Wed	17	10	3	4	30	25	1.200	5	23
5	Blackburn Rovers	18	8	6	4	40	22	1.818	18	22
6	West Bromwich A	17	9	4	4	34	22	1.545	12	22
7	**Derby County**	**17**	**10**	**2**	**5**	**35**	**28**	**1.250**	**7**	**22**

Quirk Alert: Ernald's Goal

Derby County drew their final league game of season 1912/13 at Man City, and Derby's goal-scorer was their goalkeeper, Ernald Scattergood! It was a penalty, of course, and Ernald remains the only goalkeeper to ever score for Derby in their 134-year history. Scattergood added two more the following season (1913/14), while he won his only England cap during the 1912/13 season in the 4-3 victory over Wales on 17 March 1913. He didn't score, though!

Stats Blast: Harry's Haul

At the end of the 1912/13 season, Harry Leonard was Derby's top scorer with 15 league goals. This meant that for the first time since 1893, Steve Bloomer wasn't Derby's top scorer, bar the four seasons he spent at Middlesbrough. Now aged 39, Bloomer nevertheless still managed to rattle up a 13-goal league haul in the top flight, plus one more in the FA Cup!

Perspective: Bernie Vann and Tommy Benfield

Bernie Vann, who played for Derby three times in 1907, was a Lt-Col in the Sherwood Foresters during World War I. His conduct during the war earned him a Military Cross and Bar as well as the French Croix de Guerre with Palm Leaves. However, he then received the Victoria Cross – the highest award for gallantry – for his bravery during the crossing of the Canal du Nord in September 1918. Tragically, he was killed by a sniper, five weeks before Armistice.

Meanwhile, Tommy Benfield also scored 15 league goals for Derby during season 1914/15. A sergeant with the Leicestershire Regiment, he was also tragically killed in France by a sniper, this time in September 1918 – less than two months before the end of World War I.

RAMS CHRONOLOGY: Between The Wars
The 1920s

Year	Event	Pos
Season 1919/20 (Division One)		
1919	For the 1919/20 season, Division One was increased from 20 to 22 teams	
1919	For this and the next five seasons, teams generally played each other back-to-back	
1919	06/09: Man Utd vs. Derby (W 0-2) – J Moore 2 – Rams unbeaten after 3	6
1919	08/09: Derby vs. Aston V (W 1-0) – Ritchie – Rams 3rd on same pts as leaders, WBA	3
1919	13/09: Derby vs. Bradford C (W 3-0) – Leonard 2, Bagshaw – RAMS TOP OF DIV 1	1
1919	20/09: Bradford City vs. Derby (L 3-1) – Wightman – Derby drop to 5th place	5
1919	24/09: Newcastle United vs. Derby County (D 0-0) – Derby climb back up to 3rd	3
1919	11/10: Derby vs. Notts Co (W 3-1) – Burton 2, Quantrill – first win in 5	9
1919	18/10: Notts Co vs. Derby (D 2-2) – Baker, Wightman – Rams are 4 points off top	6
1919	08/11: Derby vs. Sheffield Wed (W 2-1) – Leonard 2 – first win in 4	7
1919	20/12: West Brom vs. Derby (L 4-0) – 6 without win (D2, L4); Rams drop to 19th	19
1919	25/12: Derby vs. Arsenal (W 2-1) – Burton 2 – Rams move up to 17th	17
1920	24/01: Derby vs. Sheff Utd (W 5-1) – Lyons 2, Wightman, Thornewell, Barbour	16
1920	06/03: Preston NE vs. Derby (D 1-1) – Burton – 6 w/o win (D2, L4); Rams in trouble	20
1920	02/04: Everton vs. Derby (L 4-0) – Rams 21st and into relegation zone for first time	21
1920	03/04: Liverpool vs. Derby (L 3-0) – Rams are 1 pt behind Blackburn and Notts Co	21
1920	05/04: Derby vs. Everton (W 2-1) – Atkin, Lyons – 1 point above drop-zone	19
1920	10/04: Derby vs. Liverpool (W 3-0) – Burton 2, Leonard – 3 points clear of 21st	19
1920	24/04: Derby vs. Chelsea (W 5-0) – Burton 2, Lyons, Leonard, Thornewell	18
1920	Derby take 9 points out of 10 from last five games, and only just avoid relegation	18
1920	Derby finish season 18th (18:22), on 38 points, two points above the drop-zone	18
1920	Noah Burton/Harry Leonard top scorers with 12 league goals (Burton 13 all comps)	
Season 1920/21 (Division One)		
1920	02/10: West Brom vs. Derby County (L 3-0) – Rams bottom after 8 (W0, D4, L4)	22
1920	Derby sign striker Tewfik Abdallah only the second Egyptian to play in England	22
1920	09/10: Derby vs. Man City (W 3-0) – Burton, Murray, Abdallah – Derby up to 19th	19
1920	23/10: Derby vs. Arsenal (D 1-1) – Thornewell (W1, D6, L4)	18
1920	27/12: Derby vs. Bradford City (D 1-1) – Atkin – 12 without a win – Rams bottom	22
1921	01/01: Derby vs. Huddersfield (W 2-1) – Atkin, Thornewell – Rams out bottom 2	20

Year	Event	Pos
1921	23/02: Derby vs. Burnley (D 0-0) – another 6 without a win – Rams bottom again	22
1921	26/02: Sheff Utd vs. Derby (W 0-1) – Paterson – Rams are 4 points behind 20th	21
1921	12/03: Bradford PA vs. Derby (L 2-1) – Murray – Park Avenue leap-frog Rams	22
1921	19/03: Derby vs. Bradford PA (W 1-0) – Paterson – tit-for-tat – 2 pts from safety	21
1921	02/04: Newcastle vs. Derby (W 0-1) – Lyons – Rams three points behind Oldham	21
1921	16/04: Back-to-back draws against 2nd-placed Liverpool, but now 4 points adrift	21
1921	30/04: Back-to-back defeats to Aston Villa see Derby relegated with two to play	21
1921	Derby finish season 21st (21:22), on 26 points, 4 pts from safety; RAMS RELEGATED	21
1921	Bill Paterson is Derby's top scorer with 8 league goals (8 goals in all competitions)	
1921	Derby use 32 players during the 1920/21 season, equalling record set in 1905/06	
1921	Derby's 32 league goals was also the lowest number of goals in a season to date	
Season 1921/22 (Division Two)		
1921	10/09: Derby vs. Bristol City (W 5-1) – Paterson 3, Moore, Thornewell	10
1921	17/09: Bristol City vs. Derby (W 1-2) – Moore 2 – (W3, D1, L2)	7
1921	01/10: Derby lose back-to-back games to Nottingham Forest and drop to 12th	12
1921	22/10: Barnsley vs. Derby (L 2-1) – Wightman – Rams sink to 17th – (W4, D1, L6)	17
1921	19/11: Derby vs. Bury (W 1-0) – Paterson – 4 straight wins; Rams 5 points off top	10
1922	04/03: Leeds Utd vs. Derby (L 2-1) – Murphy – Rams now 5 points above drop-zone	16
1922	29/04: Derby vs. Rotherham County (W 4-0) – Lyons 4 – (W15, D9, L17)	11
1922	Derby finish 12th on 39 points, 6 pts clear of relegation; Rams' lowest finish to date	12
1922	Jimmy Moore is Derby's top scorer with 16 league goals (17 goals in all comps)	
1922	30/06: Jimmy Methven retires as manager after 31 years' service as player and manager, and is replaced by Cecil Potter – who arrives from Hartlepools – a path to be repeated somewhat more significantly, some 45 years later!	
Season 1922/23 (Division Two)		
1922	16/09: Derby vs. Sheffield Wed (D 1-1) – Paterson – Rams are unbeaten (W2, D4)	8
1922	07/10: Blackpool vs. Derby (L 3-2) – Storer, Wightman – three straight defeats	15
1922	28/10: Derby vs. Coventry City (W 4-0) – Paterson 2, Wightman, Lyons	13
1922	25/12: Derby vs. Crystal Palace (W 6-0) – Moore 5, Lyons – 4 wins on the trot	6
1923	13/01: FA Cup 1st Rd: Derby vs. Blackpool (W 2-0) – Moore, Lyons	7
1923	20/01: Derby vs. Fulham (W 2-0) – Lyons, Murphy – Rams now 4 pts behind 2nd	6
1923	03/02: FA Cup 2nd Rd: Bristol City vs. Derby (W 0-3) – Moore 2, Lyons	8
1923	24/02: FA Cup 3rd Rd: Derby vs. Sheffield Wednesday (W 1-0) – Moore	10
1923	26/02: Port Vale vs. Derby (W 2-3) – Stokoe, Murphy, Lyons - Rams 4 pts off 2nd	8
1923	10/03: FA Cup Quarter Final: Tottenham Hotspur vs. Derby (W 0-1) – Galloway	10
1923	17/03: Derby vs. Rotherham Co (W 1-0) – Lyons – Rams 5 pts off 2nd with 2 GIH	10
1923	24/03: FA Cup Semi-Final: Derby vs. West Ham United (L 2-5) – Moore, (og)	11
1923	Defeat knocks Rams sideways and their last 10 games result in W1, D2, L7	14
1923	Derby finish 14th (14:22), on 39 pts, 4 pts clear of relegation; a new lowest finish	14
1923	Jimmy Lyons/Jimmy Moore top scorers with 11 league goals (Moore 16 all comps)	
1923	21/05: Jimmy Moore, aged 34, makes England debut in a 4-2 win over Sweden in Stockholm, joined in side by Derby's George Thornewell; both players score!	
Season 1923/24 (Division Two)		
1923	25/08: Derby vs. Stockport County (W 4-1) – Galloway 2, Storer, Whitehouse	1
1923	22/09: Derby vs. Bristol City (L 2-3) – Galloway, Storer – (W3, D1, L3)	10

Year	Event	Pos
1923	29/09: Bristol C vs. Derby (W 0-8) – Storer 4, Galloway 2, Thornewell, Plackett	6
1923	29/09: Bristol C vs. Derby (W 0-8) – Derby's record league away victory	6
1923	06/10: Hull C vs. Derby (W 0-1) – Storer – Rams 3 pts behind leaders South Shields	3
1923	13/10: Derby vs. Hull City (W 4-1) – Murphy, Storer, Galloway, Whitehouse	2
1923	01/12: Derby vs. Crystal Palace (W 5-0) – Whitehouse 2, Galloway 2, Murphy	2
1923	08/12: Crystal Pal vs. Derby (W 0-1) – Galloway – Rams are 2 points behind Leeds	2
1923	15/12: Derby vs. Blackpool (W 2-0) – Storer, Whitehouse – RAMS GO TOP OF DIV 2	1
1923	26/12: Derby vs. Nelson (W 6-0) – Storer 4, Whitehouse 2 – Rams 1 point off Leeds	2
1923	29/12: Derby vs. Sheffield Wed (D 1-1) – Whitehouse – RAMS BACK ON TOP	1
1923	12/01: FA Cup 1st Rd: Derby vs. Bury (W 2-1) – Murphy, Whitehouse	2
1924	19/01: Derby vs. South Shields (W 6-1) – Storer 3, Plackett, Galloway, Murphy	1
1924	02/02: FA Cup 2nd Rd: Derby vs. Newcastle United (D 2-2) – Storer 2	3
1924	06/02: FA Cup 2nd Rd Replay: Newcastle United vs. Derby (D 2-2 AET) – Galloway, og	4
1924	09/02: Bury vs. Derby (L 1-0) – Rams drop to 6th but with games in hand	6
1924	11/02: FA Cup 2nd Rd, 2nd Replay: Derby vs. Newcastle (D 2-2 AET) – G'way, Th'well	6
1924	13/02: FA Cup 2nd Rd, 3rd Replay: Newcastle vs. Derby (L 5-3) – Galloway 2, Storer	6
1924	16/02: Derby vs. Man Utd (W 3-0) – Whitehouse 2 – Rams 4 points off top, 2 GIH	4
1924	15/03: Bradford C vs. Derby (W 1-2) – Galloway, Keetley – Rams 4 points off top	3
1924	29/03: Port Vale vs. Derby (L 2-0) – Rams have 40 points; Leeds/Bury have 47/45	5
1924	05/04: Derby vs. Port Vale (W 2-0) – Galloway, Bromage – Rams 3 points off Bury	3
1924	12/04: Leeds Utd vs. Derby (D 1-1) – Storer – Leeds/Bury/Derby; 49/47/43 points	3
1924	19/04: Derby vs. Leeds (W 2-0) – Storer, Whitehouse – LEE/BUR/DER; 50/49/45	3
1924	21/04: Derby vs. Coventry (W 1-0) – Whitehouse – LEE/BUR/DER; 52/49/47	3
1924	22/04: Coventry vs. Derby (W 0-1) – Galloway – LEE/BUR/DER; 52/49/49	3
1924	26/04: Leicester City vs. Derby (L 3-0) – LEE/BUR/DER; Pl: 41, 42, 41; Pts: 54, 51, 49	3
1924	Derby need to beat Leicester at home by 5 goals to pip Bury on Goal Average	3
1924	03/05: Derby vs. Leicester (W 4-0) – Moore 2, Storer, Galloway – Gypsy's again!	3
1924	Derby finish season 3rd (3:22), on 51 points, missing promotion by one goal	3
1924	Harry Storer is Derby's top scorer with 24 league goals (27 in all competitions)	
Season 1924/25 (Division Two)		
1924	Derby County buy the Baseball Ground from Sir Francis Ley for £10,000	
1924	30/08: Derby vs. Hull City (W 4-0) – Whitehouse 3, Storer	2
1924	01/09: Sheffield Wednesday vs. Derby (W 0-1) – Storer – RAMS TOP AFTER TWO	1
1924	13/09: Derby vs. Fulham (W 5-1) – Fairclough 4, Storer – 4 wins out of 5	1
1924	15/09: Blackpool vs. Derby (L 5-1) – Storer – Blackpool go top; Derby drop to 2nd	2
1924	20/09: Derby vs. Wolves (W 4-0) – Fairclough 2, Murphy, Storer – RAMS BACK TOP	1
1924	25/10: Derby vs. Clapton Orient (W 3-0) – Fairclough 2, Murphy – 9 wins from 12	1
1924	01/11: Crystal Palace vs. Derby (L 2-0) – Manchester United go top above Derby	2
1924	08/11: Derby vs. Southampton (W 3-0) – Storer, Galloway, Whitehouse – BACKTOP	1
1924	15/11: Chelsea vs. Derby (D 1-1) – Murphy – Man Utd win and go above Derby	2
1924	22/11: Derby vs. Stockport Co (W 2-0) – Fairclough 2 – Derby leap-frog Man Utd	1
1924	29/11: Man Utd vs. Derby (D 1-1) – Fairclough – Derby & Man Utd stay 1st and 2nd	1
1924	06/12: Derby vs. Leicester (L 0-3) – crucial defeat – Utd go top again; Leicester 4th	2
1924	20/12: Derby vs. Coventry (W 5-1) – Fairclough 2, Moore, Murphy, Whitehouse	2

Year	Event	Pos
1924	25/12: Oldham vs. Derby (W 0-1) – Whitehouse – United draw; DERBY GO TOP	1
1924	26/12: Derby vs. Oldham (W 1-0) – Fairclough – still top, United 2nd, Leicester 4th	1
1925	03/01: Derby vs. Portsmouth (W 6-1) – Fairclough 3, Moore 2, Whitehouse	2
1925	17/01: Fulham vs. Derby (W 0-2) – Moore, Whitehouse – RAMS TWO PTS CLEAR	1
1925	07/02: Derby vs. M'brough (W 3-1) McIntyre, Whitehouse, Moore – still 2 pts clear	1
1925	14/02: Port Vale vs. Derby (L 1-2) – Thornewell – Leicester now 2nd, 2 pts behind	1
1925	25/02: Derby vs. Bradford C (W 2-0) – Fairclough, Whitehouse – 3 points clear	1
1925	28/01: Clapton O vs. Derby (W 0-1) – Thornewell – Rams still 3 points clear at top	1
1925	07/03: Derby vs. Crystal Pal (W 3-0) – Whitehouse, Moore, (og) – 5 POINTS CLEAR	1
1925	14/03: Southampton vs. Derby (L 2-0) – 2 defeats on bounce; LEI 2 points behind	1
1925	21/03: Derby vs. Chelsea (W 1-0) – Storer – clinging on, one point ahead of Leicester	1
1925	28/03: Stockport vs. Derby (D 0-0) – Leicester go top; Rams 3 points ahead of Utd	2
1925	04/04: Derby vs. Man Utd (W 1-0) – Wightman – 5 pts clear of United with 6 to go	2
1925	11/04: Leicester vs. Derby (D 0-0) – LEI, DER, MAN on 52, 52, 50 points	2
1925	13/04: Derby vs. South Shields (D 0-0) – all three clubs draw – now 53, 53, 51 pts	2
1925	18/04: Derby vs. Stoke (L 1-2) – Murphy – LEI, MAN, DER; 55, 53, 53 points	3
1925	Rams draw last two games and finish 3rd – LEI, MAN, DER; 59, 57, 55 points	3
1925	From 5 points clear on 7th March, Rams win only 2 of last 11 scoring just 5 goals	3
1925	Derby finish season 3rd (3:22), on 55 points, two points short of promotion	3
1925	Albert Fairclough is Derby's top scorer with 22 league goals (22 in all comps)	
Season 1925/26 (Division Two)		
1925	Cecil Potter leaves Derby and George Jobey becomes the new manager	
1925	24/09: Derby sign inside-forward Harry Bedford from Blackpool for £3,500	11
1925	26/09: Nottingham Forest vs. Derby County (W 1-2) – Thoms, Murphy	8
1925	03/10: Derby vs. Swansea Town (W 5-0) – Bedford 3, Storer, Whitehouse	4
1925	17/10: Sheffield Wed vs. Derby (W 1-4) – Bedford 2, Murphy, Whitehouse	4
1925	24/10: Derby vs. Stoke (W 7-3) – Bedford 3, Storer 2, Whitehouse, Murphy	3
1925	05/12: Derby (4th) vs. M'brough (2nd) (W 2-0) – Haley, Thornewell – RAMS GO TOP	1
1925	14/12: Oldham vs. Derby (L 2-0) – Rams drop to 3rd behind Sheff Wed and Chelsea	3
1925	19/12: Derby vs. Stockport (W 4-0) – Murphy 2, Storer, Bedford – Chelsea top	2
1925	25/12: Port Vale vs. Derby (W 0-1) – Bedford – RAMS GO BACK TO THE TOP	1
1925	26/12: Derby vs. Port Vale (W 2-0) – Bedford, Storer – same points as Sheff Wed	1
1925	28/12: Derby (1st) vs. Chelsea (3rd) (W 4-2) – Bedford 2, Storer, Thoms	1
1926	02/01: Derby vs. Hull City (W 3-1) – Bedford 2, Murphy – 2 pts clear of Sheff Wed	1
1926	23/01: Derby vs. Blackpool (W 5-2) – Hart, Bromage, Keetley, Storer, Thornewell	1
1926	06/02: Derby vs. Nottm F (W 2-0) – Hart, Murphy – Rams & Owls 5 points clear	1
1926	13/02: Swansea T vs. Derby (L 2-0) – Rams now two points behind Sheff Wed	2
1926	27/02: Derby vs. Sheff Wed (W 4-1) – Bedford 3, Murphy – Rams 1 pt behind Owls	2
1926	06/03: Stoke C vs. Derby (W 0-1) – Gill – RAMS GO BACK TO THE TOP	1
1926	20/03: Wolves vs. Derby (L 2-0) – 2 defeats on bounce; WED, DER, CHE; 45, 44, 42	2
1926	27/03: Derby vs. Fulham (W 3-1) – Bacon 2, Gill ; WED, DER, CHE; 47, 46, 43	2
1926	06/04: Derby vs. Barnsley (W 4-0) – Bedford 2, Murphy, Thornewell; 53, 51, 47	2
1926	17/04: M'brough vs. Derby (W 1-2) – Bedford, Thornewell; 56, 55, 50; 3 to play	2
1926	24/04: Derby vs. Oldham (W 1-0) – Bedford – RAMS PROMOTED TO DIVISION ONE	2

Year	Event	Pos
1926	Derby finish season 2nd (2:22), on 57 points; WED, DER, CHE; 60, 57, 52 points	2
1926	Harry Bedford is Derby's top scorer with 27 league goals (28 in all competitions)	
Season 1926/27 (Division One)		
1926	The new main stand on Shaftesbury Crescent is opened	
1926	04/09: Derby vs. Liverpool (W 2-1) – Gill, Bedford – (W1, D0, L1)	13
1926	13/09: Sheffield Utd vs. Derby (L 1-0) – Rams have narrowly lost 3 out of 4	21
1926	02/10: Derby vs. Cardiff City (W 6-3) – Storer 2, Bedford 2, Gill, Murphy	15
1926	23/10: Derby vs. Tottenham H (W 4-1) – Bedford 2, Gill, McLaverty	16
1926	06/11: Derby vs. Leicester (W 4-1) – Bedford 2, Gill 2 – (W5, D1, L7)	17
1926	20/11: Derby vs. Blackburn (L 4-5) – Bedford, Gill 2, Storer – Rams drop to 20th, but with narrow defeats and big wins, Rams have a positive Goal Avg (1.038)	20
1926	04/12: Derby vs. Sunderland (W 4-2) – Mee 2, Gill, Storer – (W6, D1, L10)	21
1926	27/12: Derby vs. Bolton (W 2-0) – Gill, F'clough – Rams' first 30K gate (30,557)	20
1927	01/01: West Ham vs. Derby (W 1-2) – Murphy 2 – 3rd win on the spin	17
1927	08/01: FA Cup 3rd Rd: Bradford C vs. Derby (W 2-6) – Bedford 4, W'house, Murphy	17
1927	29/01: FA Cup 4th Rd: Derby vs. Millwall (L 0-2)	18
1927	12/02: Derby vs. Burnley (W 4-1) – Bedford 3, Gill – (W11, D1, L15)	18
1927	19/03: Derby vs. Sheff W (W 8-0) – Whitehouse 4, Bedford 3, Gill – Rams GD +10	17
1927	Derby then draw 6 in a row and win the last three, thus going 10 without defeat	12
1927	This includes two 4-4 draws at Blackburn away and Huddersfield at home	12
1927	Derby finish season 12th (12:22), on 41 points, scoring 86 league goals; Goal Avg is 1.178 and Goal Diff +13, better than 5th placed Burnley	12
1927	Harry Bedford/Jimmy Gill top scorers with 22 league goals (Bedford 26 all comps)	
Season 1927/28 (Division One)		
1927	10/09: Sammy Crooks makes Derby debut vs. Leicester (W 2-1) – Gill, Whitehouse	14
1927	24/09: Derby vs. Arsenal (W 4-0) – Gill, Whitehouse, Murphy, Crooks	14
1927	08/10: Derby vs. Bury (W 5-2) – Crooks 2, Murphy, Bedford, McIntyre	12
1927	19/11: Cardiff C vs. Derby (D 4-4) – Stephenson 2, Crooks, Bedford – 6 w/o win	20
1927	26/11: Derby vs. Sheffield Wed (L 4-6) – Whitehouse 2, Mee, Stephenson	21
1927	10/12: Derby vs. Blackburn (W 6-0) – Bedford 2, Stephenson 2, Crooks, Whitehouse	21
1927	24/12: Derby vs. Birmingham (W 4-1) – Stephenson, Mee, Crooks, Bedford	19
1927	26/12: Derby vs. Aston V (W 5-0) – Bedford 2, Whitehouse 2, Stephenson	19
1927	26/12: George Stephenson scores in a sixth consecutive game, matching John Goodall (1891/92), Alf Bentley (1909/10) and Horace Barnes (1913/14)	19
1928	02/01: Bolton vs. Derby (W 1-3) – Whitehouse 2, Stephenson – unbeaten in 7	14
1928	04/02: Arsenal vs. Derby (W 3-4) – Gill 3, Crooks – (W9, D7, L10)	13
1928	18/02: Bury vs. Derby (L 3-0) – 3 defeats on spin – but now cue a storming finish	17
1928	28/03: Derby vs. Man Utd (W 5-0) – Bedford 2, Stephenson 2, Whitehouse	12
1928	31/03: Derby vs. Cardiff City (W 7-1) – Bedford 4, Whitehouse 2, Crooks	7
1928	06/04: Sunderland vs. Derby (W 0-1) – Bedford – 5 wins in 7 – (W14, D9, L13)	6
1928	09/04: Derby vs. Sunderland (W 1-0) – Stephenson – Rams only 6 points off top	4
1928	14/04: Derby vs. Bolton (W 1-0) – Whitehouse – Rams now 5 points off top	4
1928	26/04: Ten-game unbeaten run ends at Blackburn and Derby lose 2 of last 3	4
1928	Derby finish season 4th (4:22), on 44 points, 9 points behind Champs, Everton	4

Year	Event	Pos
1928	Harry Bedford is Derby's leading scorer with 27 league goals (28 in all comps)	
1928	Derby finish with 96 goals, a club record for Div One matched again in 1936/37	
Season 1928/29 (Division One)		
1928	25/08: Derby vs. Blackburn (W 5-1) – Whitehouse 2, Bedford, Ramage, Crooks	1
1928	29/08: Arsenal vs. Derby (W 1-3) – Crooks, Bedford, Mee – RAMS TOP AFTER TWO	1
1928	15/09: Derby vs. Sheffield Wed (W 6-0) – Stephenson 3, Bedford 2, Whitehouse	2
1928	06/10: Birmingham vs. Derby (W 1-4) – Bedford 2, Whitehouse 2 – RAMS TOP	1
1928	27/10: Derby vs. Burnley (W 4-0) – Bedford 3, Storer – 2 points behind Blackburn	2
1928	03/11: Aston V vs. Derby (W 2-3) – Bedford, JC Robson, (og) – RAMS BACK ON TOP	1
1928	10/11: Derby vs. Leicester (W 5-2) – Whitehouse 2, McIntyre, Steph'son, JC Robson	1
1928	17/11: Man Utd vs. Derby (W 0-1) – Bedford – Rams 1 point ahead of Sheff Wed	1
1928	24/11: Derby vs. Leeds (L 3-4) – Whitehouse 2, Stephenson – Rams drop to 2nd	2
1928	08/12: Derby vs. West Ham (W 6-0) – Bedford 4, Whitehouse, Davison	2
1928	22/12: Derby vs. Bury (W 3-1) – Bedford, Stephenson, JC Robson – 3 points off top	2
1928	26/12: Derby vs Hudd'field (L 1-2) – JC Robson – new BBG record gate (30,651)	2
1929	19/01: Cardiff vs. Derby (L 3-0) – 6 w/o a win – Rams now 8 points off Owls at top	8
1929	02/02: Derby vs. Bolton (W 2-1) Bedford, Bowers – Jack scores on his debut	7
1929	09/02: Portsmouth vs. Derby (W 1-5) – Bowers 3, Crooks, Whitehouse	5
1929	23/02: Man C vs. Derby (W 2-3) – Stephenson 2, Crooks – Rams 5 points off Owls	6
1929	16/03: Derby vs. Aston Villa (W 1-0) – Barclay – but Rams now 7 points off Owls	3
1929	30/03: Derby vs. Man Utd (W 6-1) – Ruddy 2, Stephenson 2, Bedford 2	4
1929	02/04: Derby vs. Everton (W 3-0) – Ruddy, Stephenson, Bedford – 6 points off top	4
1929	06/04: Leeds United vs. Derby (D 1-1) – Ruddy – Rams 5 points behind Owls/top	3
1929	04/05: Bury vs. Derby (D 3-3) – Mee 2, Barclay; Rams no win in last 5 (D3, L2)	6
1929	Derby finish season 6th (6:22), on 46 points, 6 points behind Champs, Sheff Wed	6
1929	Harry Bedford is Derby's leading scorer with 27 league goals (30 in all comps)	
Season 1929/30 (Division One)		
1929	31/08: Derby vs. Sunderland (W 3-0) – Barclay 2, Bedford – a good start	8
1929	04/09: Derby vs. Aston V (W 4-0) – Stephenson 2, Bedford, Barclay – 2 out of 2	3
1929	07/09: Bolton vs. Derby (W 1-2) – Bedford, Stephenson – only Rams have max pts	1
1929	09/09: Aston Villa vs. Derby (D 2-2) – Bedford, Davison – Rams still lead the way	1
1929	14/09: Derby vs. Everton (W 2-1) – Bedford, Fereday – Rams 1 pt clear of Arsenal	1
1929	28/09: Manchester City vs. Derby (L 3-0) – 3 defeats on the bounce	7
1929	02/11: Derby vs. Blackburn (W 4-3) – Bedford 2, Barclay, Ramage – (W6, D3, L4)	5
1929	30/11: Derby vs. Birmingham (W 3-1) – Bedford, Stephenson, Crooks	4
1929	14/12: Derby vs. Grimsby T (W 5-4) – Stephenson 4, Bedford – Rams 2 pts off top	4
1929	21/12: Newcastle vs. Derby (W 2-3) – Bedford 2, Crooks – 2 pts behind Man City	2
1929	26/12: Derby vs. Leeds (W 3-0) – Bedford 3 – still 2 points behind leaders Man City	3
1929	28/12: Sunderland vs. Derby (L 3-1) – Derby exit the 1920s in 4th place in Div One	4

Stats Blast: A Great Ten-Game Season!
Derby won 3 and drew 2 of their first 5 games of the 1919/20 season. They also won 4 and drew 1 of their last 5 games, too. However, in between those two spells, the season was pretty poor, and that late run just kept them in Division One!

Quirk Alert: Potential Demise of the BBG

In 1923, Derby came close to moving to a stadium funded by the Derby Corporation in return for an annual rent of £500. The site was the Municipal Sports Ground on Osmaston Road...but, of course, the move came to nothing and the BBG was soon being further developed.

Quirk Alert: Works Like An Egyptian

On 4 September 1920 for an away game at Chelsea, Derby had to deploy 40-year-old Harry Maskrey in goal due to a goalkeeping injury crisis – having plucked Maskrey from the mid-week Works League where he played for British Cellulose! Meanwhile, one month later, Derby fielded only the second Egyptian to play in English football, when Tewfik Abdallah ran out for the Rams against Manchester City. Nicknamed "The Toothpick" because of his ability to dribble through defences, Abdallah also scored on his debut – although that proved to be his only goal in 12 games for the Rams. His excuse was perhaps that his football boots took some getting used to – on account of the fact that he preferred to play barefoot!

Quirk Alert: Insubordination and a very Merry Christmas

Jimmy Moore and Jimmy Lyons were Derby's joint top league scorers during season 1922/23. Now according to Gerald Mortimer's "Derby County The Complete Record", Jimmy Lyons was once suspended by Derby for "insubordination". The account doesn't enlarge on why.

Meanwhile, more than half of Jimmy Moore's 11 league goals came on Christmas Day and Boxing Day, when he bagged 6 in the double-header against Crystal Palace!

Quirk Alert: Neutral White Horses

During season 1922/23, Derby were 6th in January, and about to embark on a strong FA Cup run which saw them field the same 11 players in all five games. The Rams were eventually beaten by West Ham in the Semi-Final which was played at Stamford Bridge! Neutral? London? Just saying. Anyway, it was interesting that in Derby's 2-5 defeat, a Moore should score for Derby (that being Jimmy Moore, of course) – although, remarkably, Billy Moore did bag two for West Ham as well!

One also wonders at how close Derby came to being remembered for the White Horse Final, too; this being named after massive overcrowding resulted in mounted police being brought in to clear the Wembley pitch of overspilling spectators. The official attendance of this first-ever football match at Wembley was 126,047. The unofficial estimate is up to 300,000! West Ham lost 0-2 to Bolton – and a Moore didn't score in the Final either!

Quirk Alert: The Very Finest of Margins #2

Derby County finished third on the same points as Bury at the end of the 1923/24 season, with the ruling on who got promoted decided by Goal Average (goals scored divided by goals conceded). This system was used from the formation of the Football League in 1888 until 1976, when Goal Average was abolished in favour of the more attack-minded Goal Difference. It didn't help Derby in 1924 though, as they missed out by one of the finest margins ever recorded of 0.014 – a factor which is twice as unfortunate today, as they actually had a much better Goal Difference than

Bury, as the Top Three Table below reveals. Even more frustrating for Rams players and fans alike back in 1924, is had they scored just one more goal, their Goal Average would have been 1.810!

Pos	Team	Pld	W	D	L	GF	GA	GAvg	GD	Pts
1	Leeds United	42	21	12	9	61	35	1.743	+26	54
2	Bury	42	21	9	12	63	35	1.800	+28	51
3	Derby County	42	21	9	12	75	42	1.786	+33	51

Quirk Alert: Sanguine Directors

Derby's 2nd round FA Cup tie against Newcastle United during the 1923/24 season was the most extraordinary in the club's history. Over four games and 420 minutes, 20 goals had been scored, and both sides had rescued late replays, especially Newcastle in extra time of the second replay – and through a disputed free-kick, too! Derby were also the victim of some poor refereeing in the third replay – but despite being knocked out, the four games had been watched by 128,000 fans, and Derby pocketed £3,000. As the County Onlooker reported, this was "beyond the dreams of the most sanguine Derby director." However, the tie came at a cost; those four games took place inside 11 days, during which time Derby played both league games against Bury, losing them both!

Quirk Alert: Cecil Potter and the Philosopher's New Home

Cecil Potter was Derby County manager for three seasons between 1922 and 1925. With the Rams having twice missed promotion by a whisker (they finished third in his last two seasons), Potter had decided to retire to his native Sussex where he intended to take over a dairy business and talk philosophy with old friends. However, he was instead persuaded to take up the managerial position at Huddersfield Town which had been vacated by the great Herbert Chapman who, having guided Huddersfield to back-to-back Division One titles, had been tempted away to Arsenal – where his record would be just as spectacular. As for Cecil Potter, he completed the first ever Division One hat-trick of titles for Huddersfield in the 1924/25 season, and also became the first ex-Derby County manager to win a League Championship. Another would follow several decades later…

Stats Blast: Next Due in Season 2065/66

When George Jobey won promotion in his first season (1925/26), he became the first of only two Rams managers to achieve this. The other was Jim Smith – exactly 70 seasons later!

Stats Blast: Sight for Sore Eyes

Check out the Division Two table below after Derby had beaten Crystal Palace 3-0 on 7 March 1925. Alas, Derby only won two of their last 11 games and finished third!

Pos	Team	Pld	W	D	L	GF	GA	GAvg	GD	Pts
1	Derby County	31	20	6	5	66	26	2.538	+40	46
2	Manchester United	31	17	7	7	45	21	2.143	+24	41
3	Leicester City	29	17	6	6	72	27	2.667	+45	40
4	Chelsea	32	13	12	7	43	29	1.483	+14	38

Quirk Alert: Harry Bedford and the Bootlet of Fire

When Derby won promotion back to Division One in 1926, they finished runners-up, three points behind Sheffield Wednesday – whom they had beaten 4-1 both home and away. Inevitably, top scorer Harry Bedford (27 league goals; 28 in all) scored five of those eight goals against The Wednesday. At the end of his football career, Bedford settled in Derby and was initially Derbyshire County Cricket Club's masseur before working for the Rolls-Royce Fire Service between 1941 and 1964.

Stats Blast: Good Value 1

During the 1926/27 season, Derby's two games against Blackburn Rovers yielded 17 goals! Derby lost the home game 4-5 on 20th November, but ground out a 4-4 draw at Ewood Park on 9 April. The Blackburn defeat was also the only game that season missed by goalkeeper Ben Olney, when Bill Cowell stood in. Bet Bill enjoyed that! Bet he had high shorts as well!

Stats Blast: Good Value 2

During his early tenure as Derby manager, George Jobey signed three of his most important players for a mere £725 – Sammy Crooks for £300 from Durham City, Jack Barker for £275 from Denaby United and Jack Bowers for £150 from Scunthorpe and Lindsey United. Mind you, Johnny McIntyre cost only £10 – and he played 369 games for the Rams!

Stats Blast: Good Value 3

Between 19 November and 26 December 1927, George Stephenson scored in all six league games (7 goals), equalling a club record previously achieved by John Goodall (1891/92), Alf Bentley (1909/10) and Horace Barnes (1913/14). All six of the 1927 games were ridiculously high-scoring: Cardiff C (D 4-4), Sheff Wed (L 4-6), Blackburn R (W 6-0), M'brough (D 3-3), Birmingham (W 4-1) and Aston V (W 5-0). Mind you, Derby did rattle up a club record of 96 goals in that season helped by Bedford (27), Whitehouse (21) and Stephenson (17).

Quirk Alert: Dirty Leeds

During World War I, a number of internal wrangles over money at Leeds City led to both players and officials threatening to blow the whistle on illegal wages paid to players. In the end, the FA found out anyway, and ordered that Leeds City be disbanded before the commencement of the 1919/20 season. City's players passed to the FA, who then auctioned them, one of whom was George Stephenson who was sold to Aston Villa (pictured right, courtesy of W.W. Winter Ltd). He then joined Derby from Villa in November 1927 and made an immediate impact by notching the record described in "Good Value 3", above!

As an addendum to this story, you would have thought that with such a great strike rate aligned to such a great name, George Stephenson must have been nicknamed "The Rocket"...

George Stephenson.

Quirk Alert: Jobey Signs a Born Coal-scorer
George Jobey signed Sammy Crooks in September 1927 when he was playing for Durham City in the Third Division North, meeting him as he came off his coal lorry to clinch the signing! Outside right Crooks went on to score 110 goals in 445 appearances for the Rams. Sadly for Sammy, one of those 445 appearances wasn't in the FA Cup Final of 1946, when he missed out through injury. Between the wars, Sammy Crooks played 26 times for England, a feat only surpassed by Arsenal's Eddie Hapgood.

Sammy Crooks. PHOTO: W.W. Winter Ltd

The 1930s

Year	Event	Pos
1930	04/01: Derby vs. Bolton W (W 2-1) – Bedford, Crooks – Rams now 3 pts off top	3
1930	01/02: Derby (3rd) vs Man City (2nd) – (W 4-2) – Bedford 2, Crooks, Bowers	3
1930	05/02: Derby vs. West Ham (W 4-3) – Hope, Stephenson, JC Robson, Crooks	3
1930	19/02: Derby vs. Arsenal (W 4-1) – Bowers, Stephenson, Bedford, Crooks	2
1930	22/02: Liverpool vs. Derby (D 2-2) – Crooks, Barclay – Rams 3 points behind Owls	2
1930	01/03: Derby vs. M'brough (W 3-1) – Barclay 2, Bedford – 1 point behind Owls	2
1930	08/03: Blackburn vs. Derby (W 0-3) – Mee, Stephenson, Bedford – RAMS GO TOP	1
1930	15/03: Derby vs. Man Utd (D 1-1) – Crooks – Rams drop to 2nd on GAvg	2
1930	05/04: Birmingham vs. Derby (W 2-4) – Bedford 3, Barclay – 1 point behind Owls	2
1930	21/04: Derby vs. Sheffield Wed (W 4-1) – Barclay 3, JC Robson – 3 pts behind Owls	2
1930	22/04: Sheff Wed vs. Derby (L 6-3) – Barclay, Bedford, JC Robson – Owls crowned	2
1930	Derby finish season 2nd (2:22), on 50 points, 10 points behind Champs, Sheff Wed	2
1930	Harry Bedford is Derby's leading scorer with 30 league goals (31 in all comps)	
1930	Harry Bedford equals Alf Bentley's club record of 30 league goals set in 1909/10	
Season 1930/31 (Division One)		
1930	03/09: Derby vs. Leeds U (W 4-1) – Barclay 2, Crooks, Stephenson – W1 D1 L0	3
1930	17/09: Derby vs. Sunderland (W 4-1) – Bedford 3, Crooks – W3, D3, L0	4
1930	20/09: Derby vs. Grimsby T (W 1-0) – Bedford – Rams still unbeaten	3
1930	11/10: Derby (3rd) vs. Arsenal (1st) (W 4-2) – Stephenson 2, Bedford, Bowers	3
1930	11/10: Derby's victory over eventual Champions Arsenal was their 23rd at home without defeat; the run ended two weeks later with a 2-3 loss to Sheffield Wed	3
1930	18/10: Newcastle vs. Derby (W 2-5) – Crooks 2, Bedford, Bowers, Stephenson	3
1930	15/11: Aston Villa (4th) vs. Derby (3rd) (W 4-6) – Crooks 2 – leaders are Arsenal	2
1930	06/12: Derby vs. Chelsea (W 6-2) – Bowers 4, Stephenson 2 – (W9, D6, L3)	3
1930	Harry Bedford is sold to Newcastle due to the emergence of prolific Jack Bowers	3
1930	20/12: Derby vs. Huddersfield (W 4-1) – Bowers 2, Stephenson, Crooks	3
1931	17/01: Derby vs. Sheff Utd (W 4-3) – Bowers 3, Ramage – Rams 2 pts off top (ARS)	3
1931	07/02: Derby vs. Portsmouth (W 5-1) – Bowers 4, Crooks – Rams now 6 pts off top	4
1931	Derby lose 4 games either side of Portsmouth victory; Man City (4-3), Grimsby (5-3), Arsenal (6-3), Newcastle (1-5); overall 10-20; Bowers scores 7 of 10 goals	4

Year	Event	Pos
1931	14/02: Jack Bowers scores in 6th consecutive game, matching Goodall (1891/92), Bentley (1909/10), Barnes (1913/14) and Stephenson (1927/28)	4
1931	07/03: Derby vs. Bolton (W 4-1) – Bowers 2, Crooks, N Robson	4
1931	28/03: West Ham Utd vs. Derby (W 0-1) – Randall – (W16, D9, L9)	4
1931	04/04: Derby vs. M'brough (L 1-2) – Bowers – Rams drop to lowest placing/season	7
1931	18/04: Derby vs. Man Utd (W 6-1) – Bowers 4, N Robson, Crooks – Rams up to 5th	5
1931	18/04: This is Jack Bowers' third four-goal haul of the season, to add to two hat-tricks and five braces; see Quirk Alerts "The Powers of Bowers" for more...	5
1931	Derby finish season 6th, on 46 points, scoring 94 goals – 20 pts behind Arsenal	6
1931	Jack Bowers is Derby's leading scorer with a blockbusting 37 league goals (39 in all comps) – and he didn't get in the team until October! ; 37 league goals remains a club record, matched by Ray Straw in 1957/58, albeit in Division 3 North	
Season 1931/32 (Division One)		
1931	12/09: Blackburn R vs. Derby (L 3-2) – Crooks, Ruddy – Rams lose 4 of first 5	21
1931	16/09: Jack Nicholas ("Owd Nick"), plays first of 328 league games of next 331	17
1931	19/09: Derby vs. Portsmouth (W 2-1) – Bowers, Lewis – (W3, D0, L4)	13
1931	03/10: West Brom vs. Derby (L 4-0) – three defeats on the bounce	19
1931	28/11: Derby vs. Bolton W (W 5-1) – N Robson 2, Crooks, Bowers, Ramage	15
1932	02/01: Derby vs. Blackpool (W 5-0) – Crooks 2, Bowers, Ramage, Neal	14
1932	Derby sign Scottish left-winger Dally Duncan from Hull City for £2,000	
1932	06/02: Derby vs. M'brough (W 5-2) – Bowers 2, Crooks, Cooper, Nicholas	17
1932	02/04: Derby vs. Huddersfield (W 3-2) – Bowers 2, Ramage – (W12, D10, L16)	14
1932	Derby finish season 15th (15:22) on 38 points, but were never close to the drop	15
1932	Jack Bowers is Derby's leading scorer with 25 league goals (26 in all competitions)	
Season 1932/33 (Division One)		
1932	27/08: Leeds United vs. Derby (W 0-2) – Bowers, Duncan	6
1932	31/08: Derby vs. Blackburn R (W 2-1) – Bowers 2 – RAMS TOP OF INFANT TABLE	1
1932	03/09: Derby vs. Sheff Wed (W 2-0) – Ramage, Duncan – 3 wins in 3	2
1932	01/10: Derby vs. Man City (W 4-0) – Bowers 2, Crooks, Duncan – (W5, D2, L1)	3
1932	08/10: Arsenal vs. Derby (D 3-3) – Crooks 2, og – Rams/Arsenal remain 3rd/2nd	3
1932	15/10: Derby vs. Everton (W 2-0) – Bowers 2 – Rams 2 pts off leaders Aston Villa	3
1932	22/10: Chelsea vs. Derby (W 1-3) – Bowers 2, Duncan – top three all win	3
1932	26/10: Dally Duncan becomes first Derby player to play for Scotland (vs. Wales)	3
1932	12/11: Derby vs. Bolton (W 4-1) – Duncan 2, Bowers, Jessop – 3 points off top	3
1932	26/11: Derby vs. Leicester (W 3-2) – Bowers 3 – Rams 3 pts off leaders, Arsenal	3
1932	27/12: Blackpool vs. Derby (L 4-1) – Bowers – 6 w/o win – Rams now 8 pts off top	6
1932	31/12: Derby vs. Leeds Utd (W 5-1) – Bowers 2, Crooks, Duncan, Jessop	5
1933	14/01: FA Cup 3rd Rd: Wolves vs. Derby (W 3-6) – Bowers 3, Duncan 2, Crooks	6
1933	28/01: FA Cup 4th Rd: Southend United vs. Derby (W 2-3) – Bowers 2, Fabian	6
1933	04/02: Derby vs. Sunderland (W 3-0) – Bowers 3 – Rams 9 pts off top (Arsenal)	5
1933	18/02: FA Cup 5th Rd: Derby vs. Aldershot (W 2-0) – Bowers 2	6
1933	04/03: FA Cup Quarter-Final: Derby vs. S'land (D 4-4) – Duncan 2, Ramage, Bowers	6
1933	04/03: A new Baseball Ground record attendance is set of 34,218	6
1933	08/03: FA Cup Quarter-Final Replay: Sunderland vs. Derby (W 0-1 AET) – Ramage	6

Year	Event	Pos
1933	08/03: New Roker Park record att. of 75,118; 4 trainloads from Derby sent back!	6
1933	18/03: FA Cup Semi-Final : Manchester City vs. Derby (L 3-2) – Fabian, Crooks	8
1933	14/04: Portsmouth vs. Derby (L 2-0) – 10 leagues games w/o win (D5, L5)	8
1933	17/04: Derby vs. Portsmouth (W 2-0) – Bowers 2 – (W14, D14, L11)	6
1933	Derby finish season 7th (7:22), on 44 points, 14 points behind Champs, Arsenal	7
1933	Jack Bowers is Derby's leading scorer with 35 league goals (43 in all comps)	
1933	Jack Bowers' 43 goals in the 1932/33 season remains a Derby County record	
1933	Jack Bowers is also the league's leading scorer with those 35 goals	
Season 1933/34 (Division One)		
1933	The new double decker stand at the Osmaston End is opened	
1933	16/09: Derby vs. Leeds (W 3-1) – Bowers 3 – Rams first win at 5th attempt	14
1933	23/09: Stoke City vs. Derby (W 0-4) – Bowers 3, Crooks – (W2, D3, L1)	9
1933	23/09: Jack Bowers equals 1930/31 record of scoring in 6 consecutive league games, this time first 6 games of season; he is the only Ram to achieve this twice	9
1933	07/10: Derby vs. Birmingham (W 4-0) – Bowers 3, Ramage – Rams 3 pts off top	12
1933	18/11: Derby vs. Liverpool (W 3-1) – Bowers, Nicholas, Duncan – (W6, D5, L3)	6
1933	25/11: Tottenham (1st) vs. Derby (W 1-2) – Bowers, Duncan – 4 wins on spin	4
1933	02/12: Derby vs. Wolves (W 3-1) – Bowers 2, Groves – Rams 4 pts off top (Arsenal)	3
1933	09/12: Aston V vs. Derby (W 0-2) – Crooks, Groves – Rams 2 pts off top with GIH	3
1933	16/12: Derby vs. Sheff Utd (W 5-1) – Crooks 2, Bowers 2, Duncan – 7 straight wins	2
1933	25/12: Derby vs. Man City (W 4-1) – Bowers 2, Ramage 2 – Rams 3 pts off top, GIH	2
1934	01/01: Everton vs. Derby (W 0-3) – Bowers, Duncan, Alderman – 2 points off top	2
1934	27/01: FA Cup 4th Rd: Derby vs. Wolves (W 3-0) – Bowers 2, Crooks	2
1934	27/01: A new Baseball Ground record attendance is set of 37,727	2
1934	31/01: Leeds vs. Derby (W 0-2) – Bowers, Duncan – DERBY GO TOP OF DIV ONE	1
1934	03/02: Derby vs. Stoke (W 5-1) – Ramage 2, Duncan, Bowers, Crooks – 2 pts clear	1
1934	From here, Derby only win another 2 league games and start to go backwards	
1934	05/02: FA Cup 5th Rd: Arsenal vs. Derby (L 1-0)	1
1934	24/03: Derby vs. Chelsea (W 1-0) – first win in 7, but still only 3 points off top	3
1934	02/04: Derby vs. Arsenal (L 2-4) – Groves, Dobbs – Rams 8 points behind Arsenal	4
1934	07/04: Derby (4th) vs. Tottenham (3rd) (W 4-3) – Bowers 4 – Rams remain 4th	4
1934	Derby finish season 4th (4:22), on 45 points, 14 points behind Champs, Arsenal	4
1934	Jack Bowers is Derby's leading scorer with 34 league goals (37 in all competitions)	
1934	Jack Bowers finishes as the league's leading scorer with those 34 goals	
Season 1934/35 (Division One)		
1934	25/08: Derby vs. Chelsea (W 3-0) – Crooks, Bowers, Ramage	5
1934	22/09: Sunderland vs. Derby (W 1-4) – Bowers 3, Duncan – (W3, D1, L3)	10
1934	29/09: Derby vs. Tottenham (W 2-1) – Stockill 2 – Bowers serious knee injury	7
1934	06/10: Preston vs. Derby (W 0-1) – Rams 3 points behind leaders, Man City	5
1934	27/10: Derby vs. M'brough (W 2-0) – Ramage, Duncan – 2 points off top (Stoke)	5
1934	George Jobey signs striker Hughie Gallacher from Chelsea for £2,750	
1934	01/12: Leeds vs. Derby (L 4-2) – Ramage, Stockill – five without a win	13
1934	08/12: Derby vs. West Brom (W 9-3) – Crooks 3, Stockill 3, Gallacher 2, Nicholas	11
1934	15/12: Blackburn vs. Derby (W 2-5) – Hughie Gallacher bags all 5!	9
1934	22/12: Derby vs. Arsenal (W 3-1) – Stockill 2, Gallacher – (W10, D2, L8)	8

Year	Event	Pos
1935	31/01: Leicester vs. Derby (W 0-1) – Gallacher – Rams just 5 pts off top (Arsenal)	6
1935	02/02: Derby vs. Sunderland (W 3-1) – Gallacher, Groves – Rams 5 pts off top	5
1935	23/02: Grimsby Town vs. Derby (W 1-3) – Gallacher 3 – Rams still 5 pts off top	5
1935	20/03: Derby vs. Sheff Wed (W 4-0) – Groves, Ramage, Duncan, Gallacher	5
1935	06/04: Liverpool vs. Derby (W 1-3) – Crooks, Bowers, Bird – (W16, D8, L12)	5
1935	Derby finish season 6th (out of 22), on 45 points, 13 points behind Champs, Arsenal	6
1935	Hughie Gallacher is leading scorer with 23 league goals in 27 apps (24 in all comps)	
Season 1935/36 (Division One)		
1935	The new double decker stand at the Normanton End is opened	
1935	11/09: Derby vs. Preston NE (W 2-0) – Groves, Gallacher – (W2, D0, L2)	10
1935	21/09: Derby vs. Middlesbrough (W 3-2) – Napier 2, Gallacher – (W4, D1, L2)	5
1935	28/09: Aston Villa vs. Derby (W 0-2) – Boyd, Gallacher – 2nd to 5th on 11 points	5
1935	05/10: Derby vs. Wolves (W 3-1) – Nicholas, Ramage, Bird – Rams 1 pt off top	3
1935	19/10: Derby vs. Blackburn (W 1-0) – Duncan – Rams 1 pt behind Huddersfield	2
1935	02/11: Derby vs. Man City (W 3-0) – Napier 2, Gallacher – RAMS TOP OF DIV ONE	1
1935	30/11: Derby vs. West Brom (W 2-0) – Napier, Jessop – just 1 defeat in 15	2
1935	14/12: Derby vs. Grimsby (W 2-0) – Crooks, Bowers – Rams 3 pts behind Sun'land	2
1935	21/12: Sunderland (1st) vs. Derby (2nd) (L 3-1) – Bowers – Rams now 5 pts behind	2
1936	04/01: Bolton W vs. Derby (W 0-2) – Gallacher, Crooks – Rams 7 pts behind	2
1936	18/01: Derby (3rd) vs. H'field (2nd) (W 2-0) – Ramage, Halford – still 7 pts off top	2
1936	25/01: FA Cup 4th Rd: Derby vs. Forest (W 2-0) – new attendance record (37,830)	2
1936	29/01: Middlesbrough vs. Derby (W 0-3) – Bowers 2, Halford – gap now 5 points	2
1936	05/02: Derby County captain, Jack Barker, captains England (L 2-1 to Wales)	3
1936	15/02: FA Cup 5th Rd: Bradford City vs. Derby (W 0-1) – Bowers	2
1936	19/02: Derby vs. Sheff Wed (W 3-1) – Bowers 2, Crooks – now 8 points off top	2
1936	29/02: FA Cup Quarter-Final: Fulham vs. Derby County (L 3-0)	3
1936	07/03: West Brom vs. Derby (W 0-3) – Gallacher 2, Nicholas – still 8 pts behind	2
1936	21/03: Birmingham vs. Derby (W 2-3) – Gallacher 2, Duncan – 7 points off top	2
1936	04/04: Man City vs. Derby (L 1-0) – Sunderland win and go 8 points clear	2
1936	11/04: Derby vs. Leeds (W 2-1) – Hagan 2 – Rams close gap to 7 pts with 4 to go	2
1936	13/04: Derby vs. Chelsea (D 1-1) – Gallacher – Sunderland win and are Champs	2
1936	25/04: Derby vs. Sunderland (W 4-0) – Stockill 2, Halford, Gallacher – bit late!	2
1936	Derby finish season 2nd (2:22) on 48 points, 8 points behind Champs, Sunderland	2
1936	Hughie Gallacher is Derby's leading scorer with 15 league goals (16 in all comps)	
1936	Derby County reserves win the Central League Championship for the first time	
Season 1936/37 (Division One)		
1936	Former Ram Harry Storer becomes only man to play in a County Championship-winning side (Derbyshire) whilst also manager of a football club (Coventry)	
1936	05/09: Derby vs. Man U (W 5-4) – Rams 1-4 down, then Bowers bags 4 in 15 mins	9
1936	09/09: Derby vs. Sunderland (W 3-0) – Keen, Napier, Hagan – (W2, D0, L1)	3
1936	12/09: Sheff Wed vs. Derby (W 2-3) – Bowers, Napier, Duncan – (W4, D0, L1)	2
1936	23/09: Derby vs. Wolves (W 5-1) – Duncan 2, Bowers 2, Crooks – RAMS GO TOP	1
1936	At varying stages, Derby County have now been top of Division One during 6 out of 9 seasons, having also risen to 2nd in one of the other 3 seasons (1930/31)	

Year	Event	Pos
1936	26/09: Arsenal vs. Derby (D 2-2) – Stockill, Bowers – RAMS REMAIN TOP	1
1936	03/10: Derby vs. Brentford (L 2-3) – Bowers, Crooks – Rams 2nd behind P'mouth	2
1936	17/10: Jack Barker captains England against Wales (L 2-1); Crooks/Keen also play	2
1936	Derby sign striker Dai Astley from Aston Villa and sell Jack Bowers to Leicester	
1936	14/11: Charlton Athletic vs. Derby (L 2-0) – five games without a win	9
1936	21/11: Derby vs. Grimsby (W 3-1) – Astley 2, Stockill – Rams only 3 pts off top	6
1936	05/12: Derby vs. Leeds (W 5-3) – Astley 2, Ramage, Duncan, Keen – 2 pts off top	5
1936	12/12: Birmingham vs. Derby (W 0-1) – Ramage – Rams 1 point behind Charlton	2
1936	25/12: Everton vs. Derby (L 7-0) – Merry Christmas! – (W9, D4, L8)	9
1936	26/12: Derby vs. West Brom (W 1-0) – Stockill – Rams back up to 6th, 2 pts off top	6
1936	28/12: Derby vs. Everton (W 3-1) – Astley 3 – Rams 2 points off top (Arsenal)	5
1937	02/01: Man Utd vs. Derby (D 2-2) – Astley, Ramage – Rams now 4 points off top	6
1937	09/01: Derby vs. Sheff Wed (W 3-2) – Napier, Ramage, Astley – 3 points off top	5
1937	23/01: Preston vs. Derby (L 5-2) – Stockill 2 – 5 points off top – (W12, D5, L9)	6
1937	03/02: Derby vs. Arsenal (W 5-4) – Astley 3, Stockill 2 – Rams 4 points off top	4
1937	06/02: Brentford vs. Derby (L 6-2) – Astley 2 – Rams drop to 8th; Brentford are 3rd	8
1937	Derby sign striker Ronnie Dix from Aston Villa	8
1937	13/02: Derby vs. Bolton W (W 3-0) – Astley 2, Napier – 5 pts off top (Charlton)	7
1937	24/02: Derby vs. Man City (L 0-5) – home hammering from Champs-in-waiting	8
1937	20/03: Derby (7th) vs. Charlton (2nd) (W 5-0) – Crooks, Napier, Duncan, Astley, Dix	6
1937	27/03: Grimsby vs. Derby (W 3-4) – Crooks 2, Astley, Dix – Rams are 4 pts off top	6
1937	03/04: Derby vs. Liverpool (W 4-1) Nicholas, Napier, Astley, Dix – 4 pts off top	4
1937	Derby finish season 4th (4:22), on 49 points, 8 pts behind Champs, Man City	4
1937	Derby score 96 league goals, equalling their record (but also let in 90...)	
1937	Dai Astley is Derby's leading scorer with 25 league goals in 27 games (29 goals in all comps); includes 16 in first 14 games, while the 29 goals includes 3 hat-tricks	
Season 1937/38 (Division One)		
1937	11/09: Stoke vs. Derby (L 8-1) – Astley – Rams are without a win (W0, D3, L2)	20
1937	18/09: Manchester City vs. Derby (L 6-1) – Dix – but Rams still 3rd from bottom	20
1937	25/09: Derby vs. Arsenal (W 2-0) – Napier, Duncan – (W2, D3, L3)	17
1937	30/10: Derby vs. West Brom (W 5-3) – Crooks 2, Dix 2, (og) – (W3, D5, L5)	18
1937	04/12: Liverpool vs. Derby (W 3-4) – Dix, Astley, Napier, Nicholas – (W5, D7, L6)	16
1937	11/12: Derby vs. Chelsea (W 4-0) – Dix 2, Astley, Griffith (og) – (W6, D7, L6)	12
1937	27/12: Derby vs. Bolton W (W 4-2) – Astley 2, Duncan 2 – (W7, D8, L6)	12
1938	15/01: Tim Ward replaces Errington Keen, and is ever-present to end of season	15
1938	29/01: Derby vs. Man C (L 1-7) – Derby's equal-heaviest-ever home defeat	13
1938	02/02: Derby vs. Stoke (W 4-1) Duncan 2, Astley, Crooks – (W9, D8, L9)	9
1938	02/04: Derby vs. Portsmouth (W 1-0) – Dix – Rams only 6 pts off leaders, Arsenal	9
1938	16/04: Derby vs. Liverpool (W 4-1) – Nicholas, Crooks, Dix, Astley – (W15, D9, L13)	9
1938	Rams lose 4 of last 5 to finish 13th, with 40 points, 12 pts behind Champs Arsenal	13
1938	Dai Astley is Derby's leading scorer with 17 league goals (17 goals in all comps)	
Season 1938/39 (Division One)		
1938	03/09: Aston Villa vs. Derby (W 0-1) – Travis – (W2, D1, L0)	3
1938	14/09: Arsenal vs. Derby (W 1-2) – Duncan, Stockill – (W4, D1, L1)	2

Year	Event	Pos
1938	24/09: Derby vs. Stoke C (W 5-0) – Dix 2, Stockill 2, Duncan – same pts as Everton	2
1938	Derby sign striker Dave McCulloch from Brentford for a record Rams fee of £9,500	2
1938	22/10: Derby vs. Man Utd (W 5-1) – McCulloch 2, Dix, Crooks, Vose (og)	2
1938	29/10: Chelsea vs. Derby (W 0-2) – Dix, Astley – RAMS TWO POINTS CLEAR AT TOP	1
1938	26/11: Leeds vs. Derby (W 1-4) – McCulloch 2, Dix, Crooks – Rams 3 points clear	1
1938	10/12: Leicester vs. Derby (W 2-3) – McCulloch 2, Dix – Rams are 2 points clear	1
1938	17/12: Derby vs. M'brough (L 1-4) – McCulloch – Rams are still 2 points clear	1
1938	24/12: Wolves vs. Derby (D 0-0) – Everton win to close the gap to one point	1
1938	26/12: Everton (2nd) vs. Derby (1st) (D 2-2) – Dix, McCulloch – Rams remain top	1
1938	27/12: Derby (1st) vs. Everton (2nd) (W 2-1) – Duncan, McCulloch – 3 pts clear	1
1938	31/12: Derby vs. Aston Villa (W 2-1) – Dix, Astley – RAMS GO FIVE POINTS CLEAR	1
1939	28/01: Stoke City vs. Derby (L 3-0) – Everton close the gap to one point	1
1939	01/02: Derby vs. Grimsby T (W 4-1) – Dix 2, Crooks, Duncan – still 1 point clear	1
1939	04/02: Blackpool vs. Derby (D 2-2) – Duncan, Hinchcliffe – Everton overhaul Derby	2
1939	11/03: Preston vs. Derby (L 4-1) – McCulloch – a disastrous run of 6 games without a win – Rams down to 3rd, 6 pts behind Everton and 3 pts behind Wolves	3
1939	18/03: Derby vs. Charlton (W 3-1) – Jackie Stamps scores twice on debut	3
1939	01/04: Derby vs. Leeds (W 1-0) – McCulloch – Rams now 7 pts behind Everton	3
1939	Derby lose 4 of last 5 games to finish 6th, on 46 points, 13 behind Champs, Everton	6
1939	Derby had been top of Division One for 15 weeks between October and February; alas, they then lost 9 of their last 14 games from the 11th February onwards	
1939	Ronnie Dix Dave McCulloch leading scorers with 16 league goals (16 in all comps)	
Season 1939/40 (Division One)		
1939	The 1939/40 season is three games old when World War II breaks out with Derby in 7th (W2, D0, L1); the season is cancelled as are the contracts of all players	7
1939	New signing Billy Redfearn therefore only plays 3 games for Rams, while Verdun Jones – named after World War I – has his career effectively ended by WWII!	

Stats Blast: The Powers of Bowers (1930/31)

The above early 1930s' statistics are dominated by Jack Bowers, including that hat-trick of quartets scored during the 1930/31 season. However, when Bowers bagged 4 against Portsmouth on 7 February 1931, it brought his total in five consecutive games to an astonishing FOURTEEN goals – a strike rate of 2.8 goals per game. This included a brace against Birmingham (W 2-1), a hat-trick against Sheffield United (W 4-3), a brace against Manchester City (L 3-4), another hat-trick against Grimsby Town (L 3-5), and then the four against Portsmouth (W 5-1). He also scored one in the next game against Arsenal, joining an esteemed company of Derby strikers to score in six games on the bounce.

Bowers actually scored 37 league goals during the 1930/31 season, a statistic that is all the more extraordinary when considering the fact that he didn't play in the first nine games of the season. Given his strike-rate of 37 goals in 33 games (1.12 goals per game, or a 112% strike rate) we can therefore estimate that he would have scored 47 goals had he played the full season. However, that still wouldn't have made him the league's top scorer, that particular season – as that was Aston Villa's Tom "Pongo" Waring with 49 goals!

Stats Blast: The Powers of Bowers (1932/33)
Jack Bowers was the Division One leading scorer during season
1932/33, with 35 goals from 41 league appearances. He added
another 8 in six FA Cup appearances that season.

Stats Blast: The Powers of Bowers (1933/34)
Jack is Derby's leading scorer again with 34 league goals in 37
games, adding another 3 in the FA Cup. He also matched his earlier
achievement of scoring in six consecutive games (10 goals), which also
happened to be the first six games of the season. He is the only Rams
player to score in 6 consecutive games. He later scored in 5 consecutive
games in November and December 1933, but only managed a mere
6 goals in those 5 games!

Jack Bowers is Derby
County's second top
scorer of all time, scoring
183 goals in 220 games
between 1928-1936.

PHOTO: W.W. Winter Ltd

Stats Blast: The Powers of Bowers (1934-1936)
Jack suffered a serious knee injury in September 1934 and missed
most of the 1934/35 season. In the meantime, Derby signed Hughie
Gallacher, and so the following season, Jack played a lot of games for Derby reserves – where,
naturally, he bagged 30 goals as Derby County won the Central League Championship.

Quirk Alert: Just Like That!
Derby captain Tommy Cooper captained England for the first time vs. Scotland on 14 April 1934
(England won 3-0), and did so twice more, vs. Hungary and Czechoslovakia, that summer. Not
to be outdone, Jack Bowers played in the Scotland match, too – and scored, of course. Completing
a trio of Derby County players in the England side was Sammy Crooks, while later Derby County
legend Raich Carter (1945-1948) was also in the side. Cooper's honour saw him join esteemed
company in the shape of previous Derby County and England captains, John Goodall and Steve
Bloomer.

Perspective: Tommy Cooper
Tragically, Tommy Cooper was killed in a motorcycle accident in Aldeburgh in June 1940, while
serving as a sergeant with the Military Police. He died from a head-on collision with a double
decker bus, and the outcome from the resulting enquiry meant that it became illegal for despatch
riders to not wear a crash helmet. Tommy was 36 years old.

Quirk Alert: Lost 18-2
On 24 February 1937, Derby lost 0-5 at home to eventual 1936/37 Champions, Manchester
City. It got even worse the following season (1937/38) when they lost 6-1 at Maine Road on
18th September 1937 and by a record 1-7 at home on 29th January 1938. But even more remarkable, is the fact that REIGNING CHAMPIONS, Manchester City, having slaughtered Derby
13-2 on aggregate that season – WERE RELEGATED!

Quirk Alert: Merry Christmas, Ken

Goalkeeper Ken Scattergood made his debut for Derby on Christmas Day 1936, away at Everton. He didn't enjoy his festive afternoon though – the Rams lost 7-0, which was the First Division's biggest defeat that season! Poor Ken was dropped for the next game! Remarkably, despite finishing fourth, Derby also contrived to be on the wrong end of the biggest **home** defeat of the season, too – 0-5 at home to Manchester City on the 24 February 1937.

Quirk Alert: #Fearless

One final call-out for Jack Bowers. Gerald Mortimer in Derby County The Complete Record, describes Jack as "fearless, prepared to go in where there was every chance of being hurt if there was a sniff of a goal". It is rather appropriate, therefore, that when he left Derby County in November 1936, he went to #Fearless Leicester City!

Stats Blast: Rams International

In November 1938, Ronnie Dix played for England against Norway. This meant that Derby fielded an all-star international strike-force for part of the 1938/39 season, including Sammy Crooks (Eng), Dai Astley (Wal), Dave McCulloch (Sco), Ronnie Dix (Eng) and Dally Duncan (Sco – pictured right).

Stats Blast: Men For All Season

At the end of the 1938/39 season, four Derby County players had played in all 42 league games – a joint record for the Rams along with seasons 1893/94 and 1895/96. The four players in 1938/39 were full back Jack Nicholas, centre half Ralph Hann, inside forward Ronnie Dix and winger Dally Duncan. Ralph Hann was also the father of Tomorrow's World presenter Judith Hann!

Dally Duncan.
PHOTO: W.W. Winter Ltd

Stats Blast: Lovely Jobey

In the 14 seasons under George Jobey, from 1925/26 to 1938/39, Derby County averaged fractionally under 80 league goals per season, and banged in more than 90 league goals in four of those seasons! In their 13 pre-war Division One seasons, Derby also finished in the top half of the table ten times and supplied two England captains: Jack Barker and Tommy Cooper.

Jack Stamps, signed by George Jobey in 1939, and destined to become a Derby County legend. PHOTO: W.W. Winter Ltd.

RAMS CHRONOLOGY: Finally – FA Cup Glory

The 1940s

Year	Event
1941	Derby found guilty of financial irregularities during George Jobey's tenure, relating to illegal sign-on inducements and paying salaries over max wage; Jobey banned for 10 years
1941	The Osmaston End is damaged by German bombs and is not fully repaired until 1946
1945	Derby win League North (Second Period) & Midland Cup, beating Aston Villa 9-0 on agg
Season 1945/46 (FA Cup)	
1945	Qualifying rounds played Sep to Nov 1945; First Round takes place on 17th & 24th Nov
1945	All games from the First Round to the Quarter Finals are played over two legs
1945	Derby sign Peter Doherty from Man City and Raich Carter from S'land for £6,000 each
1946	Stuart McMillan (son of Derby legend, Johnny McMillan), becomes Rams manager, taking over from Ted Magner who has moulded a superb team during the war
1946	DERBY COUNTY WIN THE FA CUP FOR THE FIRST (AND ONLY) TIME – HERE'S HOW...

Rd	Date	Rams Opponents (Venue)	Result	Agg	Goalscorers	Att.
3	05/01	Luton Town (A)	W 0-6		Stamps 4, Crooks, Carter	16,792
	09/01	Luton Town (H)	W 3-0	W 9-0	Carter 2, Morrison	16,629
4	26/01	West Bromwich Albion (H)	W 1-0		Doherty	31,795
	30/01	West Bromwich Albion (A)	W 1-3	W 1-4	Carter, Stamps (pen), Harrison	37,734
5	09/02	Brighton & Hove Albion (A)	W 1-4		Doherty 2 (1 pen), Carter 2	22,000
	13/02	Brighton & Hove Albion (H)	W 6-0	W 10-1	Carter 3, Doherty 2, Crooks	32,000
QF	02/03	Aston Villa (A)	W 3-4		Doherty 2, Carter, Crooks	76,588
	09/03	Aston Villa (H)	D 1-1	W 5-4	Carter	32,000
SF	23/03	Birmingham City[1]	D 1-1		Carter	65,000
	27/03	Birmingham City[2]	W 4-0 (AET)		Doherty 2, Stamps 2	80,407[4]
F	27/04	Charlton Athletic[3]	W 4-1 (AET)		Turner (og), Doherty, Stamps 2	98,215

[1]Hillsborough; [2]Maine Road; [3]Wembley; [4]A record attendance for a midweek game outside of the FA Cup Final

Jack Nicholas introduces King George VI to Chick Musson before the commencement of the 1946 FA Cup Final. Next in line are Raich Carter, Peter Doherty and Dally Duncan. PHOTO: PA Images

As an aside, back in January 1946, Carter was within an hour of NOT becoming a Derby County player. Carter and Derby secretary, Jack Catterall, missed their train connection at York, and had to take a taxi to Sunderland where the appropriate forms were signed with an hour to spare before the third-round deadline.

Quirk Alert: A Turner for the Worse

Derby's opening goal in the FA Cup Final was an own goal scored by Charlton's Bert Turner, in the 85th minute. Remarkably, though, Turner scored at the other end a minute later from a free-kick. He therefore became the first player to score at both ends in an FA Cup Final – a feat which would be later replicated by Tommy Hutchison in 1981 and Gary Mabbutt in 1987. Turner made two records that day, though, as he also became the oldest player to score in an FA Cup Final (aged 36 years and 312 days).

Quirk Alert: Don't Even Think It!

When Derby took the lead in the FA Cup final, in the 85th minute, superstitious Rams fans perhaps began to think that the Gypsy's Curse was a load of old tosh after all. Imagine how they then felt a minute later – after Turner equalised with a heavily deflected shot that ricocheted into the opposite corner of the net to which goalkeeper Vic Woodley was diving!

Quirk Alert: Bursting the Myth

Jackie Stamps might have wrapped the game up inside the ninety minutes, after Turner's equaliser, but when clean through, the ball burst when Stamps shot for goal. Those gypsies must have shared a knowing look, right there and then! Thankfully, Stamps went on to score twice with the new ball as Derby beat Charlton 4-1 in extra-time. But incredibly, one week earlier, Derby had beaten Charlton Athletic 3-1 in a Football League South game as well – and the ball had burst in that game following a Jackie Stamps shot, too!

As for the Gypsies Curse, rumour has it that captain Jack Nicholas had crossed the palm of a local gypsy with silver prior to the FA Cup Final!

Jack Stamps' effort in the second minute of extra-time is parried by Charlton goalkeeper Sam Bartram, and Peter Doherty puts the loose ball into the net to give Derby a 2-1 lead.
PHOTO: PA Images

Quirk Alert: Under-Cover Operation

It would appear that the 1946 FA Cup Final was under threat in the days leading up to it – the reason being that the Derby County players' wives had been allocated some of the cheapest seats that weren't under cover. Apparently, Derby's senior players issued an ultimatum: sort it or there will be no match. Happily, the players' wives were moved to covered seating!

Jack Nicholas receives the FA Cup from King George VI. PHOTO: PA Images

Quirk Alert: Double Bubble

The players of both Derby and Charlton received two medals for appearing in the 1946 FA Cup Final. This was due to a shortage of gold following the end of World War II, and hence on the day, the players were presented with bronze medals. These were subsequently upgraded to gold medals a few months later when supplies became more plentiful.

Stats Blast: Perfect Ten

During Derby's FA Cup run of 1946, Peter Doherty wore the number 10 shirt, played 10 of the 11 games …and scored 10 goals along the way, with his 10th goal putting Derby 2-1 up in the Final.

Stats Blast: Striking it Hot

Check out the phenomenal Cup strike rates of Derby's 1946 FA Cup strike-force:

Player	Games	Goals	Strike Rate (Goals per Game)
Raich Carter	11	12	1.10
Peter Doherty	10	10	1.00
Jackie Stamps	8	9	1.13

Quirk Alert: Goalkeeper's Union

Three different goalkeepers played in Derby's eleven-game FA Cup run of 1946. Poor Frank Boulton was so badly clattered by Swansea Town's Trevor Ford in a Football League South game on 16th February 1946 that he was ruled out for the season, opening the way for Bill Townsend to play the Quarter Final games, and Vic Woodley to play the Semi-Final and Final.

Perspective: Tim Ward

As Tim Ward wasn't formally demobbed from the British army, he missed all-but one of Derby's FA Cup games, including the Final. However, far from being bitter, Tim's response was: "So many of my friends were killed in the war and I regarded myself as lucky to emerge from it, rather than unlucky to miss Wembley."

Derby County's FA Cup winning team of 1946. Back Row: Jim Bullions, Jack Nicholas, Vic Woodley, Leon Leuty, Jack Howe, Chick Musson; Front Row: Stuart McMillan (manager), Reg Harrison, Raich Carter, Jackie Stamps, Peter Doherty, Dally Duncan, Dave Willis (Trainer). PHOTO: W.W. Winter.

As a quirky aside, Reg Harrison won an FA Cup winners medal before he had played a league game!

RAMS CHRONOLOGY: From Glory to Obscurity

The 1940s

Year	Event	Pos
Season 1946/47 (Division One – NB: Fixtures the same as for the 1939/40 season)		
1946	04/09: Derby vs. Portsmouth (W 2-0) – Carter, Stamps – (W1, D0, L1)	7
1946	14/09: Stoke vs. Derby (L 3-2) – Carter, Doherty – 3 defeats on the spin	18
1946	21/09: Arsenal vs. Derby (W 0-1) – Broome – Rams drop 2 as others win bigger	20
1946	Dally Duncan leaves Derby to become player-coach at Luton Town	
1946	12/10: Derby vs. Blackburn (W 2-1) – Stamps 2 – two wins on the spin	14
1946	23/11: Bolton vs. Derby (L 5-1) – Broome – 6 games without a win	20
1946	14/12: Derby vs. Grimsby (W 4-1) – Morrison 2, Broome 2 – (W7, D2, L9)	15
1946	21/12: Leeds vs. Derby (W 1-2) – Carter, Stamps – four wins on the bounce	12
1946	26/12: Derby vs. Everton (W 5-1) – Doherty 2, Harrison 2, Ward – (W9, D2, L10)	12
1946	28/12: Derby vs. Sunderland (W 5-1) – Carter 2, Stamps 2, Morrison	10
1946	Peter Doherty leaves Derby to join Huddersfield Town	
1947	18/01: Derby vs. Stoke City (W 3-0) – Carter, Stamps, Harrison – (W11, D2, L11)	10
1947	15/03: Derby vs. Manchester United (W 4-3) – Broome 2, Carter, Antonio	11
1947	08/04: Wolves vs. Derby (L 7-2) – Carter 2 – (W14, D4, L16)	14
1947	03/05: Derby vs. Huddersfield Town (W 1-0) – Broome – (W17, D4, L17)	11
1947	31/05: Portsmouth vs. Derby (W 1-2) – Carter, Broome – the "latest" league game Derby ever play – although the last game sees Sheff Utd beat Stoke – on 14th June!	14
1947	Derby finish season in 14th place (14:22) on 41 points, 16 pts off top/from drop	14
1947	Raich Carter is Derby's leading scorer with 19 league goals (21 in all competitions)	
Season 1947/48 (Division One)		
1947	Derby sign Billy Steel from Morton for £15,500, a British transfer record	
1947	26/08: Burnley vs. Derby (W 0-2) – Carter, Stamps – (W1, D1, L0)	2
1947	27/09: Sunderland vs. Derby (D 1-1) – Harrison – no win in 5	16
1947	04/10: Derby vs. Grimsby (W 4-1) – Morrison 2, Broome, Antonio – (W3, D4, L4)	11
1947	25/10: Liverpool vs. Derby (D 2-2) – Steel (2) scores first goals for Derby	9
1947	01/11: Derby vs. Middlesbrough (W 4-2) – Morrison 2, Broome, Carter	7
1947	08/11: Derby vs. Sheffield United (W 2-1) – Broome, Carter – (W6, D6, L4)	5
1947	22/11: Charlton Ath vs. Derby (W 1-5) – Harrison 3, Carter, Oliver – 9 w/o defeat	4
1947	29/11: Derby vs. Arsenal (W 1-0) – Harrison – Derby end Arsenal's unbeaten start	3
1947	06/12: Preston vs. Derby (L 7-4) – Morrison 3, Howe – 1st defeat in 11 games	6
1947	25/12: Blackburn vs. Derby (W 3-4) – Carter 2, Steel, Morrison – 1st of 6 wins	4
1947	27/12: Derby vs. Blackburn (W 5-0) – Carter 2, Harrison 2, Morrison	4
1948	03/01: Derby vs. Chelsea (W 5-1) – Stamps 2, Steel 2, Carter – 3rd win on bounce	5
1948	10/01: FA Cup 3rd Rd: Derby vs. Chesterfield (W 2-0) – Stamps, Harrison	5
1948	17/01: Everton vs. Derby (W 1-3) – Stamps 2, Steel – (W12, D8, L6)	4
1948	24/01: FA Cup 4th Rd: Crewe vs. Derby (W 0-3) – Steel 2, Harrison	4
1948	07/02: FA Cup 5th Rd: Middlesbrough vs. Derby (W 1-2) – Harrison, Stamps	4
1948	14/02: Derby vs. Sunderland (W 5-1) – Carter 4, Morrison – games in hand, too	3
1948	21/02: Grimsby vs. Derby (W 2-3) – Stamps 2, Morrison – 9 straight wins (6L, 3FA)	3
1948	06/03: FA Cup QF Replay: Derby vs. QPR (W 5-0) – Stamps 2, Carter 2, Steel	5

Year	Event	Pos
1948	13/03: FA Cup Semi-Final: Man Utd vs. Derby (L 3-1) – Steel – yep, at Hillsborough	5
1948	29/03: Derby vs. Blackpool (W 1-0) – Carter – Rams are 5th but with 4 GIH on top 4	5
1948	29/03: Raich's last goal for Derby before joining Hull as player & assistant manager	5
1948	14/04: Derby vs. Wolves (L 1-2) – Stamps – 4 defeats in 5 – season implodes again	7
1948	17/04: Arsenal vs. Derby (W 1-2) – Stamps, Steel – Rams double over leaders	6
1948	21/04: Bolton W vs. Derby (W 0-3) – Broome, Harrison, Aspinall (og)	5
1948	28/04: Derby vs. Portsmouth (W 2-1) – Broome, Stamps – (W19, D12, L10)	3
1948	Derby finish season 4th (4:22) on 50 points, 9 points behind Champions, Arsenal	4
1948	Raich Carter & Reg Harrison are top scorers with 15 league goals (Reg 18 all comps)	
Season 1948/49 (Division One)		
1948	21/08: Manchester United vs. Derby (W 1-2) – Harrison, Broome	2
1948	21/08: Jack Howe becomes the first professional player to wear contact lenses!	2
1948	25/08: Derby vs. Huddersfield T (W 4-1) – Powell 2, Steel, Thompson	1
1948	28/08: Derby vs. Sheffield Utd (W 2-1) – Broome, Howe – RAMS TOP OF DIV ONE	1
1948	15/09: Derby vs. Blackpool (W 3-1) – Broome 2, Stamps – (W4, D4, L0)	2
1948	16/10: Everton vs. Derby (W 0-1) – Stamps – Rams still unbeaten – (W7, D6, L0)	2
1948	23/10: Derby vs. Chelsea (W 2-1) – Stamps, Broome – Rams level with Portsmouth	2
1948	30/10: Birmingham vs. Derby (W 0-1) – Steel – RAMS GO TOP OF DIVISION ONE	1
1948	06/11: Derby vs. Middlesbrough (W 2-0) – Stamps, Steel – RAMS 3 POINTS CLEAR	1
1948	13/11: Newcastle (3rd) vs. Derby (1st) (L 3-0) – Rams finally lose in their 17th game of season but remain two points clear of both Portsmouth and Newcastle	1
1948	20/11: Derby (1st) vs. Portsmouth (2nd) (W 1-0) – Steel – 2 pts clear of Newcastle	1
1948	04/12: Derby vs. Charlton (W 5-1) – Stamps 2, Steel 2, Broome – 3 points clear	1
1948	18/12: Derby vs. Manchester United (L 1-3) – Mozley – back-to-back defeats	3
1948	25/12: Arsenal vs. Derby (D 3-3) – Harrison, Broome, Powell – (W12, D7, L4)	3
1948	27/12: Derby vs. Arsenal (W 2-1) – Steel, Broome – POR/NEW/DER all win	3
1949	22/01: Sunderland vs. Derby (L 2-1) – Powell – Rams passed by Manchester United	4
1949	05/02: Derby vs. Wolves (W 3-2) – Broome 2, Powell – Rams 5 points off top; 1 GIH	3
1949	26/02: FA Cup QF: Portsmouth vs. Derby (L 2-1) – Fratton Park record (51,385)	4
1949	Derby sign Johnny Morris from Man Utd for £24,500 – a British transfer record	4
1949	12/03: Derby vs. Everton (W 3-2) – Stamps, Steel, Broome –6 points off top; GIH	3
1949	19/03: Portsmouth vs. Derby (L 1-0) – Portsmouth are now 8 points ahead	3
1949	26/03: Derby vs. Man City (W 2-0) – Morris, Walsh (og) – Rams 6 points off top	3
1949	09/04: Derby (3rd) vs. Newcastle (2nd) (L 2-4) – Morris, Stamps – title has gone!	4
1949	15/04: Burnley vs. Derby (L 3-1) – Morris – Rams drop to lowest position all season	7
1949	16/04: Chelsea vs. Derby (W 0-3) – Steel, Broome, Morris – (W17, D8, L11)	5
1949	18/04: Derby vs. Burnley (W 2-0) – Stamps, Steel -2 wins on the spin	4
1949	23/04: Derby vs. Birmingham (W 1-0) – Stamps – 3 wins on the spin	3
1949	30/04: Charlton vs. Derby (W 1-5) – Morris 3, Stamps, Steel – Rams 2 pts off 2nd	3
1949	04/05: Derby vs. Liverpool (W 3-0) – Morris 2, Steel – Rams go above Newcastle, but Man Utd leapfrog both Derby and Newcastle by winning their game in hand	3
1949	07/05: Derby vs. Stoke (W 4-1) – Morris 3 – Rams finish 3rd on GAvg from Man Utd	3
1949	Derby finish season 3rd (3:22) on 53 points, 5 points behind Champions, Portsmouth	3
1949	Frank Broome/Billy Steel leading scorers with 14 league goals (Steel 15 all comps)	

Year	Event	Pos
1949	Johnny Morris plays last 13 games of season and scores 13 goals, inc. 8 in last 3	
Season 1949/50 (Division One)		
1949	31/08: Derby vs. Aston Villa (W 3-2) – Morris 2, Stamps – (W2, D1, L1)	7
1949	17/09: Derby vs. Sunderland (W 3-2) – Broome 2, Morris – (W4, D2, L2)	5
1949	21/09: Derby-born right-back, Bert Mozley, makes England debut vs. Rep of Ireland	5
1949	15/10: Portsmouth vs. Derby (L 3-1) – Stamps – four defeats on the spin	17
1949	29/10: Everton vs. Derby (W 1-2) – Harrison, McLaren – (W6, D2, L6)	13
1949	05/11: Derby vs. Middlesbrough (W 1-0) – Harrison – three wins on the spin	10
1949	03/12: Derby vs Man City (W 7-0) – Morris 2, Stamps 2, McLaren 2, Steel	9
1949	17/12: Manchester United vs. Derby (W 0-1) – Stamps – 3 more wins on the spin	9
1949	27/12: Derby vs. Birmingham City (W 4-1) – Stamps 3, Mozley – (W11, D5, L7)	8
1949	31/12: Stoke vs. Derby (W 1-3) – Harrison, Morris, Stamps – Rams only 6 pts off top	7

Quirk Alert: Irish Obstinacy

Despite only making 25 peacetime appearances for Derby County (along with 60 during World War II), Peter Doherty is a recognised Derby County legend. Alas, he left for Huddersfield Town in December 1946 under a cloud, after directors blocked his plans to take over the Arboretum Hotel, fearing ownership would affect his game. Doherty was announced in the Huddersfield Town line-up on Boxing Day, but as the deal hadn't been completed, he was "summoned by police message to the Baseball Ground", according to The Book of Derby County *(Breedon Books). Typical of the man, he obliged, and also scored twice in a 5-1 victory over Everton. Apparently, the directors pressed him to change his mind, but as he said himself: "My Irish obstinacy would never have permitted me to change my mind." Doherty was also a studious and forward-thinking footballer as well as being exceptionally articulate – all of which comes over in spades in Ian Hall's chapter on Doherty in* The Legends of Derby County.

Quirk Alert: Feast Your Eyes

Derby County topped Division One at some time during most seasons in the decade or so before World War II. In fact, they were still top during February in seasons 1933/34 and 1938/39, while they were still top in mid-March during season 1929/30; during season 1938/39, they were actually FIVE points clear at the top on 31st December, 1938. However, the Rams had never before made an unbeaten start to a top flight season like they did in 1948/49:

League Division One Table – 6th November 1948								
Pos	Team	Pld	W	D	L	GF	GA	GAvg	Pts
1	**Derby County**	**16**	**10**	**6**	**0**	**26**	**12**	**2.167**	**26**
2	Portsmouth	16	9	5	2	28	12	2.333	23
3	Newcastle United	16	8	6	2	34	22	1.545	22
4	Arsenal	16	8	5	3	26	11	2.364	21
5	Charlton Athletic	16	6	7	3	30	23	1.304	19
6	Stoke City	16	7	5	4	27	22	1.227	19

Quirk Alert: Steel Broome
I missed a trick here in the Barmy Yarny, as we could have had the wife tooled up with one of these! But for the record, there were many occasions in the late 1940s when Derby scored twice through Billy Steel and Frank Broome!

Quirk Alert: Pegged Back
Billy Steel's £15,500 transfer from Morton to Derby County in 1947 broke the British transfer record. He was one of Scotland's finest-ever strikers, with great ball control and a lethal left foot. However, although he did well for Derby (35 goals in 124 appearances), Steel wasn't always popular with his team-mates. Some pointed to Steel as the reason for Derby's decline in the early 1950s, feeling he reserved his best performances for London games or the Scotland selectors; it is also thought that Leon Leuty and Jack Howe left Derby prematurely because of him. This combined with special treatment – tolerance of moonlighting and writing articles for newspapers – caused resentment. Indeed, one dressing room incident ended in Billy being hoisted onto a cloakroom peg by Jack Howe!

The 1950s

Year	Event	Pos
1950	07/01: FA Cup 3rd Rd: Man City vs. Derby (W 3-5) – Stamps 3, Steel, Powell	7
1950	14/01: Derby vs. Burnley (D 1-1) – Rams still only 5 points off leaders Man Utd	7
1950	21/01: Sunderland vs. Derby (L 6-1) – Powell – but not likely to catch 'em this way	9
1950	01/02: FA Cup 4th Rd Replay: Derby vs. Bury (W 5-2) – Stamps 3, Morris, Powell	9
1950	11/02: FA Cup 5th Rd: Derby vs. Northampton (W 4-2) – McLaren 2, Morris, Steel – and a new Baseball Ground attendance record is set (38,063)	9
1950	25/02: Wolves vs. Derby (L 4-1) – Wilkins – no win in 5 – Rams 9 points off top	11
1950	04/03: FA Cup Quarter Final: Derby vs. Everton (L 1-2) – Powell	12
1950	08/03: Derby vs. Portsmouth (W 2-1) – Stamps 2 – Rams beat Champs-in-waiting	10
1950	06/05: Derby vs. Bolton (W 4-0) – Stamps 3, Barrass (og) – (W17, D10, L15)	11
1950	Derby finish season 11th (11:22) on 44 points, 9 points behind Champs, Portsmouth	11
1950	Jack Stamps is Derby's leading scorer with 22 league goals (29 in all competitions)	
Season 1950/51 (Division One)		
1950	Derby sign striker Jack Lee from Leicester City in June	
1950	Billy Steel leaves Derby for Dundee for £23,000, a Scottish record transfer fee	
1950	06/09: Derby vs. Charlton Athletic (W 5-0) – Lee 3, Stamps, Powell – (W3, D0, L3)	11
1950	30/09: Derby vs. Blackpool (W 4-1) – Stamps 4 – (W5, D0, L5)	12
1950	07/10: Jack Lee scores in his one England appearance vs. Ireland (W 1-4)	10
1950	21/10: Derby vs. Sheffield Wed (W 4-1) – Stamps 2, Morris, McLaren	12
1950	04/11: Derby vs. Huddersfield (W 3-0) – Harrison, Stamps, McLaren – (W7, D1, L7)	9
1950	04/11: Jack Stamps' goal is his 100th for Derby, the 6th player to reach this milestone	9

Year	Event	Pos
1950	25/11: Chelsea vs. Derby (W 1-2) – Morris, Lee – 4 without defeat	9
1950	16/12: Derby vs. Sunderland (W 6-5) – Lee 4, McLaren 2 – (W10, D3, L8)	8
1951	20/01: Fulham vs. Derby County (W 3-5) – Lee 3, Stamps 2 – (W11, D6, L10)	11
1951	17/03: Derby vs. Arsenal (W 4-2) – Lee 2, McLaren 2 – (W13, D7, L12)	11
1951	31/03: Derby vs. Middlesbrough (W 6-0) – Morris 2, Harrison, Lee, McLaren, Mays	12
1951	Derby finish season 11th (11:22) on 40 points, 20 points behind Champs, Tottenham	11
1951	Jack Lee is Derby's leading scorer with 28 league goals (29 in all competitions)	
Season 1951/52 (Division One)		
1951	01/09: Derby vs. Stoke (W 4-2) – Stamps 2, Powell, Mountford (og) – (W2, D0, L3)	16
1951	06/10: Manchester Utd vs. Derby (L 2-1) – Stamps – 5 without a win	21
1951	13/10: Derby vs. Tottenham (W 4-2) – Parry 2, McLaren, Willis (og) – (W4, D1, L7)	16
1951	10/11: Derby vs. Fulham (W 5-0) – Harrison, McLaren, Parry, Wilkins, McLachlan	13
1951	24/11: Derby vs. West Brom (W 2-1) – Oliver, McLaren – 7 without defeat	11
1951	08/12: Derby vs. Bolton (W 5-2) – Morris 2, Harrison, McLaren, Wilkins	11
1952	Derby finish season 17th (17:22) on 37 points, 9 points above the trap-door	17
1952	Nevertheless, this is Derby's lowest finish since promotion from Div Two in 1926	
1952	Jack Parry is Derby's leading scorer with 11 league goals; J Morris 11 in all comps	
Season 1952/53 (Division One)		
1952	30/08: Derby vs. Aston Villa (L 0-1) – Rams are bottom after three games	22
1952	03/09: Derby vs. Chelsea (W 3-2) – Lee, Straw, Parry – (W1, D1, L2)	18
1952	20/09: Charlton vs. Derby (L 3-1) – Harrison – Rams back on bottom (W1, D1, L6)	22
1951	27/09: Derby vs. Arsenal (W 2-0) – Straw, Stamps – Rams climb off bottom	21
1952	04/10: Burnley vs. Derby (W 1-2) – Straw, Stamps – (W3, D1, L6)	19
1952	22/11: Derby vs. Liverpool (W 3-2) – McLaren 2, Dunn – first win in 7	20
1952	26/12: Derby vs. Portsmouth (W 3-0) – Lee, Dunn, McLaren – 3 wins in 4	17
1953	17/01: Derby vs. Sunderland (W 3-1) – Lee 2, Stamps – Rams a season-high 17th	17
1953	21/02: Derby vs. Burnley (L 1-3) – Lee – 3 defeats in 4 drops Rams to 2nd bottom	21
1953	14/03: Cardiff City vs. Derby (L 2-0) – Rams sink to the bottom – (W9, D6, L18)	22
1953	18/04: Derby vs. Man City (W 5-0) – Lee 2, McLaren 2, Stamps – 3 points adrift	22
1953	25/04: Stoke vs. Derby (W 1-2) – Lee, Stamps – Rams give themselves a chance	22
1953	25/04: Jack Stamps' goal is his 100th and final league goal for Derby	22
1953	29/04: If Derby (32 pts) win last game and Chelsea (33) don't, Rams will stay up; alas, Derby are playing Preston, tied with Arsenal at the top – and need to win...	22
1953	29/04: Derby vs. Preston (L 0-1) – RAMS ARE RELEGATED TO DIV TWO	22
1953	Derby finish season 22nd (22:22), on 32 points, three points from safety	22
1953	Relegation brings an end to 27 years in the top tier of English football for Derby	
1953	Jack Lee is Derby's top scorer with 16 league goals (17 in all competitions)	
Season 1953/54 (Division Two)		
1953	22/08: Derby vs. Brentford (W 4-1) – Lee 3, Powell – (W1, D1, L0)	5
1953	19/09: Derby vs. Hull City (W 2-0) – Harrison, McLaren – (W4, D4, L1)	6
1953	17/10: Derby vs. West Ham (W 2-1) – McLaren, Powell – Rams are 5 points off top	8
1953	01/11: Stuart McMillan is sacked & replaced by former Derby captain, Jack Barker	14
1953	21/11: Plymouth vs. Derby (L 3-2) – Dunn, Nielson – 5 defeats on the spin	16
1953	12/12: Derby vs. Leicester (W 2-1) – Parry 2 – Rams beat leaders, Leicester	16

Year	Event	Pos
1954	01/01: Blackburn vs. Derby (W 0-3) – Parry 2, Harrison – (W10, D5, L10)	11
1954	13/02: Derby vs. Everton (L 2-6) – Dunn 2 – no win in 5 – (W10, D7, L13)	15
1954	10/04: Derby vs. Nottm F (L 1-2) – Powell – 13 without a win; 5 straight defeats	18
1954	16/04: Doncaster R vs. Derby (W 1-3) – Law, Harrison, Wilkins – 3 points above 21st	18
1954	17/04: Luton Town vs. Derby (L 2-1) – Bell – Rams 1 pt above 21st-placed Brentford	19
1954	19/04: Derby vs. Doncaster (W 2-0) – Barrowcliffe 2 – Rams safe with one to go	18
1954	Derby finish season 18th (18:22), on 35 points; lowest-ever league placing to date	18
1954	Hugh McLaren is Derby's leading scorer with 11 league goals (11 in all comps)	
Season 1954/55 (Division Two)		
1954	21/08: Notts County vs. Derby (W 2-3) – Barrowcliffe, Parry, Dunn – a good start	4
1954	28/08: Derby vs. Liverpool (W 3-2) – Barrowcliffe, Powell, Dunn – (W2, D0, L1)	9
1954	18/09: Port Vale vs. Derby (L 3-0) – 5 defeats in 6; Rams drop to second bottom	21
1954	25/09: Derby vs. Doncaster (W 5-0) – Dunn 2, Parry, Powell, Bell – (W3, D1, L6)	19
1954	30/10: Birmingham vs. Derby (D 1-1) – McQuillan – 5 more w/o win; Rams bottom	22
1954	06/11: Derby vs. Ipswich Town (W 2-0) – Upton, Powell – (W4, D3, L9)	19
1954	27/11: Stoke City vs. Derby (L 3-1) – Pye – 3 straight defeats – Rams bottom again	22
1954	04/12: Derby vs. Lincoln City (W 3-0) – Jesse Pye hat-trick – (W5, D3, L12)	21
1955	05/02: Derby vs. Port Vale (W 6-1) – Buchanan 2, Parry, Dunn, Imlach, (og)	21
1955	26/03: Ipswich (22nd) vs. Derby (21st) (L 2-1) – K Harrison – 8 without a win	22
1955	01/04: Jack Barker resigns as Derby County manager	22
1955	16/04: Derby vs. Stoke (L 1-2) – K Harrison – 6th straight defeat – RAMS RELEGATED	22
1955	Derby finish season 22nd (22:22), with 23 points and are relegated to third tier for first time; clearly Derby's lowest-ever league placing at this stage	22
1955	Jimmy Dunn/Tommy Powell top scorers with 8 league goals; Jesse Pye 8 all comps	
Season 1955/56 (Division Three North)		
1955	01/06: Harry Storer Jr becomes 3rd successive former player to manage the Rams	
1955	Storer signs Reg (Paddy) Ryan from West Brom for £3,500 and makes him captain	
1955	20/08: Derby vs Mansfield Town (W 4-0) – Ackerman 2, Mays, Pye	
1955	23/08: Southport vs. Derby (W 2-5) – Ackerman 2, Parry, Pye, Powell – RAMS TOP	1
1955	03/09: Derby vs. Halifax Town (W 4-1) – Parry 2, Buchanan 2 – (W4, D0, L1)	1
1955	24/09: Oldham vs. Derby (D 1-1) – Tate – 6 games without a win (W4, D3, L4)	14
1955	08/10: Derby vs. Chesterfield (W 3-0) – Pye, Powell, Cresswell	6
1955	22/10: Derby vs. Bradford PA (W 4-0) – Parry 2, Mays, Buchanan – 4th win in 5	3
1955	12/11: Chester vs. Derby (W 2-5) – Mays 2, Parry, Pye, Todd – Rams 5 points off top	3
1955	26/11: Accrington Stanley (2nd) vs. Derby (3rd) (L 2-0) – Rams 7 points off top	3
1955	03/12: Derby vs. Darlington (W 6-2) – Parry 3, Todd 2, Powell – 5 points off top	3
1955	10/12: FA Cup 2nd Rd: Derby vs. Boston U (L 1-6) – Boston include SIX former Rams, including FA Cup winner Reg Harrison, and Geoff Hazledine who bags a hat-trick!	3
1956	28/01: Rochdale vs. Derby (W 0-5) – Woodhead 2, Parry, Powell, Straw – 1 pt off top	3
1956	11/02: Workington vs. Derby (W 0-3) – Powell, Straw, Woodhead – 4 wins on spin	3
1956	18/02: Chesterfield vs. Derby (L 2-0) – Rams drop to 4th, but very tight at top	4
1956	07/03: Derby vs. Barrow (W 2-1) – Parry, Woodhead – Rams jump from 4th to 1st	1
1956	10/03: Grimsby Town (2nd) vs. Derby (1st) (L 3-1) – Powell – Grimsby go top	3
1956	19/03: Derby vs. Oldham (W 2-0) – Straw 2 – RAMS BACK ON TOP	1

Year	Event	Pos
1956	30/03: Tranmere vs. Derby (W 0-1) – Barrowcliffe – RAMS 3 POINTS CLEAR AT TOP	1
1956	31/03: Carlisle vs. Derby (W 0-3) – Ryan, Powell, Straw – 12th win in 14	1
1956	07/04: Derby (1st) vs. Accrington (3rd) (W 6-2) – Ackerman 4, Straw 2 – 2 pts clear	1
1956	14/04: Darlington vs. Derby (L 1-0) – Grimsby win and go above Rams with 2 GIH	2
1956	Derby lose 2 of last 4 games, while Grimsby take 11 points from the last 12	2
1956	Derby finish season 2nd (2:24), on 63 points, their highest points haul to date	2
1956	Derby also rack up 110 league goals during season 1955/56, a new club record	
1956	Jack Parry is Derby's leading scorer with 24 league goals (27 in all comps)	
Season 1956/57 (Division Three North)		
1956	18/08: Derby vs. Gateshead (W 5-2) – Parry 2, Woodhead 2, Ackerman	
1956	19/09: Derby vs. Rochdale (W 3-0) – Straw 2, Barrowcliffe – 3rd straight win	3
1956	22/09: Derby vs. Workington (L 1-2) – Straw – Ray Straw becomes Derby's 6th player to score in 6 consecutive games, joining John Goodall, Alf Bentley, Horace Barnes, George Stephenson, and Jack Bowers (twice)	4
1956	26/09: Rochdale vs. Derby (L 3-1) – Ryan – two defeats on spin (W6, D3, L3)	6
1956	29/09: Derby vs. Halifax T (W 6-0) – Straw 3, Mays, Crowshaw, Pye	5
1956	13/10: Bradford C vs. Derby (L 2-0) – Rams are 8 points behind leaders Hartlepools	8
1956	10/11: Derby vs. Tranmere (W 4-0) – Straw 3, Parry – Rams 4 points off Hartlepools	4
1956	22/12: Derby vs. Bradford PA (W 6-1) – Crowshaw 2, Buchanan 2, Wyer, Woodhead	5
1956	25/12: Derby vs. Scunthorpe United (W 4-0) – Woodhead 2, Ryan, Barrowcliffe	3
1956	26/12: Scunthorpe U vs. Derby (W 1-4) – Straw 2, Ryan, (og) – Rams 3 points off top	2
1957	05/01: Crewe vs. Derby (W 2-5) – Crowshaw 2, Buchanan 2, Straw – RAMS GO TOP	1
1957	19/01: Hull City vs. Derby (D 3-3) – Ryan, Straw, Brown – Hartlepools back to top	2
1957	02/02: Derby (2nd) vs. Workington (3rd) (L 2-3) – Straw, Woodhead – both now level	2
1957	09/02: Halifax Town vs. Derby (L 1-0) – Rams passed by Workington	3
1957	16/02: Derby (3rd) vs. Hartlepools Utd (1st) (W 2-0) – Ryan, Brown – 1 point off top	3
1957	02/03: Derby vs. Mansfield Town (W 4-0) – Straw 2, Brown 2 – still 1 point off top	3
1957	09/03: Carlisle U vs. Derby (W 1-3) – Brown 2, Woodhead – RAMS GO TOP AGAIN	1
1957	13/04: Derby vs. Stockport (W 2-0) – Woodhead, Straw – 5th win on spin	1
1957	20/04: Southport vs. Derby (L 3-2) – Straw, Woodhead – DER, ACC, HAR; 58, 58, 57	1
1957	22/04: Derby vs. Chesterfield (W 7-1) – Straw 3, Powell, Ryan, Woodhead	1
1957	The Easter double-header with Chesterfield (D 2-2 on 19th) attracts 56,398 fans	
1957	27/04: Derby vs. Southport (W 2-0) – Straw 2 – DERBY PROMOTED TO DIV TWO	1
1957	Derby finish season 1st (1:24), on 63 points, 4 points clear of Hartlepools	1
1957	63 points is Derby's joint-highest total to date while Derby also go one better than the previous season & score 111 league goals, a new club record, never beaten	
1957	Ray Straw is Derby's leading scorer with 37 league goals (37 goals in all competitions), equalling the record set by Jack Bowers during season 1930/31	
Season 1957/58 (Division Two)		
1957	31/08: Derby vs. Barnsley (L 1-4) – Powell – welcome back – 3 straight defeats	21
1957	18/09: Derby vs. Lincoln (W 3-2) – Mays, Ryan, Parry – two wins on the spin	17
1957	12/10: Cardiff vs. Derby (L 3-2) – Parry, Darwin – four without a win	20
1957	19/10: Derby vs. Liverpool (W 2-1) – Woodhead, Darwin – (W4, D2, L7)	19
1957	23/11: Rotherham United vs. Derby (W 0-2) – Mays, Powell – 3 wins in 4	12

Year	Event	Pos
1957	26/12: Derby vs. Bristol C (W 5-2) – Parry 2, Ryan, Woodhead, Darwin – 1st win in 6	16
1958	08/03: Derby vs. M'brough (W 2-1) – Brown 2 – Rams 16th for almost 3 months!	16
1958	29/03: Doncaster vs. Derby (W 1-2) – Woodhead, Parry – Derby are STILL 16th	16
1958	08/04: Swansea Town vs. Derby (L 7-0) – still 16th – (W13, D7, L19)	16
1958	Derby finish season 16th (16:22) on 36 points, 6 points clear of the drop	16
1958	Reg Ryan is Derby's leading scorer with 14 league goals (14 in all competitions)	
Season 1958/59 (Division Two)		
1958	08/11: Grimsby Town vs. Derby (L 3-0) – a slow start – (W4, D5, L8)	17
1958	15/11: Derby vs. Liverpool (W 3-2) – Hannigan, Hunt, Darwin	15
1958	06/12: Bristol City vs. Derby (W1-3) – Parry, Hunt, Darwin – (W7, D5, L9)	12
1958	20/12: Derby vs. Huddersfield T (W 3-1) – Powell, Cargill, Darwin	11
1958	27/12: Swansea Town vs. Derby (D 4-4) – Hannigan, Powell, Cargill, Darwin	11
1959	03/01: Leyton Orient vs. Derby (W 1-3) – Parry 2, Powell – (W10, D6, L10)	10
1959	17/01: Derby vs. Scunthorpe United (W 3-1) – Darwin 2, Hannigan	8
1959	07/02: Derby (8th) vs. Fulham (2nd) (W 2-0) – Hannigan, Darwin – now 8 pts off 2nd	6
1959	14/02: Lincoln City vs. Derby (W 1-4) – Upton, Hannigan, Powell, Darwin	6
1959	28/02: Derby vs. Grimsby Town (W 3-0) – Parry 3 – 10th win in 13 league games	5
1959	14/03: Derby vs. Sheffield United (W 2-1) – Parry 2 – Rams still 8 points off 2nd	4
1959	30/03: Derby vs. Stoke City (W 3-0) – Thompson 2, Parry – now 7 points off 2nd	4
1959	04/04: Liverpool (3rd) vs. Derby (4th) (L 3-0) – still 4th, but promotion charge is over	4
1959	Derby finish season 7th (7:22), on 48 points, 12 points off 2nd-placed Fulham	7
1959	Jack Parry is Derby's leading scorer with 15 league goals (16 in all competitions)	
1959	Brian Clough is Div Two top goalscorer with 42 goals – including two against Derby	
Season 1959/60 (Division Two)		
1959	29/08: Derby vs. Middlesbrough (L 1-7) – Parry – amazingly, Cloughie didn't score – the defeat also equals Derby's worst-ever home league defeat	19
1959	09/09: Derby vs. Cardiff (L 1-2) – Swallow – (W1, D1, L4)	21
1959	12/09: Plymouth vs. Derby (W 0-5) – Thompson 2, Hannigan, Parry, Daykin	15
1959	26/09: Charlton vs. Derby (L 6-1) – Thompson – (W2, D1, L7)	19
1959	10/10: Derby vs. Portsmouth (W 1-0) – Swallow – two wins on the bounce	16
1959	26/12: Scunthorpe United vs. Derby (L 3-2) – Barrowcliffe, Buxton – 1 win in 11	20
1959	28/12: Derby vs. Scunthorpe United (W 3-0) – Upton, Parry, Hannigan	19

Quirk Alert: Silence in Caught
Derby signed goalkeeper Ray Middleton from Chesterfield in June 1951. He was also a Justice of the Peace, making him the only active professional footballer to also act as a magistrate!

Quirk Alert: An Interesting Table: League Division One, 11th October, 1952

Pos	Team	Pld	W	D	L	GF	GA	GAvg	GD	Pts
20	Derby County	11	3	2	6	14	18	0.778	-4	8
21	Manchester United	11	3	2	6	13	20	0.650	-7	8
22	Manchester City	11	1	3	8	14	23	0.609	-9	5

Perspective: Chick Musson and Leon Leuty
FA Cup Winners Chick Musson and Leon Leuty were born 12 days apart in October 1920. Tragically, they both died as young men in 1955, and almost inconceivably, they both died from leukaemia. Even more thought-provoking, is the fact that Leon Leuty was one of Chick Musson's coffin-bearers in April 1955; was he perhaps already suffering from the same illness which would claim him too, eight months later?

Quirk Alert: Jack's Flack
When Jack Barker resigned as Derby County manager in 1955, he was so disillusioned with football that he left the industry and became a fitter's mate at the Carriage and Wagon railway works in Derby. He later stated in 1981 that it was a "rotten experience", and that "I wouldn't be a manager for £10,000 a week". Bear in mind, that Jack was a tough ex-miner who had survived a pit disaster when a young man. However, he also went on to say: "The trouble is that the people you are working for know nothing about the game" – sentiments echoed rather more vociferously by one who would shortly follow...

Quirk Alert: All-Rounder Harry
Harry Storer appeared 274 times for Derby in the 1920s, scoring 63 goals, while he was also one of Derbyshire's finest ever opening batsmen, scoring 13,513 first-class runs for the county and taking 232 wickets. He then managed Derby between 1955 and 1962, and liked his team to be combative. One story goes that Joe Mercer once tipped Harry off about six of his players who had been putting it about in a game against Sheffield United. Storer promptly demanded their names – not to reprimand the six, but to sort out the other five! It is also interesting to know, that early in his Derby tenure, Harry Storer tried to sign a young Brian Clough!

Quirk Alert: 1-6, 1-6
Derby County lost their FA Cup 2nd Round tie 1-6 at home to non-league Boston United in December 1955. Back then, Boston played in the Midland League, and to this day, that remains the biggest FA Cup away win for a non-league side against league opponents. This was therefore a HUGE shock for the Rams – one which was repeated nearly 20 years later on 5 January 1974, when Derby were held at home 0-0 by Boston United in the FA Cup 3rd Round. This was equally shocking, given a Derby side packed full of internationals and in the middle of a three-year purple patch which included TWO Football League Championships, while Boston United were still a non-league side playing in the Northern Premier League. However, by a typically strange quirk of football fate, Derby went and won the replay at York Street 1-6. The attendance of 11,000 remains Boston United's largest ever crowd.

As an addendum to this Quirk Alert, Derby were knocked out of the FA Cup by non-league opposition the following season as well (1956/57), when they lost 1-3 at home to New Brighton – although the Rakers, as they were known, had at least previously been a football league club until they failed to seek re-election in 1951.

Quirk Alert: Contrasting Fortunes

Talking of New Brighton, they were replaced in the football league in 1951 by Workington Town who Derby played in their Third Division North days. During the 1955/56 season, Derby beat Barrow home and away, while they also did the double over Carlisle that season, too – these being the only three Cumbrian clubs to play in the football league (although Barrow was in Lancashire back in those days). But by the time Derby County were winning League Championships in the 1970s, both Workington and Barrow had disappeared from the Football League, never to return, as had Bradford Park Avenue, Gateshead and Southport, all of whom Derby did the double over during season 1955/56. In fact, of the 24 clubs in Division Three North that season, 18 have dropped out of the Football League at various stages, some permanently.

Perspective: Hughie Gallacher

Hughie Gallacher is one of the North-East's biggest legends, but he was also a big hit at Derby County, too, scoring 40 goals in 56 appearances between 1934 and 1936. He struggled financially following retirement, though, but when he lost his wife to a heart problem in 1950, it left him having to bring up his young sons alone, and he became very depressed and lonely. The turning point for Hughie was a minor dispute with his 14 year-old son, Mattie, after which he threw an ashtray at him which drew blood. Hughie then had an altercation with his eldest son, Hughie Junior, which resulted in the police being called, who subsequently reported the "assault" on the younger son to the authorities – and which resulted in Hughie Senior being denied access to Mattie. The day before he was due in court to answer the assault charge, Hughie Gallacher was seen pacing backwards and forwards on a footbridge over the London to Edinburgh railway line at Gateshead. He was openly weeping, talking to himself and occasionally pounding the bridge rail with his fists. He then stepped down from the bridge and walked in front of an oncoming express train.

Quirk Alert: Straw's Super Six

When Ray Straw left Derby County for Coventry City in November 1957, he joined the Sky Blues in what was then Division Three South – and because Coventry finished in the bottom half of that league, they then ended up in League Division Four when the regional split was merged into Divisions 3 and 4 at the end of season 1957/58. Having already played in Division's One and Two earlier in his career, as well as Division Three North with Derby, Straw thus became the first footballer to play in all SIX divisions of the Football League!

Former Ilkeston miner, Ray 'Tuffy' Straw, who holds the joint-record for the number of league goals scored for Derby in one season (37 during season 1956/57). PHOTO: Andy Ellis

Quirk Alert: Sixteenth

This one is nigh-on impossible to replicate for a mid-table side. But on 7 December 1957, Derby lost 3-2 at Grimsby, and dropped to 16th place. Matches were then played on the following dates, and on EVERY DATE BAR ONE, Derby remained in 16th place: 07-Dec (lost – 16th), 14-Dec (drew – 16th), 21-Dec (drew – 16th), 25-Dec (lost – 16th), 26-Dec (won – 16th), 28-

Dec (lost – 16th), 11-Jan (lost – 16th), 18-Jan (won – 16th), 01-Feb (lost – 16th), 08-Feb (drew – 16th), 15-Feb (won – 16th), 22-Feb (lost – 16th), 05-Mar (lost – 16th), 08-Mar (won – 16th), 15-Mar (drew – 16th), 22-Mar (lost – 16th), 29-Mar (won – 16th), 05-Apr (lost – 16th), 07-Apr (won – 16th), 08-Apr (lost – 16th), 12-Apr (drew – 16th), 19-Apr (won –15th), 26-Apr (lost – 16th).

Quirk Alert: One Swallow in the Summer

When ex-First Class cricketer Harry Storer signed current First-Class cricketer, Ray Swallow, from Arsenal in September 1958, Derbyshire CCC were very pleased with this little piece of business – as Swallow went on to play for Derbyshire between 1959 and 1963. Primarily deployed as an opening batsmen, Ray Swallow played 38 times for Derbyshire, top scoring with 115 and finishing with a batting average of 20.04. Swallow also racked up 128 appearances as a winger for the Rams between 1958 and 1963, scoring 22 goals.

Quirk Alert: Three Swallows in the Summer

Ray Swallow was joined at Derby County in season 1959/60 by two more First Class cricketers, Ian Hall and Ian Buxton. All three played for Derbyshire, with Hall and Buxton having remarkably similar batting statistics, as shown below, while all three appeared for the first time together in a Derby County shirt on 19 December 1959, when Swallow, Hall and Buxton wore the respective number 7, 8 and 9 shirts!

Derby County FC			Derbyshire County Cricket Club									
Player	Years	App	Gls	Years	Mch	Runs	Bat	C	Top	Wkt	Bwl	Best	Cat
I Buxton	1959-67	158	43	1959-73	350	11,803	23.94	5	118*	483	26.38	7/33	199
I Hall	1959-62	51	16	1959-72	270	11,666	25.86	9	136*	N/A	N/A	N/A	189
R Swallow	1958-64	128	22	1958-63	38	1,323	20.04	1	115	N/A	N/A	N/A	13

The 1960s

Year	Event	Pos
1960	02/01: M'brough vs. Derby (L 3-0) – Brian Clough scores 2 more against Derby	19
1960	20/02: Bristol City vs. Derby (W 0-1) – Swallow – three wins on the spin	17
1960	27/02: Portsmouth vs. Derby (W 2-3) – Hannigan 2, Swallow – (W10, D5, L15)	16
1960	Derby finish season 18th (18:22), on 35 points, five points above the drop-zone	18
1960	Jack Parry is Derby's leading scorer with 15 league goals (16 in all competitions)	
1960	Brian Clough is Division Two's top goalscorer for second year running with 39 goals	
Season 1960/61 (Division Two)		
1960	20/08: Derby vs. Brighton (W 4-1) – Swallow, Thompson, Darwin, Fagan	1
1960	24/08: Middlesbrough vs. Derby (W 1-2) – Thompson, Darwin	1
1960	10/09: Leyton Orient vs. Derby (L 2-1) – Newbery – 3 defeats on the spin	17
1960	Derby sign centre-forward Bill Curry from Brighton & Hove Albion for £12,000	
1960	08/10: Swansea Town vs. Derby (L 2-1) – Hall – Rams 8 games without a win	20
1960	11/10: League Cup 1st Rd: Watford vs. Derby – (W 2-5) – Buxton, Hutchinson, Hall, Cargill, Porter (og) – Derby's first-ever League Cup game	20
1960	15/10: Derby vs. Luton Town (W 4-1) – Curry 2, Hutchinson, Barrowcliffe	15

Year	Event	Pos
1960	19/10: League Cup 2nd Rd: Derby vs. Barnsley (W 3-0) – Hutchinson, Curry, B'cliffe	15
1960	22/10: Lincoln City vs. Derby (W 3-4) – Curry 3, Hall – (W5, D3, L6)	11
1960	29/10: Derby vs. Portsmouth (W 6-2) – Curry 2, Powell 2, Hall, Hutchinson	10
1960	05/11: Huddersfield vs. Derby (W 1-3) – Curry, Hall, Hutchinson – 4 points off 2nd	9
1960	14/11: League Cup 3rd Rd: Derby vs. Norwich City (L 1-4) – Hutchinson	9
1960	27/12: Leeds United vs. Derby (D 3-3) – Powell 2, Curry – 1 win in 8	10
1961	21/01: Derby vs. Leyton Orient (W 3-1) – Barrowcliffe 2, Hall – (W10, D6, L10)	11
1961	25/02: Derby vs. Swansea T (L 2-3) – Jack Parry scores his 100th Derby goal	12
1961	25/03: Derby vs. Huddersfield (D 1-1) – Hutchinson – only 1 win in last 7	14
1961	08/04: Derby vs. Plymouth (W 4-1) – Curry 2, Powell, Hutchinson (W14, D10, L13)	10
1961	15/04: Sunderland vs. Derby (W 1-2) – Curry, Hutchinson – 4 wins in 5	10
1961	Derby lose last 4 games and finish season 12th (12:22) on 40 points	12
1961	Bill Curry is Derby's leading scorer with 19 league goals (20 in all competitions)	
Season 1961/62 (Division Two)		
1961	19/08: Middlesbrough vs. Derby (W 3-4) – Curry 2, Palmer 2	5
1961	23/08: Derby vs. Luton Town (W 2-0) – Curry, Hutchinson – Rams win first two	2
1961	0€/09: Derby vs. Swansea Town (W 6-3) – Swallow 2, Curry 2, Hutchinson, (og)	6
1960	30/09: Derby vs. Huddersfield (W 1-0) – Hutchinson – (W6, D1, L4)	4
1961	Derby sign former England goalkeeper Reg Matthews from Chelsea	
1961	21/10: Derby (3rd) vs. Liverpool (1st) (W 2-0) – Curry, Hopkinson – (W7, D3, L4)	3
1961	11/11: Bristol Rov vs. Derby (W 1-4) – Havenhand 3, Thompson – same pts as 2nd	4
1961	18/11: Derby (4th) vs. Scunthorpe (2nd) (D 2-2) – Roby, Havenhand – (W9, D4, L5)	3
1961	16/12: Derby vs. Middlesbrough (W 3-2) – Curry 3 – Rams on same points as 2nd	4
1961	26/12: Derby vs. Southampton (D 1-1) – Havenhand – Rams 3 pts behind 2nd/Orient	3
1961	Rams have dismal second half of season, and only win 3 more (W3, D5, L10)	
1961	Derby finish season 16th on 39 points (from 30 points early Jan), 6 pts above 21st	16
1962	Bill Curry is Derby's leading scorer with 18 league goals (25 in all competitions)	
1962	01/06: Harry Storer is replaced by Tim Ward as Derby County manager	
Season 1962/63 (Division Two)		
1962	27/10: Derby vs. Chelsea (L 1-3) – Parry – terrible start; Rams bottom; (W1, D5, L9)	22
1962	03/11: Luton (21st) vs. Derby (22nd) (W 1-2) – Curry, Hutchinson	20
1962	10/11: Derby vs. Southampton (W 3-1) – Hutchinson 2, (og) – back-to-back wins	20
1962	15/12: Derby vs. Huddersfield Town (W 2-1) – Curry, Hutchinson – (W4, D7, L11)	19
1963	09/03: Derby vs. Swansea Town (L 0-2) – still only 4 wins – (W4, D8, L14)	19
1963	20/03: Derby vs. Plymouth (W 3-2) – Curry 2, Hutchinson – 2nd of 3 straight wins	18
1963	06/04: Derby vs. Scunthorpe (W 6-2) – Curry 2, Barrowcliffe, Young, Hutchinson	18
1963	24/04: Derby vs. Walsall (W 2-0) – Barrowcliffe, Webster – 6 wins in 10	17
1963	06/05: Derby vs. Norwich City (W 3-0) – Hutchinson 2, Curry – Rams now safe	16
1963	10/05: Derby vs. Portsmouth (W 4-0) – Curry 3, Hutchinson – only 1 defeat in 9	15
1963	Derby finish season 18th (18:22), on 36 points, 5 points above the drop-zone	18
1963	Bill Curry is top scorer with 21 league goals (Barry Hutchinson 22 in all comps)	
Season 1963/64 (Division Two)		
1963	Derby sign Alan Durban from Cardiff City for £10,000	
1963	28/08: Derby vs. Swansea (W 3-0) – Jack Parry scores 100th league goal for Derby	9

Year	Event	Pos
1963	11/09: Derby vs. Leyton Orient (W 1-0) – Hughes – Rams win 4 of first 6	5
1963	14/09: Plymouth Argyle vs Derby (D 0-0) – Rams 4 points off leaders, Swindon	4
1963	28/09: Derby vs. Grimsby Town (W 3-1) – Durban 2, Cullen – Rams 4 points off top	7
1963	08/10: Bury vs. Derby (W 1-2) – Durban, Hutchinson – Rams 5 pts off top (Swindon)	6
1963	16/11: Norwich City vs. Derby (L 3-0) – 5 games without a win – (W6, D4, L7)	13
1964	11/01: Derby vs. Northampton Town (D 0-0) – 7 more without a win	16
1964	17/02: Preston NE vs. Derby (W 0-2) – Durban, Webster – (W11, D10, L13)	13
1964	30/03: Derby vs. Southampton (W 3-2) – Parry, Durban, Buxton – (W12, D11, L14)	12
1964	01/04: Southampton vs. Derby (L 6-4) – Barrowcliffe 2, Bowers 2 (Jack's son, John)	13
1964	Derby finish season 13th (13:22), on 39 points, 7 points above the drop-zone	13
1964	Alan Durban is Derby's top scorer with 9 league goals (11 in all competitions)	
Season 1964/65 (Division Two)		
1964	22/08: Crystal Palace vs. Derby (W 2-3) – Bowers, Durban, Hughes	5
1964	Derby sign inside forward Eddie Thomas from Swansea for £3,500	5
1964	29/08: Derby vs. Bury (W 3-1) – Durban, Thomas, Atherton (og) – (W2, D0, L1)	6
1964	05/09: Leyton Orient vs. Derby (W 1-4) – Bowers 2, Buxton, Thomas – (W3, D0, L2)	8
1964	09/09: Derby vs. Coventry (1st) (W 2-1) – Bowers, Thomas – Rams 2 points off top	4
1964	12/09: Charlton vs. Derby (D 4-4) – Durban, Thomas, Cleevely, Bailey (og)	6
1964	15/09: Coventry (1st) vs. Derby (W 0-2) – Durban, Thomas – Rotherham now top	2
1964	15/09: Eddie Thomas becomes the 8th Derby player to score in 6 consecutive games, and the only one to do it in his first 6 games for the club	2
1964	26/09: Derby vs. Portsmouth (W 4-0) – B'cliffe, Durban, Curry – Rams 1 point off top	5
1964	07/10: Derby vs. Huddersfield T (W 2-0) – Durban, Thomas – Rams 1 point off top	4
1964	17/10: Derby vs. Preston NE (W 3-1) – Young, Buxton, Thomas – Rams 2 pts off top	5
1964	31/10: Derby vs. Plymouth (W 3-2) – Thomas 2, Curry – Rams now 4 points off top	3
1964	12/12: Derby vs. Crystal Palace (D 3-3) – Thomas 2, Young – 5 draws on the spin	7
1965	30/01: Derby vs. Man City (W 2-0) – Durban, Hughes – 3 straight wins	5
1965	20/02: Derby vs. Cardiff City (W 1-0) – Webster – Rams 7 points off top two	5
1965	06/03: Derby vs. Southampton (W 2-1) – Durban, Buxton – Rams are 4th on 38 points behind "three N's" – Norwich (42 points), Newcastle (43) and Northampton (44)	4
1965	27/03: Middlesbrough vs. Derby (W 1-2) – Durban, Thomas – Rams 6 points off top	5
1965	17/04: Jack Parry becomes only the third player to reach 500 games for Derby	7
1965	Rams lose 5 of last 6 games and finish 9th on 43 points, 13 points off promotion	9
1964	Alan Durban & Eddie Thomas top scorers with 22 league goals (24 in all comps)	
Season 1965/66 (Division Two)		
1965	01/09: Derby vs. Cardiff (L 1-5) – Hughes – Rams are bottom having lost 4 out of 4; GD is already -11	22
1965	01/09: 4 defeats in first 4 games equals worst start to a season (1899 same)	22
1965	07/09: Geoff Barrowcliffe becomes the 4th Rams player to reach 500 appearances; another of Derby's former miners from Ilkeston, he initially started as a part-time pro, training in the evenings after a day down the pit!	21
1965	11/09: Wolves vs. Derby (L 4-0) – Rams have lost 6 out of first 7	22
1965	25/09: Man City vs. Derby (L 1-0) – Rams have now lost 8 of their first 10	21
1965	16/10: Derby vs. Bolton (W 2-0) – Durban 2 – (W4, D1, L8)	21

Year	Event	Pos
1965	30/10: Derby vs. Birmingham (W 5-3) – Thomas 2, Upton 2, Durban	19
1965	13/11: Derby vs. Middlesbrough (W 5-0) – Hodgson 3, Durban 2 – (W6, D3, L8)	14
1965	27/11: Derby vs. Crystal P (W 4-0) – Thomas, Durban, Hodgson, Upton – 9 w/o loss	10
1965	18/12: Bolton W vs. Derby (W 0-1) – Bowers – Rams now only 6 points off 2nd place	8
1966	01/01: Derby vs. Portsmouth (W 3-1) – Buxton, Thomas, Hughes – 6 points off top	7
1966	19/02: Norwich vs. Derby (W 0-1) – Buxton – Rams are now 8 points off top	7
1966	09/04: Birmingham vs. Derby (D 5-5) – Durban 3, Buxton, Thomas (og) – 7 without a win – the result also equals Derby's biggest ever draw	10
1966	16/04: Derby vs. Huddersfield (W 4-1) – Thomas 2, Buxton, Durban – 9 pts off 2nd	8
1966	Derby finish season 8th (8:22) on 43 points, 11 points off 2nd place	8
1966	Alan Durban is top scorer with 17 league goals (Eddie Thomas 17 in all comps)	
Season 1966/67 (Division Two)		
1966	06/09: Ipswich vs. Derby – (L 4-3) – Thomas 2, Durban – Derby lose 5 of first 6	22
1966	Derby break transfer record to sign Kevin Hector for £38,000 from Bradford PA	
1966	24/09: Derby vs. Huddersfield (W 4-3) – Durban 3, Hector – Kevin's home debut	19
1966	08/10: Derby vs. Millwall (W 5-1) – Webster, Buxton, Hodgson, Hector, Jones og	15
1966	22/10: Derby vs. Preston (W 5-1) – Buxton 2, Hughes, Thomas, Hector – (W4, D4, L6)	15
1966	19/11: Derby vs. Birmingham (L 1-2) – Hector – three defeats on the spin	18
1966	26/11: Portsmouth vs. Derby (W 0-3) – Hector, Buxton, Durban – (W5, D5, L9)	16
1966	24/12: Wolves vs. Derby (L 5-3) – Durban 2, Richardson – (W6, D6, L11)	17
1966	26/12: Derby vs. Wolves (L 0-3) – Rams are now only 2 points above 21st	17
1967	07/01: Derby vs. Charlton (L 3-1) – Buxton – Rams now 2 points off the bottom	19
1967	14/01: Derby vs. Northampton (W 4-3) – Hector, Hodgson, Durban, Waller	18
1967	Very little changes as the Rams flit between 14th and 18th	
1967	Derby finish season 17th (17:22), on 36 points, 6 points above the drop-zone	17
1967	Kevin Hector is Derby's leading scorer with 16 league goals (16 in all comps)	
1967	Tim Ward's contract isn't renewed as Derby County manager	

Quirk Alert: The Third Men
Reg Matthews joined Derby from Chelsea in October 1961. Reg had previously played for Coventry City, and is one of only five post-war footballers to have been capped by England whilst playing in the third tier of English football.

Stats Blast: One and Four Symmetry
Inside forward Keith Havenhand played 26 league games for Derby between October 1961 and April 1962 and scored 14 goals. This included hat-tricks in both home and away games against Bristol Rovers, as Derby won both games 1-4 and 4-1!

Quirk Alert: The Winter of '63
Having lost 1-0 at Cardiff on 22nd December 1962, the harsh winter of 1963 meant that the Rams didn't take the field in the league again until 23 February, when they drew 2-2 at home to Sunderland – a gap of NINE WEEKS without a league game! Indeed, Derby's FA Cup Third Round tie with Peterborough was postponed SIX times!

Stats Blast: A Minute from the Guinness Book of Records
When Bobby Saxton came on as a 14th minute substitute for Geoff Barrowcliffe, on the opening day defeat to Southampton in the 1965/66 season, he was within a minute of being the first ever substitute in the English Football League. However, that "accolade" went to Keith Peacock of Charlton Athletic, who came on as a sub in the 13th minute on the same day.

Quirk Alert: Tim's Significant Victory
Fed up of being told by directors that so-and-so was being played in the wrong position, Tim Ward got Jack Parry and Mick Hopkinson to swap shirts for one game, but to play in their usual positions. Sure enough, after the 3-1 victory, a self-satisfied director approached Tim and told him that the tactical switch was what had won Derby the game!

Before Brian Clough and Peter Taylor arrived at the Baseball Ground, four of Derby County's future 1971/72 Champions were already in place. From left to right, Ron Webster made his debut for Derby in March 1962, Alan Durban signed for Derby from Cardiff City for £10,000 in July 1963, Colin Boulton made his debut in April 1965, and the King, Kevin Hector, was signed from Bradford Park Avenue for £38,000 in September 1966, a then-Derby County record transfer fee. Another mainstay of Derby's second Championship-winning side of 1974/75, Peter Daniel, was also a regular as early as the 1965/66 season. And finally, as a Stats Blast extra, Alan Durban played more than 550 league games in his career, most of it at Derby, but which saw him play on all 92 football league grounds! He also represented Glamorgan at both cricket and tennis. PHOTOS: Andy Ellis

RAMS CHRONOLOGY: The Spectacular Rise

The 1960s

Year	Event	Pos
Season 1967/68 (Division Two)		
1967	Brian Clough and Peter Taylor arrive at Derby County from Hartlepools United	
1967	Derby sign John O'Hare, Roy McFarland (both Aug) and Alan Hinton (Sep)	
1967	19/08: Derby vs. Charlton (W 3-2) – O'Hare, Hector, King (og)	2
1967	28/08: Rotherham vs. Derby (W 1-3) – Hector, O'Hare, Buxton – (W2, D0, L1)	8
1967	02/09: Derby vs. Aston Villa (W 3-1) – Durban 2, Hector – (W3, D0, L1)	6
1967	09/09: QPR (1st) vs. Derby (W 0-1) – Hector – Rams 3 pts off top (QPR) with 1 GIH	9

Year	Event	Pos
1967	13/09: League Cup 2nd Rd: Derby vs. Hartlepools U (W 4-0) – O'Hare 3, Hodgson	9
1967	23/09: Cardiff City vs. Derby (W 1-5) – Hector 3, O'Hare 2 – (W6, D0, L2)	5
1967	27/09: Derby vs. Rotherham (W 4-1) – Hector 2, O'Hare, Hughes – 1 point off top	4
1967	03/10: League Cup 3rd Rd: Derby vs. B'ham C (W 3-1) Hector, Hopkinson, O'Hare	5
1967	28/10: Bolton vs. Derby (L 5-3) – Hector, O'Hare, Durban – Rams 4 points off top	7
1967	15/11: League Cup 4th Rd Replay: Lincoln City vs. Derby (W 0-3) – O'Hare 2, Hector	7
1967	15/11: The match sees Lincoln City's record Sincil Bank attendance of 23,196	7
1967	29/11: League Cup QF: Derby vs. Darlington (W 5-4) – Durban 2, Hughes, Barker	10
1967	09/12: Blackpool vs. Derby (D 1-1) – O'Hare – one win in last 11 league games	14
1967	06/01: Aston Villa vs. Derby (L 2-1) – Hector – (W9, D5, L11)	15
1968	17/01: League Cup Semi-Final, 1st Leg: Derby vs. Leeds United (L 0-1)	15
1968	20/01: Plymouth vs. Derby (W 4-3) – Hinton 2, O'Hare, Barker – (W10, D5, L11)	13
1968	07/02: League Cup SF, 2nd Leg: Leeds vs. Derby (L 3-2) – Hector, Stewart [agg: L 4-2]	15
1968	17/02: Derby (15th) vs. QPR (1st) (W 4-0) – Hector, McFarland, Hinton, Stewart	14
1968	Derby win only two of their remaining 13 league games	
1968	04/05: Reg Matthews plays 246th & final game for Derby – club GK record at time	18
1968	Derby finish season 18th (18:22), on 36 points, 5 points above the drop-zone	18
1968	Kevin Hector is Derby's leading scorer with 21 league goals (24 in all comps)	
Season 1968/69 (Division Two)		
1968	July: Derby sign Dave Mackay, aged 34, from Tottenham for £5,000; a legendary midfielder, the canny Clough and Taylor deploy Mackay as a sweeper	
1968	14/08: League Cup 1st Rd: Derby vs. Chesterfield (W 3-0) – Hector, Hinton, (og)	13
1968	24/08: Huddersfield Town vs. Derby (L 2-0) – (W0, D2, L2)	21
1968	Derby sign midfielder Willie Carlin for £63,000 from Sheffield United	21
1968	28/08: Derby vs. Hull (D 2-2) – Barker, Hector – still no league win – (W0, D3, L2)	19
1968	31/08: Derby vs. Oxford U (W 2-0) – McFarland, O'Hare – first win at 6th attempt	17
1968	04/09: League Cup 2nd Rd: Derby vs. Stockport (W 5-1) – Hinton 4, Hector	17
1968	07/09: Derby vs. Aston Villa (W 3-1) – Hector 2, Hinton – (W2, D3, L2)	12
1968	18/09: Derby vs. Fulham (W 1-0) – Hinton – Rams only 3 pts off leaders, Blackpool	9
1968	21/09: Derby vs. Millwall (W 0-1) – Durban – Rams 3 pts off new leaders, Charlton	6
1968	Derby sign midfielder John McGovern for £7,500 from Hartlepools United	6
1968	28/09: Bolton vs. Derby (W 1-2) – Walker, Barker – Rams 1 point off top (Charlton)	5
1968	02/10: League Cup 3rd Rd Replay: Derby vs. Chelsea (W 3-1) – Mackay, Durban, Hector – an impressive Division 1 scalp!	5
1968	05/10: Middlesbrough vs. Derby (D 0-0) – Rams still one point off top spot	4
1968	09/10: Hull City vs. Derby (L 1-0) – Rams 2 points off new leaders, Blackburn	7
1968	12/10: Derby vs Preston NE (W 1-0) – Hinton – Rams 1 point off new leaders, Hull	4
1968	19/10: Portsmouth vs. Derby (W 0-1) – Hector – Rams 1 point off top (M'brough)	3
1968	23/10: League Cup 4th Rd Replay: Derby vs. Everton (W 1-0) – Hector – 2nd scalp!	3
1968	26/10: Derby vs. Birmingham (W 1-0) – Carlin – top three all win – (W8, D5, L3)	3
1968	05/11: League Cup QF Replay: Swindon vs. Derby (L 1-0) – Rams are now the scalp!	3
1968	09/11: Derby vs. Charlton (W 2-1) – O'Hare, Hector – Rams 1 point behind Millwall	2
1968	16/11: Cardiff vs. Derby (D 1-1) – Durban – Rams now 2 points behind Millwall	2
1968	23/11: Derby vs. Carlisle (D 3-3) – Mackay, O'Hare, Carlin – Rams 1 point off top	3

Year	Event	Pos
1968	30/11: Crystal Pal (2nd) vs. Derby (3rd) (W 1-2) – McFarland, Carlin – RAMS GO TOP	1
1968	21/12: Derby vs. Portsmouth (W 2-1) – Hector 2 – Rams still top – (W11, D9, L3)	1
1968	26/12: Derby (1st) vs. M'brough (2nd) (W 3-2) – Hinton 2, McFarland – 3 pts clear	1
1969	11/01: Derby vs. Bury (W 2-0) – McFarland, O'Hare – Rams still 3 pts clear at top	1
1969	14/01: Birmingham vs. Derby (D 1-1) – Hector – Rams go 4 points clear at top	1
1969	18/01: Charlton vs. Derby (L 2-0) – first league defeat in 14 – (W13, D10, L4)	1
1969	25/01: Bury vs. Derby (W 0-1) – O'Hare – Rams are 4 points clear of 2nd (Cardiff)	1
1969	01/02: Derby (1st) vs. Cardiff (2nd) (W 2-0) – Hector 2 – Rams still 4 points clear	1
1969	Due to bad weather, Rams don't play for exactly one month, but remain top	1
1969	01/03: Derby vs. Blackburn (W 4-2) – Hector, O'Hare, Carlin, Wignall – 2 points clear	1
1969	05/03: Crystal Pal vs. Derby (L 1-0) – Middlesbrough close gap to one point	1
1969	08/03: Blackpool vs. Derby (W 2-3) – McFarland, O'Hare, Hinton – still 1 point clear	1
1969	11/03: Carlisle vs. Derby (D 1-1) – Hector – Rams extend lead at top to 2 points	1
1969	15/03: Derby vs. Huddersfield (W 1-0) – McFarland – Rams 4 points clear of Cardiff	1
1969	22/03: Oxford United vs. Derby (W 0-2) – Hector 2 – Rams 4 points clear of 'Boro	1
1969	29/03: Aston Villa vs. Derby (W 0-1) – Simmons (og) – Rams 4 pts clear of Palace	1
1969	02/04: Fulham vs. Derby (W 0-1) – Wignall – Rams 6 pts clear of 2nd (C Palace)	1
1969	05/04: Derby vs. Bolton (W 5-1) – McFarland, O'Hare, Hector, Carlin, Wignall – DERBY COUNTY ARE PROMOTED TO DIVISION ONE WITH 4 GAMES TO SPARE	1
1969	19/04: Derby vs. Bristol City (W 5-0) – Durban 3, Hinton, Hector – (W26, D11, L5)	1
1969	Derby finish season 1st (1:22), on 63 points, 7 points clear of 2nd-placed C Palace	1
1969	Derby win 16 of their last 20 league games, including all of their last nine, the latter a club record for consecutive league victories	1
1969	Derby win 10 league games away from home, equalling club record set 1955/56	1
1969	Derby amass 63 points, equalling record points total achieved in Division Three North seasons 1955/56 and 1956/57 – but this time in 42 games instead of 46	1
1969	Derby win promotion by a huge margin, 13 points clear of 3rd-placed Charlton Ath	1
1969	Kevin Hector is Derby's top scorer with 16 league goals (20 in all competitions)	
1969	Roy McFarland is Derby County's inaugural Player of the Season	
1969	Dave Mackay is joint Footballer of the Year with Manchester City's Tony Book	

Derby County, Second Division Champions 1968/69. Back Row: Peter Taylor (assistant manager), Frank Wignall, John Robson, Ron Webster, Les Green, Roy McFarland, Alan Durban, Dave Mackay, Brian Clough (manager). Front Row: Jim Walker, John McGovern, John O'Hare, Willie Carlin, Kevin Hector, Alan Hinton.
PHOTO: Andy Ellis

Brian Clough (right) and Peter Taylor (left) signing new contracts under the watchful eye of chairman Sam Longson and secretary, Stuart Webb. Although Clough deserves all of the plaudits he has received over the years, one should never under-estimate the value of Peter Taylor. A Nottingham man, and former manager of Burton Albion, Taylor was aware of Derby's potential before the duo arrived. He was also brilliant at spotting potential and identifying the right sort of players whom Clough would then go and win over in his own inimitable style.
PHOTO: Andy Ellis

Year	Event	Pos
Season 1969/70 (Division One)		
1969	The Ley Stand is built during summer of 1969 and the Baseball Ground becomes one of a handful of football stadia to have standing and seating on all four sides	
1969	09/08: Derby vs. Burnley (D 0-0) – first game back in Division One for 16 years	12
1969	12/08: Ipswich vs. Derby (W 0-1) – McFarland – (W1, D1, L0)	4
1969	20/08: Derby vs. Ipswich (W 3-1) – Hinton 2, Carlin – (W2, D2, L0)	6
1969	30/08: West Brom vs. Derby (W 0-2) – Hector, Mackay – Rams 3 points off top	3
1969	03/09: League Cup 2nd Rd: Hartlepool vs. Derby (W 1-3) – McFarland, Carlin, Hinton	3
1969	06/09: Derby (3rd) vs. Everton (1st) (W 2-1) – O'Hare, Hector – Rams 2 pts off top	3
1969	10/09: Derby vs. Southampton (W 3-0) – Durban, Carlin, Hector – (W5, D4, L0)	2
1969	13/09: Newcastle vs. Derby (W 0-1) – McFarland – RAMS GO TOP OF DIV ONE	1
1969	13/09: Derby are top of English first tier for the first time since December 1948	1
1969	17/09: It only lasts for 4 days, as Everton play and win their game in hand	2
1969	20/09: Derby vs. Tottenham (W 5-0) – Durban 2, Carlin, O'Hare, Hector	2
1969	20/09: The Tottenham match sees Derby's highest-ever attendance of 41,826	2
1969	20/09: Game also marks Derby's 22nd league match without defeat – a club record	2
1969	24/09: League Cup 3rd Rd: Derby vs. Hull City (W 3-1) – O'Hare, Hector, Hinton	2
1969	27/09: Sheffield Wed vs. Derby (L 1-0) – unbeaten start (11) and run (22) both end	3
1969	04/10: Derby vs. Manchester United (W 2-0) – Hector, Fitzpatrick (og)	2
1969	25/10: Leeds (5th) vs. Derby (3rd) (L 2-0) – four games without a win	3
1969	29/10: League Cup 4th Rd Replay: Derby vs. Crystal Pal (W 3-0) – Hinton 2, Hector	4
1969	01/11: Derby vs. Liverpool (2nd) (W 4-0) – Hector 2, McGovern, O'Hare – att. 40,993	4
1969	08/11: Arsenal vs. Derby (L 4-0) – Rams are now 9 points behind leaders, Everton	4
1969	15/11: Derby vs. Sunderland (W 3-0) – Durban 2, Ashurst (og) – (W10, D5, L5)	5
1969	19/11: League Cup Quarter-Final Replay: Manchester United vs. Derby (L 1-0)	5
1969	29/11: Derby vs. Nottingham For (L 0-2) – Rams 10 points behind leaders, Everton	7
1969	13/12: Derby vs. Newcastle (W 2-0) – McGovern, Hinton – (W12, D5, L7)	5
1969	26/12: Stoke City vs. Derby (L 1-0) – Rams now 12 points behind leaders, Everton	8
1969	27/12: Derby vs. West Brom (W 2-0) – O'Hare 2 – (W13, D5, L9)	5

The 1970s

Year	Event	Pos
1970	Rams sign Terry Hennessey from Forest for £100,000 – Derby's first £100K player	
1970	11/02: Derby vs. Chelsea (D 2-2) – Durban, Hector – (W14, D6, L11)	10
1970	21/02: Derby vs. Arsenal (W 3-2) – O'Hare, Hector, Mackay – 1st of 6 straight wins	5
1970	28/02: Liverpool vs. Derby (W 0-2) – O'Hare, Hennessey – (W16, D7, L11)	4
1970	07/03: Derby vs. West Ham (W 3-0) – Durban, O'Hare, Hinton – Rams 11 pts off top	4
1970	14/03: Nottingham Forest vs. Derby (W 1-3) – Durban, O'Hare, O'Kane (og)	3
1970	21/03: Derby vs. Crystal Pal (W 3-1) – Carlin, Hector, Hinton – (W19, D7, L11)	4
1970	27/03: Man City vs. Derby (W 0-1) – McFarland – six wins on the spin	4
1970	30/03: Derby vs. Leeds (W 4-1) – McFarland, Carlin, O'Hare, Wignall	3
1970	30/03: Derby finally taste victory over Leeds, and also end Leeds' title challenge	3
1970	Derby finish season 4th (4:22), on 53 points, 13 points behind Champs, Everton...	4
1970	...but only 4 points behind Runners-Up Leeds United; the gap is closing...	4
1970	Again, Derby complete season with long unbeaten run (12 this time – W8, D4)	
1970	K Hector/J O'Hare are top scorers with 13 league goals (O'Hare 16 all comps)	
1970	John O'Hare is Derby's Player of the Season	
Season 1970/71 (Division One)		
1970	Rams fined £10,000 & banned from competing in UEFA Cup due to administrative irregularities; Birmingham City and Greek national team court Clough and Taylor	
1970	Derby win the Watney Cup, beating Fulham, Sheff Utd – and Man Utd 4-1 in final	
1970	19/08: Wolves vs. Derby (W 2-4) – McGovern 2, Durban, O'Hare – (W1, D0, L1)	8
1970	26/08: Derby vs. Ipswich Town (W 2-0) – Hector, Harper (og) – (W3, D0, L1)	5
1870	29/08: Huddersfield Town vs. Derby (D 0-0) – Rams 3 pts behind leaders, Leeds	4
1970	02/09: Derby vs. Coventry (L 3-4) – McGovern, Hector, Hinton – (W3, D1, L2)	8
1970	12/09: Southampton vs. Derby (L 4-0) – 3 defeats on the bounce	13
1970	Derby sign Archie Gemmill from Preston for £59,000; Willie Carlin sold to Leicester	
1970	14/11: Man City vs. Derby (D 1-1) – O'Hare – 8 without a win and 1 win in 13	19
1970	28/11: Nottm Forest vs. Derby (W 2-4) – McGovern, O'Hare, Wignall, Gemmill	14
1970	26/12: Derby vs. Man Utd (D 4-4) – Mackay, Hector, Wignall and Gemmill	17
1971	05/01: Derby win BBC TV's Quiz Ball, beating Crystal Palace 4-2 in the final!	17
1971	09/01: Derby vs. Wolves (L 1-2) – 5 w/o win – Taylor told to rest due to chest pains	18
1971	16/01: Ipswich Town vs. Derby (W 0-1) – O'Hare – (W7, D7, L11)	16
1971	03/02: Roy McFarland becomes Derby's first England international in 21 years	17
1971	03/02: Archie Gemmill wins first Scotland cap and plays alongside John O'Hare	17
1971	06/02: West Ham vs. Derby (W 1-4) – Hector 2, Hinton 2 – (W8, D7, L11)	15
1971	Derby smash their transfer record, signing Colin Todd for £175,000 from Sun'land	15
1971	27/02: Derby vs. Arsenal (2nd) (W 2-0) – McFarland, Hector – 5 wins on spin	13
1971	10/04: Manchester United vs. Derby (W 1-2) – O'Hare 2 – (W13, D8, L16)	12
1971	17/04: Derby vs. Everton (W 3-1) – O'Hare 2, Hector – (W14, D9, L16)	12
1971	24/04: Burnley vs. Derby (W 1-2) – McGovern, Durban – Burnley are relegated	10
1971	01/05: Derby vs. West Brom (W 2-0) Hinton, Durban – (W16, D10, L16)	8
1971	01/05: Dave Mackay, aged 36, signs off with his first ever-present league season	8
1971	Derby finish season 9th (9:22), on 42 points, 22 points behind Champs, Arsenal	9
1971	John O'Hare is Derby's leading scorer with 13 league goals (15 in all competitions)	
1971	Dave Mackay is Derby's Player of the Season	

Although Derby didn't pull up any trees in Clough and Taylor's first season (1967/68), the future Football League Championship-winning side was largely in place. Boulton, Webster, Durban and Hector were already there, but Clough made three crucial early signings in 1967, in John O'Hare (August, above left), Roy McFarland (August, centre left) and Alan Hinton (September, centre right). They cost a mere £75,000 between them. Meanwhile, John Robson (far right) was spotted in North East junior football by Peter Taylor, who signed him for nothing. So for an outlay of £75,000, the quartet went on to make a combined 1,359 appearances for the Rams, scoring 216 goals. PHOTOS: Andy Ellis

Quirk Alert: Feast Your Eyes II

Top of League Division One Table –13 September 1969									
Pos	Team	Pld	W	D	L	F	A	GAvg	GD	Pts
1	Derby County	10	6	4	0	14	4	3.500	10	16
2	Liverpool	10	7	2	1	22	10	2.200	12	16
3	Everton	9	7	1	1	17	7	2.429	10	15
4	Wolverhampton W	9	4	4	1	17	13	1.308	4	12
5	Leeds United	9	3	5	1	16	11	1.455	5	11

Everton win their game in hand and their next game; Derby beat 6th-placed Spurs 5-0 in their next game, in front of a record BBG crowd; NB: check out Derby's awesome Goal Avg, below!

Top of League Division One Table – 20 September 1969									
Pos	Team	Pld	W	D	L	F	A	GAvg	GD	Pts
1	Everton	11	9	1	1	22	8	2.750	14	19
2	Derby County	11	7	4	0	19	4	4.750	15	18
3	Liverpool	11	8	2	1	25	11	2.273	14	18
4	Wolverhampton W	11	4	6	1	19	15	1.267	4	14
5	Leeds United	10	4	5	1	18	11	1.636	7	13

Quirk Alert: The Panned United

When Derby County beat Leeds United 4-1 at the Baseball Ground on 30 March 1970, the win lifted Derby into 3rd place with two to play, but perhaps more significantly it virtually ended 2nd-placed Leeds' title challenge.

Left: Dave Mackay, Derby's captain holds aloft the Watney Cup, won before the start of the 1970/71 season. Mackay had won every honour in the game before Brian Clough talked him into choosing Derby instead of Heart of Midlothian, his home-town club. As for the Watney Cup, it was comprised of the eight highest goalscoring clubs from the previous season who hadn't qualified for Europe or achieved promotion. Derby beat Fulham 3-5 (having been 3-1 down after 14 minutes), Sheffield United 1-0, and Manchester United 4-1 in the Watney Cup Final with goals from McFarland, Hinton, Durban and Dave Mackay himself. PHOTO: Andy Ellis

Quirk Alert: All Change!
When Derby beat Nottingham Forest 4-2 at the City Ground on 28 November 1970, the Rams scorers were John McGovern, John O'Hare, Frank Wignall and Archie Gemmill. Wignall played for Forest between 1963 and 1968, while McGovern, O'Hare and Gemmill were all destined for Forest in significantly better times for the Reds!

RAMS CHRONOLOGY: Champions of England

Season 1971/72

Year	Event	Pos
1971	Derby change club badge and kit from traditional black & white to blue & white	
1971	21/08: Leicester City vs. Derby (W 0-2) – Hector, Hinton – (W2, D1, L0)	3
1971	04/09: Everton vs. Derby (W 0-2) – Wignall, Hector – (W3, D4, L0)	3
1971	11/09: Derby vs. Stoke (W 4-0) – Todd, Gemmill, O'Hare, Hinton	2
1971	15/09: Texaco Cup Rd 1: Derby vs. Dundee United (W 6-2) – six different scorers	2
1971	Roger Davies signed from Worcester City for a non-league record fee of £12,000	
1971	02/10: Newcastle United vs. Derby (W 0-1) – Hinton – Rams are 2 points off top	3
1971	09/10: Derby vs. Tottenham (D 2-2) – Todd, McFarland – Rams unbeaten after 12 games (W5, D7, L0); 18 counting the end of the previous season	4
1971	16/10: Man Utd (1st) vs. Derby (4th) (L 1-0) – Rams actually rise one place on GAvg!	3
1971	20/10: Texaco Cup Rd 2: Derby County vs. Stoke City (W 3-2) – O'Hare 2, Hector	
1971	20/10: Steve Powell becomes Derby's youngest-ever player, aged 16 yrs, 30 days	4
1971	23/10: Derby vs. Arsenal (W 2-1) – O'Hare, Hinton – Rams 4 pts behind Man Utd	2
1971	30/10: Nottm F vs. Derby (W 0-2) – Robson, Hinton – Rams close gap to 2 points	2
1971	06/11: Derby vs. Crystal P (W 3-0) – Wignall, Hector, (og) – Rams 1 pt off Man Utd	2
1971	13/11: Wolves vs. Derby (L 2-1) – O'Hare – Rams now 3 points behind Man Utd	2
1971	20/11: Derby vs. Sheffield United (W 3-0) – Hinton 2, Hector – still 3 pts off top	2
1971	24/11: Texaco Cup Semi-Final, 1st Leg: Derby vs. Newcastle (W 1-0) – O'Hare	
1971	27/11: Huddersfield T vs. Derby (L 2-1) – McGovern – Rams overtaken by Man City	3
1971	04/12: Derby (3rd) vs Man City (2nd) (W 3-1) Webster, Durban, Hinton – 5 pts off top	2

79

Year	Event	Pos
1971	08/12: Texaco Cup Semi-Final, 2nd Leg: Newcastle vs. Derby (W 2-3 AET) – McGovern, Todd, Walker – [agg 2-4]	2
1971	11/12: Liverpool vs. Derby (L 3-2) – O'Hare 2 – Rams now 6 pts behind Man Utd	4
1971	18/12: Derby vs. Everton (W 2-0) – Hinton 2 – Rams 5 points behind Man Utd	3
1971	27/12: Leeds vs. Derby (L 3-0) – Rams now 6 points behind leaders, Man Utd	5
1972	08/01: Southampton vs. Derby (W 1-2) – O'Hare, Durban – Rams now 2 pts off top	4
1972	15/01: FA Cup 3rd Rd: Derby vs. Shrewsbury Town (W 2-0) – Hector 2	4
1972	26/01: Texaco Cup Final 1st Leg: Airdieonians vs. Derby County – D 0-0	4
1972	29/01: Derby vs. Coventry (W 1-0) – Robson – 2 pts behind new leaders, Man City	3
1972	05/02: FA Cup 4th Rd: Derby vs. Notts C (W 6-0) – Durban 3, Robson, Hector, Hinton	3
1972	05/02: Kevin Hector's goal against Notts County is his 100th goal for Derby County	3
1972	12/02: Arsenal vs. Derby (L 2-0) – Rams now 3 points behind leaders, Man City	3
1972	19/02: Derby vs. Nottingham F (W 4-0) – Hinton 2, Hector, O'Hare – 3 pts off top	3
1972	26/02: FA Cup 5th Rd: Derby vs. Arsenal (D 2-2) – Durban, Hinton	3
1972	29/02: FA Cup 5th Rd Replay: Arsenal vs. Derby (D 0-0 AET)	3
1972	04/03: Derby vs. Wolves (W 2-1) – Hinton, McFarland – 5 points off City with 2 GIH	3
1972	11/03: Tottenham vs. Derby (W 0-1) – Hinton – still 5 points off top with 2 GIH	3
1972	13/03: FA Cup 5th Rd, 2nd Replay (Filbert Street): Arsenal vs. Derby (L 1-0)	3
1972	18/03: Derby vs. Leicester (W 3-0) – O'Hare, Hector, Durban – still 5 points off top	2
1972	22/03: Derby vs. Ipswich (W 1-0) – Hector – Rams close gap on Man City to 3 points	2
1972	28/03: Crystal Palace vs. Derby (W 0-1) – Walker – Rams close gap to 1 point	2
1972	01/04: Derby (2nd) vs. Leeds (3rd) (W 2-0) – O'Hare, Hunter (og) – DERBY GO TOP	1
1972	03/04: Derby vs. Newcastle (L 0-1) – Rams blow chance to extend lead at top	1
1972	05/04: West Brom vs. Derby (D 0-0) – Rams are still top by 1 point from Leeds	1
1972	08/04: Sheffield Utd vs. Derby (W 0-4) – Gemmill, O'Hare, Hector, Durban	1
1972	15/04: Derby vs. Huddersfield (W 3-0) – McFarland, O'Hare, Hector – 4 to play	1
1972	22/04: Man City vs. Derby (L 2-0) – City leap-frog Derby into first place 22/04: Derby appear to have blown it, and drop to third with one to play 22/04: Man City have now completed their fixtures, a point clear at the top 22/04: Liverpool beat Ipswich to go 2nd with 2 games to play – theirs to lose 22/04: Leeds beat West Brom and are 4th with two to play, 2 points off the top	3
1972	26/04: Texaco Cup Final, 2nd Leg: Derby vs. Airdrieonians (W 2-1) [Agg 2-1] – Hinton, Davies – DERBY WIN THE TEXACO CUP	3
1972	01/05: Derby vs. Liverpool (W 1-0) – McGovern's vital goal – another twist 01/05: Derby go back to the top; Liverpool drop to 4th, two points behind Derby 01/05: Derby have now completed their fixtures and can only wait 01/05: Leeds beat Chelsea 2-0 to go 2nd, a point behind Derby 01/05: Leeds and Liverpool still have one game each to play 01/05: So it's now Leeds' title to lose, with Liverpool waiting in the wings 01/05: Leeds' Goal Avg is better than Liverpool's; Liverpool's better than Derby's 01/05: So all Leeds need is a draw at Wolves 01/05: Liverpool need to win at Arsenal and hope Leeds lose to Wolves 01/05: Derby need Leeds to lose and Liverpool to not win 01/05: Odds are based on Leeds, Liverpool, Derby, in that order. And incredibly...	1
1972	08/05: Wolves vs. Leeds (2-1)	

Year	Event	Pos
	08/05: Arsenal vs. Liverpool (0-0)	1
1972	DERBY COUNTY ARE DIVISION ONE CHAMPIONS FOR THE FIRST TIME (58 points)	1
1972	Alan Hinton is Derby's top scorer with 15 league goals (20 in all competitions)	
1972	Colin Todd is Derby's Player of the Season	
1972	Derby County Reserves win the Central League title	
1972	27/05: Alan Durban makes his 27th appearance for Wales, becoming (at this time) Derby's most-capped international, overtaking Sammy Crooks (26 caps for England)	

Stats Blast: Unimportant!
Remarkably, Derby's home game against Nottingham Forest on 19 February saw an attendance of 31,801 – Derby's 13th highest home league attendance of that season!

The following table charts the ebb and flow of this remarkable season. Derby were always within touching distance of top spot, but didn't hit the summit until a hugely significant victory over Leeds United on April 1st 1972 – only to almost throw it away again...

#	Date	Opponents	V	Result	Top of Table	Top Pts	DER Pts	DER Pos
1	14/08/71	Manchester United	H	D 2-2	Liverpool	2	1	7
2	18/08/71	West Ham United	H	W 2-0	Sheffield United	4	3	6
3	21/08/71	Leicester City	A	W 0-2	Sheffield United	6	5	3
4	24/08/71	Coventry City	A	D 2-2	Sheffield United	8	6	3
5	28/08/71	Southampton	H	D 2-2	Sheffield United	9	7	4
6	31/08/71	Ipswich Town	A	D 0-0	Sheffield United	11	8	2
7	04/09/71	Everton	A	W 0-2	Sheffield United	13	10	3
8	11/09/71	Stoke City	H	W 4-0	Sheffield United	14	12	2
9	18/09/71	Chelsea	A	D 1-1	Sheffield United	16	13	3
10	25/09/71	West Bromwich Albion	H	D 0-0	Sheffield United	18	14	3
11	02/10/71	Newcastle United	A	W 0-1	Sheffield United	18	16	3
12	09/10/71	Tottenham Hotspur	H	D 2-2	Manchester United	19	17	4
13	16/10/71	Manchester United	A	L 1-0	Manchester United	21	17	4
14	23/10/71	Arsenal	H	W 2-1	Manchester United	23	19	3
15	30/10/71	Nottingham Forest	A	W 0-2	Manchester United	23	21	2
16	06/11/71	Crystal Palace	H	W 3-0	Manchester United	24	23	2
17	13/11/71	Wolverhampton W	A	L 2-1	Manchester United	26	23	2
18	20/11/71	Sheffield United	H	W 3-0	Manchester United	28	25	2
19	27/11/71	Huddersfield Town	A	L 2-1	Manchester United	30	25	3
20	04/12/71	Manchester City	H	W 3-1	Manchester United	32	27	2
21	11/12/71	Liverpool	A	L 3-2	Manchester United	33	27	4
22	18/12/71	Everton	H	W 2-0	Manchester United	34	29	3
23	27/12/71	Leeds United	A	L 3-0	Manchester United	35	29	5
24	01/01/72	Chelsea	H	W 1-0	Manchester United	35	31	4
25	08/01/72	Southampton	A	W 1-2	Manchester United	35	33	4
26	22/01/72	West Ham United	A	D 3-3	Leeds United	36	34	4

#	Date	Opponents	V	Result	Top of Table	Top Pts	DER Pts	DER Pos
27	29/01/72	Coventry City	H	W 1-0	Manchester City	38	36	3
28	12/02/72	Arsenal	A	L 2-0	Manchester City	39	36	3
29	19/02/72	Nottingham Forest	H	W 4-0	Manchester City	41	38	3
30	04/03/72	Wolverhampton W	H	W 2-1	Manchester City	45	40	3
31	11/03/72	Tottenham Hotspur	A	W 0-1	Manchester City	47	42	3
32	18/03/72	Leicester City	H	W 3-0	Manchester City	49	44	2
33	22/03/72	Ipswich Town	H	W 1-0	Manchester City	49	46	2
34	25/03/72	Stoke City	A	D 1-1	Manchester City	50	47	2
35	28/03/72	Crystal Palace	A	W 0-1	Manchester City	50	49	2
36	01/04/72	Leeds United	H	W 2-0	Derby County	51	51	1
37	03/04/72	Newcastle United	H	L 0-1	Derby County	51	51	1
38	05/04/72	West Bromwich Albion	A	D 0-0	Derby County	52	52	1
39	08/04/72	Sheffield United	A	W 0-4	Derby County	54	54	1
40	15/04/72	Huddersfield Town	H	W 3-0	Derby County	56	56	1

With two games to go, we now pick up the story by including the three other protagonists in this extraordinary end to an extraordinary season...

Saturday 15 April 1972

Pos	Team	Pld	W	D	L	F	A	GAvg	GD	Pts	Home		Res	Away
1	Derby County	40	23	10	7	68	31	2.194	+37	56	Derby County		3-0	Huddersfield T
2	Manchester City	40	22	11	7	74	43	1.721	+31	55	Coventry City		1-1	Manchester City
3	Liverpool	39	23	8	8	62	29	2.138	+33	54	West Ham United		0-2	Liverpool
4	Leeds United	38	22	9	7	69	28	2.464	+41	53				

Tuesday 18 April 1972

Pos	Team	Pld	W	D	L	F	A	GAvg	GD	Pts	Home		Res	Away
1	Derby County	40	23	10	7	68	31	2.194	+37	56				
2	Manchester City	41	22	11	8	75	45	1.667	+30	55	Ipswich Town		2-1	Manchester City
3	Liverpool	39	23	8	8	62	29	2.138	+33	54				
4	Leeds United	38	22	9	7	69	28	2.464	+41	53				

Wednesday 19 April 1972

Pos	Team	Pld	W	D	L	F	A	GAvg	GD	Pts	Home		Res	Away
1	Derby County	40	23	10	7	68	31	2.194	+37	56				
2	Manchester City	41	22	11	8	75	45	1.667	+30	55				
3	Liverpool	39	23	8	8	62	29	2.138	+33	54				
4	Leeds United	39	22	9	8	69	29	2.379	+40	53	Newcastle Utd		1-0	Leeds United

Saturday 22 April 1972

Pos	Team	Pld	W	D	L	F	A	GAvg	GD	Pts	Home		Res	Away
1	Manchester City	42	23	11	8	77	45	1.711	+32	57	Manchester City		2-0	Derby County
2	Liverpool	40	24	8	8	64	29	2.207	+35	56	Liverpool		2-0	Ipswich Town
3	Derby County	41	23	10	8	68	33	2.061	+35	56	Manchester City		2-0	Derby County
4	Leeds United	40	23	9	8	70	29	2.414	+41	55	West Bromwich A		0-1	Leeds United

Monday 1 May 1972

Pos	Team	Pld	W	D	L	F	A	GAvg	GD	Pts	Home	Res	Away
1	Derby County	42	24	10	8	69	33	2.091	+36	58	Derby County	1-0	Liverpool
2	Leeds United	41	24	9	8	72	29	2.483	+43	57	Leeds United	2-0	Chelsea
3	Manchester City	42	23	11	8	77	45	1.711	+32	57			
4	Liverpool	41	24	8	9	64	30	2.133	+34	56	Derby County	1-0	Liverpool

Monday 8 May 1972

Pos	Team	Pld	W	D	L	F	A	GAvg	GD	Pts	Home	Res	Away
1	Derby County	42	24	10	8	69	33	2.091	+36	58			
2	Leeds United	42	24	9	9	73	31	2.483	+43	57	Wolverhampton W	2-1	Leeds United
3	Liverpool	42	24	9	9	64	30	2.133	+34	57	Arsenal	0-0	Liverpool
4	Manchester City	42	23	11	8	77	45	1.711	+32	57			

Stats Blast: Six of the Best

When Derby beat Dundee United 6-2, in the Texaco Cup First Round, on 15th September 1971, Derby had six different scorers: Durban, Hector, Walker, O'Hare, Hinton and Robson – the Texaco Cup being a competition involving clubs from England, Scotland and Northern Ireland.

Stats Blast: Unbeaten

When Derby drew 2-2 at home with Tottenham Hotspur on 9 October 1971, there were a number of points of note. Firstly, it was the only time that central defenders Colin Todd and Roy McFarland were on the scoresheet together. Secondly, it increased Derby's unbeaten start to the 1971/72 season to 12 league games. And thirdly, it stretched Derby's overall unbeaten league run to 18 games – ironically since they'd lost 2-1 to Tottenham on 7th April, 1971. Derby lost their next game, 1-0, away to Manchester United. Already top of the league at that point, United went three points clear, while Derby remained in fourth position.

Quirk Alert: Blades of Glory

But if you think that Derby had a great start to the season, check out unfancied Sheffield United:

League Division One Table – 25 September 1971									
Pos	Team	Pld	W	D	L	F	A	GAvg	GD	Pts
1	Sheffield United	10	8	2	0	18	6	3.000	+12	18
2	Manchester United	10	6	3	1	22	13	1.692	+9	15
3	**Derby County**	10	4	6	0	17	7	2.429	+10	14

Stats Blast: Sixteen

Sixteen is the number of players that Derby used during the 1971/72 season. It is a frequent requirement for Champions to have luck with injuries, but even so, 16 players is remarkable – particularly when you consider that three of them – Tony Bailey, Steve Powell and Jim Walker – only made six appearances between them! Furthermore, Frank Wignall only appeared 11 times, before his move to Mansfield Town in November. However, he had been a valuable contributor, scoring 5 goals in those 11 league games. Of course, 16 was also the age of Steve Powell when he stood in for Ron Webster in that crucial final game of the season against Liverpool, and didn't put a foot wrong!

Quirk Alert: We got by with a little help from our friends...

From the moment that Derby lost to Newcastle on Easter Monday, 3 April 1972, they were 4th favourites to lift the Division One Championship. They may well have been top, but their rivals had games in hand, and Derby still had to play away at Manchester City. Cue Derby's "friends" as shown right ->

04/04/1972: Southampton vs. Manchester C (2-0)
15/04/1972: Coventry City vs. Manchester C (1-1)
18/04/1972: Ipswich Town vs. Manchester C (2-1)
19/04/1972: Newcastle United vs. Leeds Utd (1-0)
08/05/1972: Wolves vs. Leeds United (2-1)
08/05/1972: Arsenal vs. Liverpool (0-0)

Quirk Alert: Miserable Bar Stewards

Prior to Derby's home game with Wolves on 4 March 1972, Derby paraded their new signing. He was Ian Storey-Moore, signed from Nottingham Forest for £225,000. The player even put out a press statement stating his delight at joining Derby. However, they had all reckoned without the approval of Nottingham Forest who, angered by the pre-match unveiling, promptly refused to sign the the transfer forms, and then proceeded to sell him to Manchester United! Still, Brian had the last laugh six seasons later when Forest **didn't** block the exchange of goalkeeper John Middleton for midfield wizard Archie Gemmill. Hey, hang on a minute...

Left: John McGovern arrived at Derby in September 1968, for £7,500, from Hartlepool; Centre: Archie Gemmill was signed in September 1970 for £66,000 from Preston; Right: Colin Todd was the final piece of the jigsaw, arriving in February 1971 for a club record fee of £170,000 from Sunderland.
PHOTOS: Andy Ellis

The goal that won the title. John McGovern falls to the floor as he lashes home in the 1-0 victory over Liverpool on Monday 1st May 1972, a win which took Derby back to the top of Division One. Leeds and Liverpool weren't good enough to better Derby's 58 points and the Rams were thus crowned Champions of England for season 1971/72.
PHOTO: Andy Ellis

Derby County, Football League Champions 1971/72. Back Row: Brian Clough (Manager), Terry Hennessey, Ron Webster, Colin Boulton, Colin Todd, John Robson, Peter Taylor (Assistant Manager), Jimmy Gordon (Trainer); Front Row: John McGovern, Archie Gemmill, John O'Hare, Roy McFarland, Kevin Hector, Alan Hinton, Alan Durban. PHOTO: Andy Ellis

RAMS CHRONOLOGY: Up with the Big Boys

Season 1972/73

Year	Event	Pos
1972	August: Brian Clough and Sam Longson allegedly fall out over a pre-season tour, while Clough also faces two separate charges of bringing the game into disrepute, due to comments made about the FA and the Football League	
1972	24/08: Derby break British transfer record to sign David Nish from Leicester for £225K	12
1972	29/08: Everton vs. Derby (L 1-0) – Rams win only 1 of first 6 games (W1, D2, L3)	16
1972	02/09: Derby vs. Liverpool (W 2-1) – O'Hare, Hinton – (W2, D2, L3)	13
1972	02/09 – 04/11: Thus starts a 10-game sequence of WLWLWLWLWL (home W, away L), including heavy defeats at Man United (3-0), Leeds (5-0) and Man City (4-0)	16
1972	25/11: Derby vs. Arsenal (W 5-0) – McFarland, McGovern, Hector, Hinton, Davies	13
1972	John Robson sold to Aston V for £90,000, a record outbound fee for Derby at the time	
1972	09/12: Derby vs. Coventry (W 2-0) – Gemmill, Hinton – 4 straight wins	7
1972	16/12: Derby vs. Newcastle (D 1-1) – Hector – Rams 8 pts behind leaders, Liverpool	6
1972	23/12: Stoke City vs. Derby (L 4-0) – Rams drop down to 10th, now 10 pts off top	10
1972	26/12: Derby vs. Manchester United (W 3-1) – McFarland 2, Hinton – (W11, D4, L9)	7
1973	06/01: Derby vs. Norwich City (W 1-0) – Hinton – but Rams 11 points off top	5
1973	20/01: Liverpool vs. Derby (D 1-1) – Davies – credible draw at league leaders	6
1973	27/01: Derby vs. West Brom (W 2-0) – Hinton, Davies – Rams 9 points off top	5
1973	07/02: FA Cup 4th Rd Replay: Tottenham vs. Derby (W 3-5) – Davies 3, Hector 2	5
1973	17/02: Derby vs. Southampton (W 4-0) – Hector 2, Hinton, McCarthy (og)	5
1973	24/02: FA Cup 5th Rd: Derby vs. Queens Park Rangers (W 4-2) – Hector 3, Davies	6

Year	Event	Pos
1973	17/03: FA Cup Quarter-Final: Derby vs. Leeds United (L 0-1)	8
1973	24/03: Sheffield United vs. Derby (L 3-1) – 4 games without a win	9
1973	31/03: Arsenal vs. Derby (W 0-1) – Powell – (W15, D7, L14)	8
1973	14/04: Kevin Hector becomes 7th & last player to score 100 league goals for Derby	9
1973	18/04: Colin Boulton is suspended, bringing an end to 131 consecutive appearances	9
1973	30/04: Derby vs. Ipswich (W 3-0) – Hector 2, Davies – (W18, D8, L15)	9
1973	04/05: Derby vs. Wolves (W 3-0) – Davies 2, McFarland – Rams finish with 3 wins	7
1973	Derby finish season 7th (7:22) on 46 points, 14 points behind Champions, Liverpool	7
1973	Kevin Hector is Derby's leading scorer with 14 league goals (23 in all competitions)	
1973	Kevin Hector is also Derby's Player of the Season	

Stats Blast: Derby County's European Cup, 1972/73

Date	Match	Opponents	Country	Res	Agg	Goals
13/09/1972	1st Rd, 1st Leg	FK Željezničar	Yugoslavia	W 2-0		McFarland, Gemmill
27/09/1972	1st Rd, 2nd Leg	FK Željezničar	Yugoslavia	W 1-2	W 1-4	Hinton, O'Hare
25/10/1972	2nd Rd, 1st Leg	Benfica	Portugal	W 3-0		McFarland, Hector, McGovern
08/11/1972	2nd Rd, 2nd Leg	Benfica	Portugal	D 0-0	W 0-3	
07/03/1973	3rd Rd, 1st Leg	Spartak Trnava	Czechoslovakia	L 1-0		
21/03/1973	3rd Rd, 2nd Leg	Spartak Trnava	Czechoslovakia	W 2-0	W 2-1	Hector 2
11/04/1973	SF, 1st Leg	Juventus	Italy	L 1-3		Hector
25/04/1973	SF, 2nd Leg	Juventus	Italy	D 0-0	L 1-3	

Quirk Alert: The Old <insert noun> of Turin
And I don't mean a lady, either! Or a shroud! Yes, this was one of Brian Clough's bitter outbursts after Derby lost the first leg of their 1973 European Cup Semi-Final to Juventus under hugely controversial circumstances. The Rams lost the first leg 3-1 in Turin thanks to a number of massively questionable refereeing decisions, including the harsh bookings of Roy McFarland and Archie Gemmill that saw them both ruled out of the second leg.

Quirk Alert: "No cheating <insert another noun {plural}> will I talk to"
Yes, this was another of Cloughie's outbursts – this time to the waiting Italian reporters as he emerged from Derby's dressing room after the game. When asked what he meant, he slightly rearranged the words and said "I will not talk to any cheating bastards".

Quirk Alert: Flippancy aside...
...this is clearly no laughing matter, and it robbed Derby of what proved to be their best-ever chance of emulating Manchester United and precursoring Liverpool, Forest, Villa et al.
*   For those not familiar, Derby manager Brian Clough complained bitterly at the time, after Peter Taylor had spotted Juve's German substitute, Helmut Haller, accompanying the German referee into his dressing room both before the match in Italy, and at half time.*
*   That wasn't it for controversy, though, as the return leg at the Baseball Ground was a 0-0 draw, with Derby having to manage with 10 men following the sending off of the normally mild-*

mannered 6ft 3in centre forward, Roger Davies. Mind you, head-butting an aforementioned {alleged} cheating <insert noun> into the back of his own net must carry small levels of compensation!

Quirk Alert: Later Confirmation

After the second leg, the Portuguese referee reported to his own FA that he had been offered a bribe to favour Juventus. UEFA took no action other than to indefinitely suspend the Italian agent in question – and hence the Old Lady proceeded to the Final. The following year, the Sunday Times interviewed the Portuguese referee and printed the story – which went down badly in Turin. Well boo-hoo! Sadly, it took another 33 years for justice to catch up with them!

Stats Blast: Cold Comfort

There was one small chink of light to emerge from this tie; remarkably, Kevin Hector's equaliser in Turin was the first European Cup goal scored by any English side in Italy! Hmm...

Season 1973/74

Year	Event	Pos
1973	Summer: Brian Clough's media profile increases, with outspoken comments on the FA, directors, important figures in the game, and a call for Leeds to be demoted	
1973	26/06: Clough agrees terms with Bobby Moore unbeknown to both clubs; Derby make formal £100K offer in August for Moore & Brooking; West Ham reject bid	
1973	29/08: Derby vs. Manchester City (W 1-0) – Hinton – Rams joint-top (W2, D0, L0)	5
1973	01/09: Birmingham City vs. Derby (D 0-0) – Rams have 5 pts out of 6; Leeds 6/6	2
1973	04/09: Liverpool vs. Derby (L 2-0) – Rams still only 1 point behind leaders, Leeds	7
1973	12/09: Derby vs. Liverpool (W 3-1) – McFarland, Davies, Hector – (W4, D1, L1)	5
1973	21/09: Derby sign Henry Newton from Everton for £110K, against medical advice	6
1973	22/09: Derby vs. Southampton (W 6-2) – Hector 3, Davies 2, Hinton – 3 pts off top	2
1973	24/09: Chairman, Sam Longson, demands Brian Clough curb his media profile	2
1973	McFarland, Todd, Nish, Hector all in England squad for vital WC qualifier vs. Poland	
1973	Derby's directors suggest to Longson he should resign as Chairman; Sam declines	
1973	29/09: Tottenham vs. Derby (L 1-0) – Rams now 5 points behind leaders, Leeds	4
1973	01/10: Article in Daily Mirror questions Brian Clough's commitment to Derby Co	4
1973	Clough travels to Holland to watch Poland as prep for pending big match on ITV	4
1973	10/10: Clough criticises FA for full league programme, 4 days before vital WC game	4
1973	11/10: Longson, calls for Clough and Taylor to be sacked – motion rejected	4
1973	13/10: Manchester United vs. Derby (W 0-1) – Hector – Rams 4 points off top	3
1973	13/10: Longson accuses Clough of V sign to Sir Matt Busby; Clough strongly denies	3
1973	13/10: Board member Jack Kirkland demands to know what Peter Taylor's role at the club is, and that Taylor face the board to explain this on Monday	3
1973	14/10: Other board members again ask Longson to step down; again, Sam declines	3
1973	15/10: In response to Kirkland's insulting request, Clough and Taylor resign, as does director Michael Keeling; this time, the board accept their resignations	3
1973	17/10: Brian Clough calls Poland's goalkeeper a clown as England fail to reach	

Year	Event	Pos
	the World Cup Finals; Kevin Hector makes England debut as a "too little, too late" 88th minute substitute, but still has an effort cleared off the line	3
1973	18/10: A long and strong statement by Sam Longson appears in the Derby Evening Telegraph justifying the acceptance of Clough and Taylor's resignations	3
1973	20/10: A similar statement appears in The Ram magazine, culminating with: "No-one can be bigger than the club. No-one can put the club's interests second."	3
1973	20/10: Derby vs. Leicester (W 2-1) – McGovern, Hector – amidst angry demos	3
1973	20/10: Unbeknown to directors, Brian Clough is in the crowd and is hailed by fans, while poor Sam Longson takes the accolades, believing the applause is for himself	3
1973	20/10: Clough leaves the game early and appears on Parkinson later that evening where he attacks football directors in general	3
1973	Derby's players petition the board to reinstate Brian Clough and Peter Taylor	3
1973	Pressure mounts, with marches in Derby also demanding reinstatement, while local MP, Phillip Whitehead, also speaks out on Clough's behalf	3
1973	22/10: Clough starts legal proceedings against the club's Directors for damages for alleged libel; the matter and compensation is settled out of court two years later	3
1973	23/10: Derby appoint Dave Mackay as manager; DET reports "Clough saga is over"	3
1973	08/12: Derby have gone 8 games without a win, 6 in the league; run includes home defeats to Second Division Sunderland (0-3 in League Cup) and QPR (1-2 in league)	9
1973	15/12: Newcastle vs. Derby (W 0-2) – Davies, Hinton – Mackay's first win	7
1973	22/12: Derby vs. Tottenham H (W 2-0) – Hinton 2 – (W9, D6, L6)	4
1974	09/01: FA Cup 3rd Rd Rep: Boston U vs. Derby (W 1-6) – Gemmill 3, Bourne 2, Nish	9
1974	12/01: Derby (9th) vs. Burnley (3rd) (W 5-1) – Hector 3, Bourne 2 – (W10, D8, L7)	4
1974	02/02: Derby vs. Newcastle (W 1-0) – McFarland – Rams 13 points off top/Leeds	3
1974	Derby sign Bruce Rioch from Aston Villa for £200,000	3
1974	23/02: Norwich City vs. Derby (W 2-4) – Bourne 2, Davies, Hector	3
1974	23/03: Derby (3rd) vs. Ipswich (4th) (W 2-0) – Hector, Rioch – (W14, D13, L8)	3
1974	13/04: Derby vs. Sheffield United (W 4-1) – Hector 3, Davies	4
1974	27/04: Derby vs. Wolves (W 2-0) – Powell, Hector – Rams climb above Ipswich	3
1974	Derby finish season 3rd (3:22) on 48 points, 14 points behind Champions, Leeds	3
1974	Derby also qualify for the following season's UEFA Cup	
1974	Kevin Hector is Derby's top scorer with 19 league goals	
1974	Ron Webster is Derby's Player of the Season	

Left: Roger Davies, signed from Worcester City in Sep-71; Centre: David Nish was signed from Leicester City in August 1972 for a British transfer record at that time of £225,000; Right: Bruce Rioch was signed in February 1974 from Aston Villa for £200,000. All three were key players in Derby's next League Championship-winning side. PHOTOS: Andy Ellis

Stats Blast: Simply The Best
During the six-year tenure of Brian Clough and Peter Taylor, Derby County won the Second Division title, First Division title, Central League, Watney Cup and Texaco Cup, while they also made the semi-finals of the League Cup and the European Cup. Alas, Brian Clough's increasing media profile was to prove the pair's undoing along with a public falling out with Sam Longson and one resignation too many. Nevertheless, despite Dave Mackay doing a tremendous job in his first two and a half seasons as successor, Derby County were ultimately the big time losers from the affair. Worse still, the undoubted winners were waiting down the A52!

RAMS CHRONOLOGY: Champions Again

Season 1974/75

Year	Event	Pos
1974	15/05: Roy McFarland ruptures his Achilles tendon playing for England	
1974	Peter Daniel, at the club since 1964, deputises for Roy brilliantly	
1974	Archie Gemmill is appointed Derby captain	
1974	Derby sign Francis Lee, aged 30, from Man City for £100,000 – an inspired buy	
1974	24/08: Derby vs. Sheffield United (W 2-0) – Davies, Hector – (W1, D2, L0)	7
1974	11/09: League Cup 2nd Rd: Portsmouth vs. Derby (W 1-5) – Hector 2, Lee, Rioch	11
1974	14/09: Birmingham vs. Derby (L 3-2) – Rioch, Davies – 4 without a win	14
1974	18/09: UEFA Cup 1st Rd, 1st Leg: Derby vs. S Geneva (W 4-1) – Hector 2, Daniel, Lee	14
1974	21/09: Derby vs. Burnley (W 3-2) – Rioch, Hector, Lee – (W2, D4, L2)	10
1974	25/09: Derby vs. Chelsea (W 4-1) – Webster, Rioch, Hector, Daniel	7
1974	02/10: UEFA Cup 1st Rd, 2nd Leg: S Geneva vs. Derby (W 1-2) – Lee, Hector [agg 2-6]	8
1974	08/10: League Cup 3rd Rd: Southampton vs. Derby (L 5-0)	9
1974	12/10: Derby vs. Leicester (W 1-0) – Rioch – Rams 3 points off leaders, Ipswich	5
1974	15/10: Sheffield Utd vs. Derby (W 1-2) – Lee 2 – 1 pt off new leaders, Liverpool	3
1974	19/10: Carlisle vs. Derby (L 3-0) – (W5, D6, L3)	7
1974	23/10: UEFA Cup 2nd Rd, 1st Leg: Derby vs. Atlético Madrid (D 2-2) – Nish, Rioch	7
1974	26/10: Derby vs. Middlesbrough (L 2-3) – Hector, Hinton – Rams 5 points off top	7
1974	02/11: Leeds vs. Derby (W 0-1) – Lee – a rare win at Leeds; Rams 3 points off top	7
1974	06/11: UEFA Cup 2nd Rd, 2nd Leg: Atlético Madrid vs. Derby (D 2-2 AET) – Rioch, Hector – [agg: 4-4]; Derby win 7-6 on penalties	7
1974	09/11: Derby vs. QPR (W 5-2) – Hector 3, Lee, Rioch – Rams 2 points off top	5
1974	16/11: Arsenal vs. Derby (L 3-1) – Rioch – Rams 10th but only 2 points off top!	10
1974	23/11: Derby vs. Ipswich (W 2-0) – Rioch, Hector – Rams still 2 points off top	5
1974	27/11: UEFA Cup Rd 3, Leg1: Derby vs. Velez Mostar (W 3-1) – Bourne 2, Hinton	6
1974	07/12: Liverpool vs. Derby (D 2-2) – Davies, Bourne – 4 points off leaders, Stoke	8
1974	11/12: UEFA Cup Rd 3, Leg2: Velez Mostar vs. Derby (L 4-1) – Hector [agg: 5-4]	9
1974	14/12: Derby vs. Everton (L 0-1) – Everton go top, 5 points ahead of Derby	9
1974	21/12: Luton Town vs. Derby (L 1-0) – (W8, D7, L7) – still 5 points off top	10
1974	21/12: Ron Webster becomes the 5th player to reach 500 appearances for Derby	
1974	26/12: Derby vs. Birmingham (W 2-1) – Rioch, Bourne – Rams 4 points off top	10

Year	Event	Pos
1974	28/12: Man City vs. Derby (W 1-2) – Newton, Lee – VERY INTERESTING...	9
1975	03/01: FA Cup 3rd Rd: Orient vs. Derby (D 2-2) – Todd 2 – a very rare brace indeed!	9
1975	11/01: Derby vs. Liverpool (W 2-0) – Lee, Newton – 3 pts behind leaders, Ipswich	7
1975	18/01: Wolves vs. Derby (W 0-1) – Newton – Rams 2 points off leaders, Everton	5
1975	27/01: FA Cup 4th Rd: Derby vs. Bristol Rovers (W 2-0) – Hector, Rioch	5
1975	08/02: Derby vs. Leeds (D 0-0) – Rams & Leeds are 9th & 10th; Rams 3 pts off top	9
1975	18/02: FA Cup 5th Rd: Derby vs. Leeds United (L 0-1) – Leeds again	9
1975	22/02: Derby vs. Arsenal (W 2-1) – Powell 2- Rams 3 points behind leaders, Stoke	7
1975	25/02: Ipswich vs. Derby – (L 3-0) – but still only 4 points behind leaders, Everton	8
1975	01/03: Derby vs. Tottenham H (W 3-1) – Rioch, Daniel, Davies – 4 points off top	7
1975	08/03: Chelsea vs. Derby (W 1-2) – Daniel, Hinton – Rams still 4 points off top	3
1975	15/03: Derby vs. Stoke (L 1-2) – Hector – Rams now 5 points off top	6
1975	22/03: Newcastle vs. Derby (W 0-2) – Nish, Rioch – Rams 4 points off top	7
1975	29/03: Derby vs. Luton (W 5-0) – Roger Davies bags all 5 – Rams 3 points off top	6
1975	29/03: Roger Davies is first Ram to bag 5 in a game since Hughie Gallacher in 1934	6
1975	31/03: Burnley vs. Derby (W 2-5) – Hector 2, Davies, Nish, Rioch – 2 pts off top	5
1975	01/04: Derby vs. Man City (W 2-1) – Rioch 2 – Ipswich, Everton, Derby all on 46 pts	3
1975	05/04: Middlesbrough vs. Derby (D 1-1) – Hector – Rams 47 pts with LIV/EVE/STO	4
1975	09/04: Derby vs. Wolves (W 1-0) – Lee – RAMS FINALLY GO TOP – and two points clear, at that; also Roy McFarland returns to the side for Derby's last four games	1
1975	12/04: Derby vs. West Ham (W 1-0) – Rioch – RAMS STILL TWO POINTS CLEAR	1
1975	19/04: With two games to go, Rams can still be caught by LIV/EVE/IPS/STO	1
1975	19/04: Leicester vs. Derby (D 0-0) – incredibly LIV/EVE/IPS/STO all lose...	1
1975	19/04: ...and Derby go 3 points clear... so with one game left to play...	1
1975	19/04: ...only Ipswich (game in hand) can catch Derby if they win last 2 games...	1
1975	23/04: Man City vs. Ipswich (D 1-1) – DERBY COUNTY ARE DIV ONE CHAMPIONS	1
1975	26/04: Derby vs. Carlisle (D 0-0) – Rams receive Championship trophy before match	1
1975	Derby finish season 1st (1:22) on 53 points, 2 points ahead of Liverpool	1
1975	Bruce Rioch is top league scorer with 15 goals; Kevin Hector 21 goals in all comps	
1975	Peter Daniel is voted as Derby's Player of the Season	
1975	Colin Todd is voted Professional Footballers' Association Player of the Year	

The following table charts the ebb and flow of yet another remarkable League Championship-winning season. Like three years earlier, Derby didn't hit the top until April. However, at times they were as distant as 14th (in September), and were even 9th in February and still only 7th on 22 March. That doesn't tell the full story, though, as this season must surely have been the most compressed England's top tier has ever been, with the lead changing hands 21 times, while one crazy Saturday in November saw the Top Ten separated BY ONLY TWO POINTS!

#	Date	Opponents	V	Result	Top of Table	Top Pts	DER Pts	DER Pos
1	17/08/74	Everton	A	D 0-0	Liverpool	2	1	12
2	21/08/74	Coventry City	H	D 1-1	Manchester City	4	2	14
3	24/08/74	Sheffield United	H	W 2-0	Carlisle United	6	4	7
4	27/08/74	Coventry City	A	D 1-1	Ipswich Town	8	5	4
5	31/08/74	Tottenham Hotspur	A	L 2-0	Liverpool	9	5	11
6	07/09/74	Newcastle United	H	D 2-2	Liverpool	11	6	11
7	14/09/74	Birmingham City	A	L 3-2	Ipswich Town	12	6	14
8	21/09/74	Burnley	H	W 3-2	Ipswich Town	14	8	10
9	25/09/74	Chelsea	H	W 4-1	Ipswich Town	16	10	7
10	28/09/74	Stoke City	A	D 1-1	Ipswich Town	16	11	8
11	05/10/74	West Ham United	A	D 2-2	Ipswich Town	16	12	9
12	12/10/74	Leicester City	H	W 1-0	Ipswich Town	17	14	5
13	15/10/74	Sheffield United	A	W 1-2	Liverpool	17	16	3
14	19/10/74	Carlisle United	A	L 3-0	Liverpool	19	16	7
15	26/10/74	Middlesbrough	H	L 2-3	Liverpool	21	16	7
16	02/11/74	Leeds United	A	W 0-1	Liverpool	21	18	7
17	09/11/74	Queens Park R	H	W 5-2	Manchester City	22	20	5
18	16/11/74	Arsenal	A	L 3-1	Ipswich Town	22	20	10
19	23/11/74	Ipswich Town	H	W 2-0	Manchester City	24	22	5
20	07/12/74	Liverpool	A	D 2-2	Stoke City	27	23	8
21	14/12/74	Everton	H	L 0-1	Everton	28	23	9
22	21/12/74	Luton Town	A	L 1-0	Ipswich Town	28	23	10
23	26/12/74	Birmingham City	H	W 2-1	Liverpool	29	25	10
24	28/12/74	Manchester City	A	W 1-2	Ipswich Town	30	27	9
25	11/01/75	Liverpool	H	W 2-0	Ipswich Town	32	29	7
26	18/01/75	Wolverhampton W	A	W 0-1	Everton	33	31	5
27	01/02/75	Queens Park R	A	L 4-1	Everton	35	31	8
28	08/02/75	Leeds United	H	D 0-0	Everton	35	32	9
29	22/02/75	Arsenal	H	W 2-1	Stoke City	37	34	7
30	25/02/75	Ipswich Town	A	L 3-0	Everton	38	34	8
31	01/03/75	Tottenham Hotspur	H	W 3-1	Everton	40	36	7
32	08/03/75	Chelsea	A	W 1-2	Everton	42	38	3
33	15/03/75	Stoke City	H	L 1-2	Everton	43	38	6
34	22/03/75	Newcastle United	H	W 2-0	Everton	44	40	7
35	29/03/75	Luton Town	H	W 5-0	Liverpool	45	42	6
36	31/03/75	Burnley	A	W 2-5	Everton	46	44	5
37	01/04/75	Manchester City	H	W 2-1	Ipswich Town	46	46	3
38	05/04/75	Middlesbrough	A	D 1-1	Liverpool	47	47	4
39	09/04/75	Wolverhampton W	H	W 1-0	Derby County	49	49	1
40	12/04/75	West Ham United	H	W 1-0	Derby County	51	51	1
41	19/04/75	Leicester City	A	D 0-0	Derby County	52	52	1
42	26/04/75	Carlisle United	H	D 0-0	Derby County	53	53	1

With five games to go, the following set of tables reveal how the Top Four changed during this period, and of the extraordinary capitulation of Derby's rivals…

Saturday 5 April 1975

Pos	Team	Pld	W	D	L	F	A	GAvg	GD	Pts	Home	Res	Away
1	Liverpool	39	18	11	10	55	37	1.486	18	47	Leeds Utd	0-2	Liverpool
2	Everton	38	15	17	6	51	36	1.417	15	47	Everton	1-1	Burnley
3	Stoke City	39	17	13	9	64	46	1.391	18	47	Stoke City	3-0	Chelsea
4	Derby County	38	19	9	10	65	49	1.327	16	47	Mid'brough	1-1	Derby County

Wednesday 9 April 1975

Pos	Team	Pld	W	D	L	F	A	GAvg	GD	Pts	Home	Res	Away
1	Derby County	39	20	9	10	66	49	1.347	17	49	Derby County	1-0	Wolves
2	Liverpool	39	18	11	10	55	37	1.486	18	47			
3	Stoke City	39	17	13	9	64	46	1.391	18	47			
4	Everton	39	15	17	7	52	38	1.368	14	47	Luton Town	2-1	Everton

Saturday 12 April 1975

Pos	Team	Pld	W	D	L	F	A	GAvg	GD	Pts	Home	Res	Away
1	Derby County	40	21	9	10	67	49	1.367	18	51	Derby County	1-0	West Ham Utd
2	Liverpool	40	19	11	10	57	37	1.541	20	49	Liverpool	2-0	Carlisle United
3	Everton	40	16	17	7	53	38	1.395	15	49	Newcastle U	0-1	Everton
4	Ipswich Town	39	22	4	13	60	40	1.500	20	48	Ipswich Town	2-1	Queens Park R

Saturday 19 April 1975

Pos	Team	Pld	W	D	L	F	A	GAvg	GD	Pts	Home	Res	Away
1	Derby County	41	21	10	10	67	49	1.367	18	52	Leicester City	0-0	Derby County
2	Liverpool	41	19	11	11	57	38	1.500	19	49	Mid'brough	1-0	Liverpool
3	Everton	41	16	17	8	55	41	1.341	14	49	Everton	2-3	Sheffield Utd
4	Ipswich Town	40	22	4	14	61	42	1.452	19	48	Leeds United	2-1	Ipswich Town

Wednesday 23 April 1975

Pos	Team	Pld	W	D	L	F	A	GAvg	GD	Pts	Home	Res	Away
1	Derby County	41	21	10	10	67	49	1.367	18	52			
2	Liverpool	41	19	11	11	57	38	1.500	19	49			
3	Ipswich Town	41	22	5	14	62	43	1.442	19	49	Manchester C	1-1	Ipswich Town
4	Everton	41	16	17	8	55	41	1.341	14	49			

Saturday 26 April 1975

Pos	Team	Pld	W	D	L	F	A	GAvg	GD	Pts	Home	Res	Away
1	Derby County	42	21	11	10	67	49	1.367	18	53	Derby County	0-0	Carlisle United
2	Liverpool	42	20	11	11	60	39	1.538	21	51	Liverpool	3-1	Queens Park R
3	Ipswich Town	42	23	5	14	66	44	1.500	22	51	Ipswich Town	4-1	West Ham Utd
4	Everton	42	16	18	8	56	42	1.333	14	50	Chelsea	1-1	Everton

Stats Blast: Stats for Keeps

Although eight players appeared in both Derby County Championship-winning sides, goalkeeper Colin Boulton was the only player to play in all 84 games. Boulton also passed Reg Matthews' record of 246 goalkeeping appearances during the Championship-winning season of 1974/75, and went on to amass 344 appearances – still a Derby goalkeeping record today. Also, were it not for a two-game suspension in April 1973, Boulton would have made 248 consecutive appearances between January 1971 and January 1976! As for the suspension, that was for putting a muddy glove into the face of the referee after Derby had lost 2-3 to Leeds on 3 March 1973, this thanks to two controversial penalties awarded to Leeds!

Quirk Alert: South-Coast Symmetry

Derby had an almost symmetrical League Cup experience on the South Coast during season 1974/75, hammering Portsmouth 1-5, but then losing to Southampton 5-0!

Quirk Alert: Just Look at his Face!

The date was 28 December 1974, and legendary BBC Commentator Barry Davies was about to deliver one of his most memorable quotes. Derby were playing away at Manchester City and had taken the lead through a superb 25-yarder from Henry Newton, while Colin Bell had replied for Man City with a move and goal of top quality. Cue Francis Lee, signed by Dave Mackay from Manchester City in August. He fielded the ball under pressure on the left wing ("Lee...") and darted away from his marker in one fluid movement ("interesting..."), moving inside at pace before lashing the ball into the opposite top corner, again from 25 yards ("...very interesting! Oh! Look at his face! Just look at his face!")

Quirk Alert: Crazy Congestion

Below is the league table after the games played on Saturday 16 November 1974 – surely no Tier 1 league table has ever been this tight before? For the record, Derby had just lost 3-1 at Arsenal – who are conspicuous by their absence in the Top Ten (they were 18th), whilst Leeds were 17th, Tottenham 19th and Chelsea 20th. This was turning into one WEIRD season!

Saturday 16 November, 1974										
Pos	Team	Pld	W	D	L	F	A	GAvg	GD	Pts
1	Ipswich Town	18	10	2	6	25	12	2.083	13	22
2	Liverpool	17	10	2	5	23	12	1.917	11	22
3	Everton	18	5	12	1	23	18	1.278	5	22
4	Manchester City	18	9	4	5	21	22	0.955	-1	22
5	Sheffield United	18	8	5	5	27	29	0.931	-2	21
6	Stoke City	17	7	6	4	29	23	1.261	6	20
7	West Ham United	18	8	4	6	34	27	1.259	7	20
8	Newcastle United	17	7	6	4	25	20	1.250	5	20
9	Middlesbrough	17	7	6	4	24	21	1.143	3	20
10	Derby County	18	7	6	5	30	27	1.111	3	20

Quirk Alert: A Timely Inversion
When Derby won their first League Championship in 1972, it was Ipswich who crucially denied Manchester City in City's penultimate game, winning 2-1 at Portman Road. By a strange quirk of fate, the boot was on the other foot in 1975, and it was Ipswich requiring two wins from their last two games to win the title — but they could only manage a 1-1 draw at Maine Road on Wednesday 23 April, 1975, and the title went once again to Derby County.

Derby County, Football League Champions 1974/75. Here the Rams parade the Championship trophy around the Baseball Ground before their final match of the season against Carlisle. Pictured from left to right are Francis Lee, Alan Hinton, Colin Boulton, David Nish, Rod Thomas, Roy McFarland, Kevin Hector and Colin Todd. PHOTO: Andy Ellis

RAMS CHRONOLOGY: Up with the Big Boys (Reprise)

Season 1975/76

Year	Event	Pos
1975	Derby sign Charlie George from Arsenal for £100,000 in July 1975	
1975	09/08: FA Charity Shield: Derby vs. West Ham (W 2-0) – Hector, McFarland	
1975	09/08: Charlie George becomes the only Derby player to make debut at Wembley	
1975	16/08: Sheffield United vs. Derby (D 1-1) – Charlie George scores on league debut	11
1975	23/08: Derby vs. QPR (L 1-5) – McFarland – a big shock – Rams drop to 17th place	17
1975	27/08: Derby vs. Newcastle (W 3-2) – Lee, Hector, Craig (og) – (W1, D2, L1)	12
1975	30/08: Everton vs. Derby (L 2-0) – Rams drop to 19th position – (W1, D2, L2)	19
1975	06/09: Derby vs. Burnley (W 3-0) – Gemmill, Lee, Hector – (W2, D2, L2)	12
1975	13/09: Tottenham H vs. Derby (W 2-3) – Lee, Hector, George – Rams 3 pts off top	8
1975	17/09: European Cup 1st Rd, 1st Leg: Slovan Bratislava vs. Derby (L 1-0)	8
1975	20/09: Derby vs. Manchester City (W 1-0) – Lee – (W4, D2, L2)	7
1975	24/09: Derby (7th) vs. Man Utd (1st) (W 2-1) – George 2 – 4 wins on the spin	4

Year	Event	Pos
1975	27/09: Stoke vs. Derby (L 1-0) – Rams are, 3 points behind leaders, QPR	6
1975	01/10: European Cup 1st Rd, 2nd Leg: Derby vs. Slovan Bratislava (W 3-0) – Lee 2, Bourne – [agg: 3-1]	6
1975	04/10: Derby vs. Ipswich (W 1-0) – Lee – Rams 1 point off leaders, Man Utd	5
1975	18/10: Derby vs. Wolves (W 3-2) – Hector 2, Lee – Rams now 2 pts behind United	4
1975	22/10: European Cup 2nd Rd, 1st Leg: Derby vs. R Madrid (W 4-1) – George 3, Nish	4
1975	25/10: Liverpool vs. Derby (D 1-1) – Lee – Rams 1 point behind new leaders, QPR	4
1975	01/11: Derby vs. Leeds (W 3-2) – George, Gemmill, Davies – Rams still 1 pt off top	4
1975	05/11: European Cup 2nd Rd, 2nd Leg: R Madrid vs. Derby (L 5-1 AET) – [agg 5-6]	4
1975	08/11: Derby vs. Arsenal (W 1-0) – Hector – Rams same pts as leaders, West Ham	2
1975	15/11: Derby (2nd) vs. West Ham (1st) (W 2-1) – Rioch, George – DERBY GO TOP	1
1975	29/11: Derby vs. Middlesbrough (W 3-2) – Newton, Gemmill, Lee – (W11, D5, L3)	1
1975	Derby sign Leighton James from Burnley for a club record fee of £310,000	1
1975	06/12: Birmingham vs. Derby (L 2-1) – George – QPR go top, same pts as Derby	2
1975	13/12: QPR (1st) vs. Derby (2nd) (D 1-1) – Rioch – QPR, LIV, MNU, DER all on 28 pts	4
1975	20/12: Derby vs. Sheffield United (W 3-2) – Nish, George, Garner (og)	3
1975	26/12: Leicester vs. Derby (L 2-1) – James – Rams still only 1 point off the top	5
1975	27/12: Derby vs. Aston Villa (W 2-0) – George, Powell – Rams still 1 point off top	4
1976	03/01: FA Cup 3rd Rd: Derby vs. Everton (W 2-1) – George 2	4
1976	24/01: FA Cup 4th Rd: Derby vs. Liverpool (W 1-0) – Davies	4
1976	31/01: Derby vs. Coventry (W 2-0) – George 2 – 2 pts behind leaders, Man Utd	3
1976	07/02: Newcastle vs. Derby (L 4-3) – Rioch, George, Powell – Rams 3 pts off top	4
1976	18/02: Derby vs. Arsenal (W 2-0) – James 2 – Rams 2 pts behind leaders, Liverpool	4
1976	21/02: West Ham vs. Derby (W 1-2) – Rioch, George – still 2 pts behind Liverpool	4
1976	25/02: Man U (3rd) vs. Derby (4th) (D 1-1) – Rioch – both remain one point off top	4
1976	28/02: Derby (4th) vs. Liverpool (1st) (D 1-1) – George – clubs remain 4th and 1st	4
1976	02/03: Leeds (5th) vs. Derby (4th) (D 1-1) – Gemmill – LIV/QPR/MNU/DER all 43 pts	4
1976	06/03: FA Cup QF: Derby vs. Newcastle (W 4-2) – Rioch 2, Newton, George	4
1976	13/03: Derby vs. Norwich (W 3-1) – Rioch, Gemmill, James – 2 pts off top (QPR)	4
1976	20/03: Middlesbrough vs. Derby (W 0-2) – Hector, George – (W19, D9, L7)	4
1976	24/03: Derby vs. Stoke (D 1-1) – Rioch – George dislocates shoulder/out for season	3
1976	27/03: Derby vs. Birmingham (W 4-2) – Nish, Rioch, Davies, James – Rams 3rd, 1 pt behind leaders QPR; Rams are genuine double contenders at this point in time	3
1976	03/04: FA Cup Semi-Final: Manchester United vs. Derby County (L 2-0); a deflected free-kick and a perfectly good goal disallowed – the famous Rams Watershed	4
1976	06/04: QPR & Liverpool both win, putting them 3 pts ahead of Derby & Man Utd	4
1976	20/04: Derby fail to win any of next 4 games (D1, L3) all played inside 10 days; the last 3 in 4 days; both League and Cup gone in a handful of days	4
1976	24/04: Ipswich vs. Derby (W 2-6) – Lee 2, Hector 2, Rioch 2 – way too late	4
1976	24/04: Francis Lee becomes only player to score twice in last 2 minutes of career	4
1976	Derby finish season 4th (4:22) on 53 points, 7 points behind Champions, Liverpool	4
1976	Charlie George is Derby's top scorer with 16 league goals (24 in all competitions)	
1976	Charlie George is Derby's Player of the Season and Midlands Player of the Season	
1976	06/05: Archie Gemmill becomes the first Derby County player to captain Scotland	

Quirk Alert: Sport's Most Spectacular Dismissal

Well, that was the opinion of the Observer *in 2003. They were, of course, referring to the infamous punch-up between Francis Lee and Norman Hunter at the Baseball Ground on 1 November 1975. Derby won the match 3-2, and happily for posterity, the 24-minute BBC highlights are available on YouTube. Check it out – yes, for the punch-up, which is shamelessly entertaining, but also for how GOOD Derby and Leeds both were. John Motson also delivers a peerless commentary, and sums the quality up in his introduction by saying that "Charlie George has the chance to prove something again today, in a match with 15 full internationals on the field, a company to which he does not yet belong". He also points out that Derby are missing the injured Roy McFarland, "otherwise, the Champions are at full strength".*

Anyway, look out for a wonky team-sheet caption and listen out for strains of "We are the Rams" to Mary Hopkin's "Those Were The Days My Friend", before a struggle for the ball between Hunter and Lee sees Lee gain a corner and Hunter positively PUNCH the ball towards the corner flag. Motson notes a minute or so later that "There's quite a battle going on between Norman Hunter and Francis Lee". You reckon John?

Next, there's a stunning trademark strike from Lorimer and a great save from Boulton, Trevor Cherry heading Leeds in front, Archie Gemmill equalising, and Frannie Lee's theatrics when he gains Derby a penalty, allegedly tripped by...Norman Hunter, of course. Poor chap. Motty then closes off the first half by saying: "Well, they can say what they like about English football. I doubt whether you would see a more exciting 45 minutes than that. Leeds showing much of their old Championship form; Derby much of their new." He also points out, as the players' troop off: "Francis Lee, who has won many penalties in his time!"

The second half then commences and eventually we have "the incident". I won't spoil it for those who haven't seen it, but suffice to say that Motty is a master of the under-statement: "The fists were flying and that's been brewing for quite some time."

Nevertheless, the game continues. Great football, too and apart from the punch-up, there seemed to be a good spirit between the two sets of players as well as mutual respect.

Anyway, the score is 2-2 as the game enters the 88th minute, when Colin Todd surges forward and then plays the ball to 6ft 3in Roger Davies on the edge of the box. Davies then cuts inside and unleashes an unstoppable 20-yarder into the far top corner. As Motty says: "So much skill for a big man".

After the final whistle, Motty sums up: "But it's all over, and Derby have snatched the victory at the end, of a game eventful to say the least. And let's hope that the good football which the crowd are applauding is what's remembered most from this game, and not the unfortunate incident in which Francis Lee and Norman Hunter were sent off the field."

Erm, yes Motty. Whatever you say, mate!

Seconds out! Round Two! PHOTO: Andy Ellis

Quirk Alert: It's a Cracker!
Having just given Motty a good outing, here comes his distinguished co-commentator of the day, Barry Davies, once again. This time it was the second round of the European Cup, under the Baseball Ground flood-lights on Wednesday 22 October 1975. The visitors were Real Madrid and a slick move involving David Nish and Archie Gemmill ended up with Charlie George hammering the ball into the bottom corner. Cue Barry: "Oh, that's a cracker! Applause all around the ground and my word he deserves it!" PHOTOS: Andy Ellis

Charlie George.

And here is the goal, as Charlie George (No 11) wheels away to celebrate, as does Francis Lee in the foreground.

As for Charlie, he was stunning that season, and was nailed-on Footballer of the Year for 1975/76 until he dislocated his shoulder on 24 March. He missed the rest of the season, a period of six weeks which proved to be Derby County's watershed, when they went from genuine double contenders to Division Three in just eight years!

RAMS CHRONOLOGY: The Spectacular Fall

The 1970s

Year	Event	Pos
Season 1976/77 (Division One)		
1976	31/08: League Cup 2nd Rd: Doncaster vs. Derby (W 1-2) – George, Rioch	
1976	15/09: UEFA Cup 1st Rd, 1st Leg: Derby vs. Finn Harps (W 12-0) – Hector 5, George 3, James 3, Rioch – Derby's biggest win of all time	19
1976	25/09: Derby vs. West Brom (D 2-2) – McFarland 2 – (W0, D5, L2)	19
1976	29/09: UEFA Cup 2nd Leg: F Harps vs. Derby (W 1-4) – Hector 2, George 2 [agg 1-16]	19
1976	02/10: Birmingham vs. Derby (L 5-1) – James – Rams no win and 3rd-bottom	20
1976	04/10: League Cup 3rd Rd Replay: Notts County vs. Derby (W 1-2) – Rioch 2	20
1976	16/10: Derby vs. Tottenham H (W 8-2) – Rioch 4, George 2, Todd, Thomas – Rioch emergency striker in for injured Kevin Hector – biggest win in Div One, 1976/77	18
1976	20/10: UEFA Cup 2nd Rd, 1st Leg: AEK Athens vs. Derby (L 2-0)	19
1976	30/10: Derby vs. Bristol City (W 2-0) – George, Hector – (W2, D5, L4)	17
1976	03/11: UEFA Cup 2nd Leg: Derby vs. AEK Athens (L 2-3) – George, Rioch – [agg: 2-5]	17
1976	08/11: League Cup 5th Rd Replay: Derby vs. Brighton (W 2-1) – Todd, Hector	17
1976	17/11: Roy McFarland wins 28th (and final) England cap vs. Italy to become Derby's most-capped player, passing Alan Durban's 27 caps for Wales	18
1976	20/11: Everton vs. Derby (L 2-0) – (W2, D6, L5)	19
1976	25/11: Dave Mackay is sacked as manager of Derby County, despite having previously steered the Rams to finishes of 3rd, 1st and 4th	19

Year	Event	Pos
1976	26/11: Reserve team coach, Colin Murphy, becomes caretaker manager	19
1976	27/11: Derby vs. Sunderland (W 1-0) – James – (W3, D6, L5)	18
1976	01/12: League Cup Quarter-Final: Derby vs. Bolton (L 1-2) – George	18
1976	Derby sign striker Derek Hales from Charlton Athletic for £330,000	
1977	19/01: FA Cup 3rd Rd Replay: Derby vs. Blackpool (W 3-2) – Hales, James, George	17
1977	22/01: Derby vs. Newcastle (W 4-2) – Hales 2, McFarland, Powell	15
1977	26/02: FA Cup 5th Rd: Derby vs. Blackburn Rovers (W 3-1) – George 2, Hector	19
1977	02/03: Aston V vs. Derby (L 4-0) – Kevin Hector makes 500th appearance for Derby	20
1977	05/03: West Brom vs. Derby (L 1-0) – 5th league defeat on spin – RAMS BOTTOM	22
1977	05/03: Derby have gone from TOP to BOTTOM in just over 12 months	22
1977	Derby sign Gerry Daly from Man Utd for £175,000 – Daly gives Rams much-needed lift and scores 7 important goals in 17 league games in which Derby only lose twice	
1977	19/03: FA Cup Quarter-Final: Everton vs. Derby (L 2-0)	21
1977	23/03: Tottenham vs. Derby (D 0-0) – 4th draw on the bounce – (W5, D12, L12)	19
1977	02/04: Derby vs. Stoke (W 2-0) – James, Daly – (W6, D12, L12)	19
1977	09/04: Derby vs. Aston Villa (W 2-1) – Hales, James – (W7, D13, L12)	15
1977	23/04: Ron Webster passes Steve Bloomer's record of 525 appearances for Derby	17
1977	30/04: Derby vs. Man City (W 4-0) – Daly, Gemmill, Hector, Daniel...and the famous painted penalty spot; Rams still 1 point above 20th; defeat costs Man City the title	15
1977	11/05: Derby vs. QPR (W 2-0) – McFarland, Daly – Rams are now safe	13
1977	Derby finish season 15th (15:22), on 37 points, 3 points above the drop-zone	15
1977	Derby's 9 wins is lowest in the league that year, 3 less than bottom-placed Spurs	
1977	Leighton James is top league scorer (9); Charlie George 17 goals in all comps	
1977	Leighton James is also Derby's Player of the Season	

Quirk Alert: Bob Smith

Bob Smith was Derby's head groundsman from 1967 to 1984. He is also probably the most famous football groundsman of all time, for it was Bob who had to run onto the Baseball Ground pitch on 30 April 1977, armed with a tape measure, a tin of white paint and a thick brush. Derby had just won a penalty in a televised match against Manchester City, but the ground was so churned up, the penalty spot had

Bob Smith and Joe Corrigan appear to be checking the quality of the paintbrush, whilst the ref marks the distance to the penalty spot with a tape measure! PHOTO: Andy Ellis

completely disappeared. Bob duly obliged, and a remarkably cool Gerry Daly slotted home from 12 yards – ball, paint and all!

As for his job, it was certainly unenviable, as the notorious Baseball Ground pitch was the victim of a crucial design flaw. As Bob himself stated when interviewed: "The pitch was 4ft below street level and the drains were 2ft under the surface. The ground was built over a river and a brook so, when it rained, the water came up rather then went down!" This was presumably the story "floated" by Brian Clough when quizzed about the state of the pitch after certain European games...

Quirk Alert: Tragedy

When Derby played Everton at home on 16 April 1977, they led comfortably at half time, 2-0, Gerry Daly having scored both goals. There now follows a true account of two events that I remember vividly from this game. Firstly, Derby took to the field in the second half at the exact moment the tannoy blared out the word "Tragedy" from the Bee Gees' hit single of 1977. I turned to my Dad and said: "Well that's a good omen then!" To which he told me not to be so stupid. Except that Everton then scored three times in the second half. Furthermore, the winner, from Bob Latchford, was going wide until it hit a divot on the famous Baseball Ground pitch and thus re-directed itself inside Colin Boulton's far post!

Year	Event	Pos
Season 1977/78 (Division One)		
1977	Derby sign Billy Hughes from Sunderland for £30,000	13
1977	27/08: Nottingham Forest vs. Derby (L 3-0) – Cloughie is on the march again	20
1977	17/09: Derby vs. Leeds (D 2-2) Hughes, Gemmill (Archie's last game)	21
1977	17/09: Colin Murphy is sacked and replaced by Tommy Docherty	21
1977	24/09: Liverpool vs. Derby (L 1-0) – Rams still without a win (W0, D3, L4)	21
1977	Derby swap Archie Gemmill and £25,000 for Forest keeper John Middleton	
1977	01/10: Derby vs. Middlesbrough (W 4-1) – Daly, Hector, Hughes, Powell	18
1977	04/10: Wolves vs. Derby (W 1-2) – Hughes 2 – (W2, D3, L4)	16
1977	08/10: Newcastle vs. Derby (W 1-2) – McFarland, Hughes – 3 wins on spin	15
1977	Derby and QPR exchange Leighton James and Don Masson	
1977	12/11: Bristol City vs. Derby (L 3-1) – Rioch – five without a win (W3, D5, L7)	18
1977	26/11: Arsenal vs. Derby (W 1-3) – Powell, Ryan, Rioch	15
1977	03/12: Derby vs. Manchester City (W 2-1) – Hughes, Ryan – (W6, D5, L7)	13
1977	17/12: Derby vs. Bristol City (W 1-0) – Todd – 4 wins in 5	12
1977	26/12: QPR vs. Derby (D 0-0) – 6 games without defeat – (W7, D7, L7)	11
1977	31/12: Ipswich vs. Derby (W 1-2) – George, Ryan	12
1978	02/01: Derby vs. Coventry (W 4-2) – George 3, Daly – 6 wins in 9 – (W9, D7, L8)	10
1978	Derby sign Steve Buckley from Luton Town for £163,000	
1978	04/03: Derby vs. Newcastle (D 1-1) – George – four without a win	14
1978	08/03: Derby vs. Liverpool (W 4-2) – Daly 2, George, Crawford (19) scores on debut	12
1978	11/03: Derby vs. Chelsea (D 1-1) – Daniel – (W10, D10, L10)	10
1978	22/04: Derby vs. Leicester (W 4-1) – George 2, Rioch, Buckley – (W13, D12, L15)	13
1978	Derby sign Gordon Hill from Manchester United for £250,000	
1978	09/05: Derby vs. Arsenal (W 3-0) – Curran, Chesters, Hill (debut goal)	12
1978	Derby finish season 12th (12:22) on 41 points, 9 points above the drop-zone	12
1978	Charlie George is top league scorer with 11 goals (Gerry Daly 12 in all comps)	

Year	Event	Pos
1978	David Langan is Derby's Player of the Season	
1978	Bruce Rioch is Scotland captain during the 1978 World Cup Finals	
1978	In America, Alan Hinton sets new record in the NASL while playing for Vancouver Whitecaps, laying on 30 goals to beat mark previously set by Pelé and George Best!	
Season 1978/79 (Division One)		
1978	09/09: Bolton vs. Derby (L 2-1) – Daly – another poor start – (W0, D2, L3)	19
1978	Tommy Docherty sells Colin Todd to Everton for £300,000	
1978	16/09: Derby vs West Brom (W 3-2) – Daly, Powell, Duncan	16
1978	23/09: Derby vs. Southampton (W 2-1) – George, Carter – (W2, D2, L3)	13
1978	14/10: Liverpool vs. Derby (L 5-0); 28/10: Leeds vs. Derby (L 4-0) – (W3, D3, L6)	19
1978	04/11: Derby vs. Wolves (W 4-1) – Daly, Hill, Duncan, Caskey	16
1978	11/11: Man City vs. Derby (W 1-2) – Daly, Duncan	13
1978	18/11: Derby vs. Birmingham (W 2-1) – Buckley, Daly – 3 wins on the spin	13
1978	25/11: Derby vs. QPR (W 2-1) – Daniel, Caskey – (W7, D3, L7)	11
1978	02/12: From this point onwards, Derby only win 3 of their last 25 league games	12
1978	December: Tommy Docherty sells Charlie George to Southampton	12
1978	26/12: Nottingham Forest vs. Derby (D 1-1) – Daly – 5 w/o win (W7, D5, L10)	13
1979	Derby don't play in the league again until February, due to bad weather	
1979	03/02: Southampton vs. Derby (W 1-2) – Powell, Duncan – 5 pts clear of 20th	15
1979	13/03: Middlesbrough vs. Derby (L 3-1) – Daly – 5th loss on spin – 4 pts from 20th	17
1979	21/03: Derby vs. Bolton (W 3-0) – McFarland 2, Daly – (W9, D6, L15)	17
1979	21/04: Derby vs. Arsenal (W 2-0) – Buckley, Daly – Rams are 18th, but safe	18
1979	Derby finish 19th on 31 points, 6 pts clear of danger, despite last 12 (W1, D5, L6)	19
1979	Gerry Daly is Derby's top scorer with 13 league goals (13 in all competitions)	
1979	Steve Powell is Derby's Player of the Year	
1979	Tommy Docherty resigns in order to become manager of relegated QPR	
Season 1979/80 (Division One)		
1979	July: Colin Addison is appointed as Derby County manager	
1979	01/09: Crystal Palace vs. Derby (L 4-0) – another terrible start – (W0, D1, L3)	21
1979	08/09: Derby vs. Arsenal (W 3-2) – McCaffery, Langan, Duncan	20
1979	29/09: Southampton vs. Derby (L 4-0) – Derby sink to the bottom of the league	22
1979	06/10: Derby vs. Bolton (W 4-0) – Duncan 2, Emson 2 – (W3, D1, L5)	17
1979	27/10: Stoke vs. Derby (L 3-2) – Hill 2 – three defeats on the spin – (W3, D2, L8)	21
1979	03/11: Derby vs. West Brom (W 2-1) – Hill, Emery	19
1979	10/11: Bristol City vs. Derby (W 0-2) – Moreland, Duncan – 19th but easing away	19
1979	24/11: Derby vs. Nottingham Forest: (W 4-1) – Daly, Duncan 2, Emery	19
1979	22/12: Derby vs. Liverpool (L 1-3) – Davies – four without a win (W6, D3, L12)	21

The 1980s

Year	Event	Pos
1980	05/01: FA Cup 3rd Rd: Bristol City vs. Derby (L 6-2) – Davies, Daly	21
1980	January: Derby sign striker Alan Biley from Cambridge United for £350,000	21
1980	12/01: Derby vs. Crystal Palace (L 1-2) – Osgood – Rams now 3 points from safety	21

Year	Event	Pos
1980	16/02: Derby vs. Soton (D 2-2) – Davies, B Powell – 12 w/o win – Rams 6 pts adrift	21
1980	23/02: Derby vs. Tottenham H (W 2-1) – McCaffery, Biley – Rams now 5 pts adrift	21
1980	Derby sign striker Dave Swindlehurst from Crystal Palace, initially on loan	20
1980	15/03: Bolton vs. Derby (W 1-2) – Swindlehurst, Biley – Rams still 4 pts adrift	20
1980	22/03: Derby vs. Bristol City (D 3-3) – Biley 3 – still 4 pts adrift – (W8, D7, L19)	20
1980	05/04: Derby vs. Leeds (W 2-0) – 5 w/o defeat, but still 4 pts off Man City in 19th	20
1980	12/04: Derby vs. Brighton (W 3-0) – Biley 2, Osgood – now 3 pts adrift of Everton	20
1980	26/03: Dave Swindlehurst signs on pitch before game, Derby's first £400,000 player	20
1980	26/03: Derby vs. Man City (W 3-1) – Swindlehurst & Biley both score, but...	20
1980	...Everton also win; Derby relegated to Div Two after 11-year tenure in top flight	20
1980	Derby finish season 21st (21:22) on 30 points, 5 points adrift of Everton in 19th	21
1980	Alan Biley is Derby's top scorer with 9 league goals (in only 19 games)	
1980	Steve Buckley is Derby's Player of the Season	
1980	Derby sign goalkeeper Roger Jones from Stoke City – 12 years after Brian Clough had been interested in signing him from Bournemouth!	

Quirk Alert: The Four-Minute Orgasm!

The date was 24 November 1979, and Derby were playing Nottingham Forest at home. Derby were in decline and on their way to relegation. Conversely, Nottingham Forest had already surpassed Derby's achievements of the 1970s, by not only winning the League Championship during season 1977/78, but going on to win the European Cup of 1978/79. And as if that wasn't enough, Forest achieved all of this success with Derby's former revered management duo of Brian Clough and Peter Taylor. Throw in a handful of former (and legendary) Derby players (and even Derby's trainer), and this was bile-wrenching stuff of the highest order.

"He's dropped it! He's dropped it". Check it out on YouTube. Fan or not, you won't be disappointed! PHOTO: Andy Ellis

So, when the teams met on 24 November 1979, nothing other than further humiliation was expected; Derby were 4th from bottom, and Forest, the reigning European Champions were 4th from top. Cue three Derby goals in four first-half minutes! And if this episode is unfamiliar to you, then please check out the YouTube video highlights of the match, over-dubbed with the hilarious BBC Radio Derby commentary from the brilliant Graham Richards. You might then get what it meant!

*Of course, the joy was short-lived. Within six months, Derby were facing life in Division Two and Forest had retained (yes **retained**) the European Cup!*

Quirk Alert: "Swindles & Bi-Bi"
and "We'll be back in '81"
Despite being relegated from Division One at the end of season
1979/80, Derby had put up a real fight to stay up, largely
triggered by the twin-signings of strikers Alan Biley (shown
right) and Dave Swindlehurst. Their goals and general
improved team performance meant that an atmosphere of
optimism was present going into the next season in Division
Two, with the most-frequently heard chant from the Derby
terraces being "We'll be back in '81".

Sadly, despite a big impact at
Derby, it was Bi-Bi Alan only a year
after he signed from Cambridge.

Derby lost their first match back in Division Two, 3-0
– at Cambridge United!

PHOTO: Andy Ellis

Year	Event	Pos
Season 1980/81 (Division Two)		
1980	16/08: Cambridge United vs. Derby (L 3-0) – Oh dear!	22
1980	20/08: Derby vs. Chelsea (W 3-2) – B Powell, Biley, Chivers (og)	15
1980	23/08: Luton Town vs. Derby (W 1-2) – Swindlehurst, Osgood	8
1980	30/08: Derby vs. Bolton (W 1-0) – Swindlehurst – 3rd win on the bounce	2
1980	06/09: Derby (2nd) vs Blackburn R (1st) (D 2-2) – Biley 2 – (W3, D1, L1)	2
1980	13/09: Grimsby vs. Derby (W 0-1) – Swindlehurst – (W4, D1, L1)	2
1980	20/09: Derby vs. Wrexham (L 0-1) – curse of the MotD cameras!	6
1980	04/10: Derby vs. Sheffield Wednesday (W 3-1) – Biley, Emson, Grant (og)	5
1980	04/10: Roy McFarland becomes 7th player to reach 500 appearances for Derby	5
1980	One of Roy's predecessors, Kevin Hector, returns to Derby County, aged 35	
1980	18/10: Derby vs. QPR: (D 3-3) – Emson, Sheridan 2 – Frank (18) double on debut	9
1980	12/11: Chelsea vs. Derby (W 1-3) – Clark, Wilson, Reid – Tony (17) debut goal	8
1980	15/11: Derby vs. Cambridge (L 0-3) – a nightmare double – now 7 pts off 3rd	11
1980	26/11: Derby vs. West Ham (W 2-0) – Clark and Biley sink league leaders	8
1980	06/12: Preston vs. Derby (W 0-3) – Biley, Swindlehurst, Hector – Rams 4 pts off 3rd	5
1980	Kevin Hector makes 536th appearance for Derby, breaking Ron Webster's record	5
1980	26/12: Derby vs. Oldham (W 4-1) – Biley 2, Swindlehurst 2 – Rams 2 pts off 3rd	7
1980	27/12: Newcastle vs. Derby (W 0-2) – McFarland, Boam (og) – Rams 1 point off 3rd	5
1981	10/01: Derby vs. Bristol Rovers (W 2-1) – Biley, Gillies (og) – Rams 1 point off 2nd	4
1981	07/02: Derby vs. Grimsby (W 2-1) – Emery, Swindlehurst – Rams two pts off 2nd	4
1981	Alan Biley is sold to Everton for £300,000 – does decision cost more than £300K?	
1981	28/03: Derby vs. Bristol C (W 1-0) – Swindlehurst – first win in 6 ; still 2 pts off 3rd	5
1981	18/04: Derby vs. Newcastle (W 2-0) – McFarland, Wilson – Rams now 3 pts off 3rd	8
1981	20/04: Oldham vs. Derby (W 0-2) – Buckley, Clayton – 1 point off 3rd, two to play	5
1981	Derby finish season 6th (6:22) with 45 points, missing promotion by 5 points	6
1981	Dave Swindlehurst is Derby's top scorer with 11 league goals (11 goals all comps)	
1981	Roger Jones is Derby's Player of the Year	
1981	Roy McFarland leaves Derby after 14 years to become Bradford C player-manager	

Year	Event	Pos
Season 1981/82 (Division Two)		
1981	The 1981/82 season sees three points for a win introduced	
1981	12/09: Derby vs. Leicester (W 3-1) – Ramage, Hector, Buckley – (W2, D0, L2)	12
1981	26/09: Derby vs. QPR (W 3-1) – Hector 2, Ramage – (W3, D1, L3)	12
1981	07/10: Kevin Hector scores 200th goal for Derby in 2-3 L Cup defeat to West Ham	17
1981	04/12: Cardiff vs. Derby (L 1-0) – Rams have won only 3 of last 11 league games	15
1982	25/01: Colin Addison is sacked and assistant John Newman is asked to take over	13
1982	26/01: Watford vs. Derby (L 6-1) – Emson – a disastrous first game for Newman	13
1982	30/01: Derby vs. Sheffield Wed (W 3-1) – Wilson 2, Sheridan – (W8, D4, L10)	12
1982	10/03: Derby vs. Shrewsbury (D 1-1) – Wilson – 7 games without a win	16
1982	13/03: Derby vs. Crystal Pal (W 4-1) – Wilson 2, Buckley, Skivington	15
1982	March: Charlie George returns to Derby	
1982	10/04: Barnsley vs. Derby (D 0-0) – Rams now only 2 pts above 20th & drop-zone	16
1982	20/04: Chelsea vs. Derby (W 0-2) B Powell , George – Rams have a 4 point cushion	14
1982	15/05: Due to other results, Derby had to win final game to be certain of staying up	16
1982	15/05: Derby vs. Watford (W 3-2) – Hector, Wilson, Buckley – Rams survive	16
1982	15/05: Kevin Hector plays his final and 589th game for Derby, still a club record	16
1982	Derby finish season 16th (16:22), on 48 points, four points above the drop-zone	16
1982	Kevin Wilson is Derby's top scorer with 9 league goals (9 goals in all competitions)	
1982	Steve Buckley is voted Derby's Player of the Season for the second time	

Quirk Alert: Rammer Mark II

Derby signed centre half Alan Ramage from Middlesbrough before the 1980/81 season. Barrel-chested Ramage was well-known for taking no prisoners. His most "productive" game was on 12 September 1981 when Derby beat Leicester City 3-1 at the Baseball Ground. Ramage scored Derby's opening goal when, up in the box for a corner, a Leicester defender attempted to hack the ball clear, only to rifle it against Ramage's ample chest – from where the ball looped back up and over stranded goalkeeper Mark Wallington and into the net.

However, Ramage was also busy elsewhere in this match – as Leicester striker Alan Young will probably testify to – having made the mistake of attempting to mix it up with the big man in an off-the-ball incident! Young later came round in the Leicester dressing room!

Stats Blast: The King's Farewell

On 15 May, 1982, Kevin Hector (37), played his final and 589th game for Derby, and scored his 201st and final goal for the Rams. His appearance record is unlikely to be beaten, and neither are his 201 goals – although even The King finished 131 goals behind Steve Bloomer!

Year	Event	Pos
Season 1982/83 (Division Two)		
1982	28/08: Derby vs. Carlisle (L 0-3); 04/09: QPR vs. Derby (L 4-1); Rams bottom after 2	22
1982	06/11: Sheffield Wed vs. Derby (L 2-0) – Rams now 5 pts from safety (W1, D5, L7)	22
1982	Manager John Newman is sacked and replaced by Peter Taylor	22

Year	Event	Pos
1982	Taylor brings in Roy McFarland and Mick Jones from Bradford City as assistant manager and coach – Derby are later fined for an illegal approach	22
1982	Peter Taylor also brings 35 year-old Archie Gemmill back to Derby	22
1982	Derby sign Bobby Davison for £80,000 from Halifax Town	22
1982	04/12: Derby vs. Rotherham (W 3-0) – Swindlehurst 2, Dalziel – Rams off bottom	21
1982	29/12: Derby vs. Shrewsbury (L 2-3) – Davison 2 – 3 defeats in 4 – 6 pts from safety	22
1983	01/01: Oldham vs. Derby (D 2-2) – Swindlehurst, Gemmill – Rams now 8 pts adrift	22
1983	08/01: FA Cup 3rd Rd: Derby vs. Nottingham F (W 2-0) – Gemmill, Hill – the highs…	22
1983	15/01: Carlisle vs. Derby (L 3-0) - …and the lows – Rams now 9 points from safety	22
1983	22/01: Derby vs. Leeds (D 3-3) – Swindlehurst, Davison, Gemmill – 8 points adrift	22
1983	29/01: FA Cup 4th Rd: Derby vs. Chelsea (W 2-1) – Kevin Wilson bags both	22
1983	05/02: Chelsea vs. Derby (W 1-3) – Rams still bottom but now 6 points from safety	22
1983	19/02: FA Cup 5th Rd: Derby vs. Manchester United (L 0-1) – Whiteside (offside?)	22
1983	26/02: Derby vs. Grimsby (W 2-0) – Davison, Moore (og) – now only 3 pts adrift	22
1983	Dave Swindlehurst is sold to First Division West Ham for £160,000	22
1983	26/03: Bolton vs. Derby (W 0-2) – Brolly, Wilson – 8 w/o defeat; finally off bottom	21
1983	04/04: Derby vs. Newcastle (W 2-1) – Hooks, Wilson – Rams now out of bottom 3	19
1983	09/04: Middlesbrough vs. Derby (W 2-3) – Davison 2, Gemmill – (W8, D16, L11) *	16
1983	30/04: Derby vs. Burnley (W 2-0) – Wilson, Davison – Rams unbeaten in 15	14
1983	02/05: Blackburn vs. Derby (L 2-0) – Derby's unbeaten run ends at 15	14
1983	07/05: Crystal Palace vs. Derby (L 4-1) – Rams 2 pts above 20th; 1 to play; not safe	15
1983	14/05: Derby vs. Fulham (W 1-0) – Davison – the Great Escape is completed	13
1983	Bottom for most of season, Derby finish 13th with 49 points and 4 points to spare	13
1983	Dave Swindlehurst & Bobby Davison top league scorers (8); (Swindles 11 all comps)	
1983	Goalkeeper Steve Cherry is Derby's Player of the Season	

PHOTO: Andy Ellis

Quirk Alert: The Great Escape
This is what season 1982/83 became known as. Derby went into 1983 bottom of the table, eight points from safety, which later became nine points. However, they went on a remarkable 15-game unbeaten run from 22 January to 30 April and actually finished in 13th position. Key to this revival were the inspired signings of Archie Gemmill and Bobby Davison (right). Gemmill was already a Derby legend when he returned, aged 35 – but he provided much-needed graft and guile in midfield. Davison was only 23 when he signed, but would also go on to forge legendary status among Derby fans, eventually exceeding 100 goals, placing him 10th in Derby's all-time scorers list; he also played 105 consecutive league games between September 1983 and December 1985.

Quirk Alert: Seating Plan
Spare a thought for the company who provided Derby County's new seating in 1983. The seats had gone in at the Osmaston (Ossie) End during January 1983, but most of them came out when Derby rescued a late point against Leeds United on 22nd January. The seats were replaced for

Derby's FA Cup Fourth Round tie against Chelsea a week later, and Derby fans were switched from the Ossie End standing area to the Pop Side – the logic being that Chelsea fans surely wouldn't rain seats down onto their own supporters. Erm, wrong! Kevin Wilson was the party-pooper on this occasion with two late goals knocking Chelsea out. Still, in went the third batch of seats, although the seat company were probably already moulding replacements, as Leeds and Chelsea were followed by Manchester United in the FA Cup Fifth Round! Fortunately, Derby succumbed in the 84th minute, and the seats stayed put!

Year	Event	Pos
Season 1983/84 (Division Two)		
1983	27/08: Chelsea vs. Derby (L 5-0) – Rams go straight to the foot of the table	22
1983	03/09: Derby vs. Swansea (W 2-1) – Davison, Campbell – (W1, D1, L1)	12
1983	10/09: Blackburn vs. Derby (L 5-1) – Campbell – (W1, D1, L3)	18
1983	01/10: Derby vs. Carlisle (L 1-4) – Davison – (W1, D2, L5)	21
1983	08/10: Derby vs. Barnsley (L 0-2); Rams spend all of October second bottom	21
1983	05/11: Cambridge United vs. Derby (W 0-1) – Davison	19
1983	12/11: Derby vs. Middlesbrough (W 1-0) – Davison	18
1983	19/11: Derby vs. Leeds (D 1-1) – Davison scores for 4th consecutive game	18
1983	03/12: Derby vs. Newcastle (W 3-2) – Davison 2, Gemmill – five without defeat	19
1983	17/12: Derby vs. Shrewsbury Town (W 1-0) – Plummer – Rams 8 pts above 20th	17
1983	26/12: Fulham vs. Derby (D 2-2) – Wilson 2 – 1 defeat in 8, and 8-point cushion	15
1984	07/01: FA Cup 3rd Rd: Cambridge vs. Derby (W 0-3) – Wilson, Plummer, McAlle	19
1984	01/02: FA Cup 4th Rd: Derby vs. Telford U (W 3-2) – Davison hat-trick – but financial storm-clouds gathering; Rams unable to pay Telford their share of match takings	20
1984	04/02: Carlisle vs Derby (L 2-1) – Powell – 6 league defeats on the bounce	20
1984	18/02: FA Cup 5th Rd: Derby vs. Norwich (W 2-1) – Gemmill, Davison	20
1984	21/02: Grimsby vs. Derby (L 2-1) – Garner – Rams are now 6 points from safety	20
1984	10/03: FA Cup Quarter-Final: Plymouth vs. Derby (0-0) – Rams miss key chances	20
1984	Elsewhere, Derby are now in dire financial trouble and face a winding up order in the High Court. Robert Maxwell is on the verge of bailing Derby out...	20
1984	14/03: ...but his financial rescue package is withdrawn minutes before the kick-off of Derby's FA Cup Quarter Final replay against Plymouth Argyle	20
1984	14/03: FA Cup QF Replay: Derby vs. Plymouth (L 0-1) – financial ruin, rooted in bottom 3, dog on pitch, knocked out by goal direct from corner – Happy Days!	20
1984	31/03: Barnsley vs. Derby (L 5-1) – Davison – Rams now 7 points from safety	20
1984	Stuart Webb saves club with financial backing of Maxwell who installs son, Ian, as Rams chairman; Taylor resigns as manager; Roy Mac takes over for last 9 games	20
1984	07/04: Derby vs. Crystal P (W 3-0) – Garner (18) bags hat-trick – still 5 pts adrift	20
1984	21/04: Derby vs. Fulham (W 1-0) – Garner – Rams only 2 pts behind Oldham (19th)	20
1984	28/04: Derby vs. Man City (W 1-0) – Watson – Rams still 2 points behind Oldham	20
1984	05/05: Newcastle vs. Derby (L 4-0) – Oldham win – Rams now 5 pts adrift; 2 to go	20
1984	Derby finish season 20th (20:22) on 42 points, five points from safety	20
1984	Rams relegated to third tier, only 9 years after winning the League Championship	
1984	Bobby Davison is Derby's top scorer with 14 league goals (18 in all competitions)	
1984	37-year-old Archie Gemmill retires as Derby's Player of the Season	

Quirk Alert: Mark My Words and The Spectacular Fall

Derby took a couple of five-goal hammerings early in season 1983/84 season. At which point Peter Taylor came out with one of his most memorable one-liners: "Top Six by Christmas. Mark my words". Well we did. Enough said. Meanwhile, on Saturday 5 May 1984, Arthur Cox's Newcastle United all-but clinched promotion to Division One with a 4-0 hammering of Derby County – and all-but consigned Arthur's next club to Division Three! As it happened, Derby were relegated without kicking a ball, when Oldham Athletic won two days later, thus consigning the League Champions of 1975 to Division 3 in 9 years. The Spectacular Fall indeed!

RAMS CHRONOLOGY: Arthur and Roy

The 1980s

Year	Event	Pos
Season 1984/85 (Division Three)		
1984	28/05: Derby appoint Arthur Cox as manager – a huge coup (interestingly, Robert Maxwell wanted Jim Smith!); Roy McFarland is named as Arthur's assistant	
1984	July: Arthur Cox signs Rob Hindmarch from Sunderland on a free transfer	
1984	Derby begin their centenary season in Division Three, but are financially sound	
1984	29/08: League Cup 1st Rd: Derby vs. Hartlepool (W 5-1) – Wilson 4, Powell	19
1984	01/09: Derby vs. Bolton (W 3-2) – Wilson 3 – Kevin Wilson on fire – (W1, D0, L1)	9
1984	25/09: League Cup 2nd Rd: Ipswich vs. Derby (L 4-2) – Wilson 2 (Ipswich remember)	12
1984	Kevin Wilson already has 13 goals, but suffers broken arm and is out for 2 months	
1984	Sep-Nov – Derby remain mid-table, largely winning at home and losing away	
1984	24/11: Derby vs. Wigan (D 2-2) – Davison 2 – Rams 15th but only 9 points off top	15
1984	28/11: Derby vs. Doncaster (W 3-1) – Davison 3 – Davison now has 11 goals	12
1984	15/12: Derby vs. Orient (W 1-0) – Garner – 3 wins on bounce – Rams 3 pts off 3rd	7
1984	29/12: Swansea vs. Derby (W 1-5) – Davison, Wilson, Buckley, Garner, Palmer	8
1985	01/01: Derby vs. York City (W 1-0) – Davison – Rams only 4 points off 3rd place	7
1985	The returning Kevin Wilson is sold to Ipswich for £150,000 – good business, as...	
1985	February: Derby sign Trevor Christie from Nottingham Forest for £92,500	
1985	February: Derby sign Gary Micklewhite from QPR for £92,500	
1985	02/03: Derby vs. Rotherham (D 1-1) – Christie – 6 games w/o win – 12 pts off 3rd	13
1985	16/03: Plymouth vs. Derby (W 0-1) – Davison – 3 wins in 4 – now 10 points off 3rd	11
1985	March: Derby sign Geraint Williams from Bristol Rovers for £43,500	
1985	03/04: Millwall vs. Derby (L 2-1) – Micklewhite – 3 without a win – 18 points off 3rd	12
1985	Derby finish strongly (W5, D4, L1) as promotion team starts to take shape	
1985	Derby finish season 7th (7:24), on 70 points, but still some 17 points shy of 3rd	7
1985	Bobby Davison is Derby's top scorer with 24 league goals (26 in all competitions)	
1985	Bobby is first Ram to pass 20 league goals since Kevin Hector in 1967/68, and his 26 goals in all comps is highest in a season since Ray Straw's 37 during 1956/57	
1985	Bobby Davison is also Derby's Player of the Season	

Perspective: Rob and Gary, RIP

One upsetting statistic of the 1984/85 season is that Rob Hindmarch played a handful of games alongside a very young Gary Ablett, who was at Derby on loan from Liverpool when still aged only 19. Big Rob died tragically young in 2002, of motor neurone disease at the age of only 41. Just as tragic was Gary Ablett's death in 2012 of non-Hodgkin's lymphoma, aged only 46. It seems impossible, even now, that both have gone; it would have been unthinkable back in 1985.

Big Rob Hindmarch.

PHOTO: Andy Ellis

Stats Blast: Ships in the Night

During season 1984/85, Kevin Wilson scored 14 goals for Derby and Bobby Davison 26. Remarkably, though, they only ever scored in the same game ONCE – this being the 5-1 win at Swansea on 29 December 1984.

One month into the 1984/85 season, and Kevin Wilson had already bagged a dozen goals.

PHOTO: Andy Ellis

Year	Event	Pos
Season 1985/86 (Division Three)		
1985	Summer: Arthur Cox signs Jeff Chandler, Ross MacLaren and Steve McClaren	
1985	17/08: Derby vs. Bournemouth (W 3-0) – Chandler 2, Christie – great start	2
1985	26/08: Derby vs. Wolves (W 4-2) – Christie 2, Lewis, Davison – (W2, D0, L1)	4
1985	21/09: Derby vs. Chesterfield (D 0-0) – 5 without a win – Chesterfield are 5th	13
1985	02/10: Derby vs. Swansea (W 5-1) – Davison 2, Christie, Micklewhite, Chandler	6
1985	22/10: Gillingham vs. Derby (W 1-2) – fifth win on spin – Rams are now 2nd, but...	2
1985	22/10: Rams are on 25 pts from 13 games; Reading are top on 39 points from 13!	2
1985	Derby sign Michael Forsyth from West Bromwich Albion for £26,000	
1985	09/11: Derby vs. Lincoln (W 7-0) – H'march 2, M'white 2, Chandler, Davison, Garner	4
1985	Derby sign John Gregory from QPR for £100,000	4
1985	16/11: FA Cup 1st Rd: Derby vs. Crewe (W 5-1) – Davison 2, Christie 2, Chandler	4
1985	09/12: FA Cup 2nd Rd: Derby vs. Telford (W 6-1) – Chandler 3, M'white 2, Gregory	7
1985	15/12: Doncaster vs. Derby (W 0-3) – Davison 2, Micklewhite – (W10, D7, L3)	3
1985	22/12: Derby vs. Wigan (W 1-0) – Christie – Rams 2nd – 16 points behind Reading!	2
1985	28/12: Wolves vs. Derby (W 0-4) – Williams, Christie, Davison, Gregory – 4 wins in 5	2
1986	13/01: FA Cup 3rd Rd: Derby vs. Gillingham (W 3-1 AET) – M'white, Garner, Christie	2
1986	25/01: FA Cup 4th Rd: Sheff Utd vs. Derby (W 0-1) – Hindmarch – 10,000 away fans	6
1986	08/02: York City vs. Derby (W 1-3) – Micklewhite 2, Christie – 7 wins in 9, but...	3
1986	08/02: ...due to pp's and FA Cup run, Derby have SEVEN games in hand on some	3
1986	22/02: Chesterfield vs. Derby (L 1-0) – first league defeat in 12 – Rams 4 pts off 3rd	4
1986	26/02: FA Cup 5th Rd: Derby vs. Sheffield Wed (D 1-1) – Davison	4
1986	05/03: FA Cup 5th Rd Replay: Sheffield Wed vs. Derby (L 2-0)	4
1986	08/03: Notts County vs. Derby (W 0-3) – Davison 2, Micklewhite – (W16, D8, L4)	4
1986	12/03: Derby vs. Walsall (W 3-1) – Chandler, Williams, Hart (og) – many GIH	3
1986	19/03: Derby vs. Bristol C (W 2-0) – Gregory, Christie – 3 pts clear of 4th with 5 GIH	3

Year	Event	Pos
1986	19/03: In fact, Rams now only 13 pts behind Reading with 3 GIH, and a Goal Diff of +38 vs. Reading's +16... but as games come thick & fast, victories harder to buy...	3
1986	...and it doesn't help that Plymouth come from nowhere, winning 13 out of 15	
1986	22/03: Plymouth vs. Derby (W 4-1) – Christie – Rams 1 pt above Plymouth; 4 GIH	3
1986	05/04: Derby vs. Brentford (D 1-1) – Micklewhite – 4 w/o win; Rams down to 5th	5
1986	07/04: Derby (5th) vs. Gillingham (2nd) (W 2-0) – Davison, Micklewhite – up to 4th	4
1986	12/04: Lincoln vs. Derby (W 0-1) – Davison – up to 3rd but only 2 GIH now	3
1986	19/04: Derby vs. Bolton (W 2-1) – Buckley, Williams – same pts as WIG/PLY; 3 GIH	2
1986	03/05: Derby vs. Doncaster (D 1-1) – Hindmarch – no win in 4 (D3, L1) – down to 5th	5
1986	Most teams have finished their season; can the exhausted Rams prevail...	5

Pos	Team	Pld	W	D	L	GF	GA	GD	Pts
1	Reading	45	28	7	10	65	51	14	91
2	Plymouth Argyle	46	26	9	11	88	53	35	87
3	Wigan Athletic	46	23	14	9	82	48	34	83
4	Gillingham	46	22	13	11	81	54	27	79
5	**Derby County**	**43**	**21**	**15**	**7**	**74**	**38**	**36**	**78**
6	Walsall	46	22	9	15	90	64	26	75

Year	Event	Pos
1986	06/05: Swansea vs. Derby (W 0-3) – Christie 2, Chandler – vital victory – up to 4th	4

Pos	Team	Pld	W	D	L	GF	GA	GD	Pts
1	Reading	46	29	7	10	67	51	16	94
2	Plymouth Argyle	46	26	9	11	88	53	35	87
3	Wigan Athletic	46	23	14	9	82	48	34	83
4	**Derby County**	**44**	**22**	**15**	**7**	**77**	**38**	**39**	**81**

Year	Event	Pos
1986	09/05: Derby vs. Rotherham (W 2-1) – Gee, Christie – Rams crawl over finish line	3
1986	Derby finish season 3rd (3:24), on 84 pts; DERBY ARE PROMOTED TO DIV TWO	3
1986	Steve Buckley, Ross MacLaren and Gary Micklewhite play all 60 games of season	
1986	Bobby Davison is leading scorer again with 17 league goals; 23 in all competitions	
1986	Ross MacLaren is Derby's Player of the Season	

Stats Blast: Lucky 13

When Derby won their fifth game on the bounce at Gillingham on 22 October 1985, the Rams moved up to 2nd, on 25 points from 13 games. However, they were FOURTEEN POINTS behind leaders Reading – as the Royals had won all 13 of their first 13 league games!

Quirk Alert: All In Hand

When Derby beat York City on 8 Feb 1986, they were 3rd in Div Three, but had only played 25 games, and had as many as SEVEN games in hand on some teams. They somehow had to fit 21 league games into 3 months, and eventually crawled over the finish line in mid-May.

Stats Blast: Pools Win
In the back-to-back Division Three seasons of 1984/85 and 1985/86, Derby actually played Hartlepool United FIVE times in the League Cup and FA Cup, winning three and losing one.

Stats Blast: Central Control
Derby County won the Central League again during season 1985/86, and became the first (and only) Third Division club to achieve this.

Stats Blast: Staying Power
When Derby completed their marathon 1985/86 season, 32 year-old left back Steve Buckley played in all 60 games. In fact, his last game for Derby was his 366th and also his 122nd consecutive game. Having completed an earlier century of consecutive Rams appearances, Bucko became the only player in Derby's history to complete two separate centuries of league appearances. Small surprise, therefore, that Bucko had also been an ever-present on FIVE other occasions, and won Derby's Player of the Season award twice.

Steve (Bucko) Buckley.

PHOTO: Andy Ellis

Stats Blast: Bucko and Brucie
Steve Buckley had also been Derby's regular left back for eight and a half seasons when he left Derby at the end of the 1985/86 season. However, his immediate successor, Michael Forsyth (right), also played for Derby for NINE seasons and hence the pair spanned 17.5 seasons, from 1978 to 1995, making 748 appearances between them and weighing in with a useful 34 goals from the left back position, too! Like Buckley, Forsyth also had long unbroken stints in the side, his longest being 124 consecutive appearances between April 1988 and January 1991.

Bruuucie!

PHOTO: Andy Ellis

Year	Event	Pos
Season 1986/87 (Division Two)		
1986	Summer: Derby sign right-back Mel Sage from Gillingham for £60,000	
1986	Summer: Derby sign striker Mark Lillis from Manchester City for £200,000	
1986	23/08: Derby kick off the season with a home defeat to Oldham Athletic (L 0-1)	18
1986	23/08: Little do they know that they won't lose at home again all season!	18
1986	30/08: Birmingham vs. Derby (D 1-1) – Gregory grabs Derby's first goal and point	17
1986	06/09: Derby vs. Crystal Palace (W 1-0) – Gregory again, seals Derby's first win	15
1986	13/09: Mark Lillis' knee injury sees Phil Gee promoted to number 8	
1986	13/09: Grimsby vs. Derby (W 0-1) – Davison secures first away win	11
1986	27/09: West Brom vs. Derby (L 2-0) – Rams are 9 points behind leaders, Oldham	16
1986	01/10: Derby vs. Sunderland (W 3-2) – Forsyth, Davison, Sage – from 0-2 down	8
1986	11/10: Derby vs. Hull (D 1-1) – Phil Gee's first goal of the season – (W3, D3, L3)	13
1986	25/10: Derby vs. Brighton (W 4-1) – Gee 2, Gregory, Sage	8
1986	01/11: Stoke City vs. Derby (W 0-2) – Williams, Gee – (W6, D3, L4)	7
1986	08/11: Derby vs. Ipswich (W 2-1) – Micklewhite, Davison – 3 wins on the spin	6

Year	Event	Pos
1986	15/11: Barnsley vs. Derby (W 0-1) – Gee – 4 wins on spin and only 4 pts off top	4
1986	22/11: Derby vs. Sheffield U (W 2-0) – Micklewhite, Gregory – 5th win on the spin	4
1986	06/12: Derby vs. Reading (W 3-0) – Davison 3 – Rams 4 pts behind leaders, Oldham	4
1986	13/12: Plymouth (3rd) vs. Derby (4th) (D 1-1) – Plymouth equalise in 90th minute	4
1986	21/12: Derby vs. Grimsby (W 4-0) – Davison 2, Micklewhite, Gee – 3 pts off top	3
1986	26/12: Bradford City vs. Derby (W 0-1) – Gregory's 84th min pen – 2 points off top	3
1986	27/12: Derby vs. Barnsley (W 3-2) – Gee, Gregory, Davison – Rams come from 0-2 down again AND GO TOP OF DIVISION TWO	1
1986	03/01: Crystal Palace vs. Derby (L 1-0) – Rams 5 points behind leaders Portsmouth	3
1987	24/01: Oldham (2nd) vs. Derby (3rd) (W 1-4) – Davison, Gregory, Gee, Micklewhite	2
1987	24/01: This win on Oldham's synthetic pitch starts a run of 13 games w/o defeat	2
1987	Derby sign former England-U21 winger Nigel Callaghan from Watford for £140,000	2
1987	07/02: Derby vs. Birmingham (D 2-2) – Gee 2 – Rams now 7 pts behind Portsmouth	2
1987	28/02: Millwall vs. Derby (W 0-1) – Callaghan – Rams 6 points behind Portsmouth	2
1987	04/03: Derby vs. Portsmouth (D 0-0) – Rams remain 6 points behind Pompey	2
1987	07/03: Brighton vs. Derby (W 0-1) – Gee – Rams close gap on Pompey to 3 points	2
1987	14/03: Derby vs. Shrewsbury (W 3-1) – Davison 2, Callaghan – Rams 1 point off top	2
1987	18/03: Derby vs. Blackburn (W 3-2) – Davison 2, Keeley (og) – RAMS GO TOP	1
1987	04/04: Ipswich vs. Derby (W 0-2) – Callaghan, Davison – Rams remain top on GD	1
1987	08/04: Derby vs. Huddersfield (W 2-0) – Gregory, Gee – Rams go 3 points clear	1
1987	17/04: Blackburn vs. Derby (L 3-1) – Hindmarch – Keeley crocks Bobby	2
1987	18/04: Portsmouth draw 2-2 at Reading, and go above Derby on Goal Difference	2
1987	20/04: Derby vs. Bradford (W 1-0) – Lillis diving header – Rams 3 points clear at top	1
1987	25/04: Sheff U vs. Derby (W 0-1) – Gee – Rams 3/12 pts clear of Pompey/Oldham	1
1987	25/04: Derby's win is their 11th league away win of the season, a new club record	1
1987	02/05: Derby vs. Leeds (W 2-1) – Gee, Davison – DERBY ARE PROMOTED TO DIV 1	1
1987	09/05: Derby vs. Plymouth (W 4-2) – Davison, Callaghan, Micklewhite, Gregory	1
1987	09/05: DERBY COUNTY ARE DIVISION TWO CHAMPIONS	1
1987	Derby finish season 1st (1:22) on 84 points, 6 points clear of Portsmouth in 2nd	1
1987	Bobby Davison is again Derby's top scorer with 19 league goals (22 in all comps)	
1987	Geraint Williams is Derby's Player of the Season	
1987	With Derby now in the First Division, Robert Maxwell takes over as club chairman	

Derby County celebrate promotion to Division One on 2 May 1987 after goals from Phil Gee and Bobby Davison secure a 2-1 win over Leeds United. Pictured are: Back Row: Lillis, Gregory, Williams, Forsyth, MacLaren, Pratley, Blades, Cross, Sage, McFarland; Front Row: Guthrie, Steele, Gee, Cox, Hindmarch, Davison, Callaghan, Micklewhite and Harbey. PHOTO: Andy Ellis

Stats Blast: Longevity

Most of the players signed by Arthur Cox in his first three years at Derby, went on to make many appearances for the Rams, as shown by the table below. Bobby Davison and Paul Blades were already at Derby when Cox arrived in the summer of 1984, but have been included below, as they were both mainstays of the Rams' back-to-back promotion seasons of the mid-1980s. The statistics speak for themselves, but two things need to be emphasised: a) remarkable business was done in those three years; b) Arthur Cox was a brilliant manager!

Arthur Cox.

PHOTO: Andy Ellis

Gary Micklewhite.

PHOTO: Andy Ellis

Geraint Williams.

PHOTO: Andy Ellis

Player	Signed	Fee	When	Apps	Gls
Nigel Callaghan	Feb-86	£140,000	1987-1990	95	12
Michael Forsyth	Oct-85	£26,000	1986-1995	382	9
Phil Gee	Sep-85	£10,000	1986-1992	144	31
John Gregory	Nov-85	£100,000	1985-1988	120	23
Rob Hindmarch	Jul-84	Free	1984-1990	190	10
Ross MacLaren	Jul-85	£67,000	1985-1988	144	5
Gary Micklewhite	Feb-85	£85,000	1985-1993	278	37
Mel Sage	Jul-86	£60,000	1986-1991	167	4
Geraint Williams	Mar-85	£43,500	1985-1992	321	9
Totals ->		£531,500		1,841	140
Paul Blades	Appren.	N/A	1982-1989	200	1
Bobby Davison	Dec-82	£80,000	1982-1991	248	105
Totals ->		£611,500		2,289	246

Year	Event	Pos
Season 1987/88 (Division One)		
1987	Summer: Derby sign England goalkeeper Peter Shilton from Southampton	
1987	Summer: Derby also sign England defender Mark Wright from Southampton	
1987	Summer: Mark Wright arrives for a Rams record transfer fee of £760,000	
1987	15/08: Derby vs. Luton (W 1-0) – Gregory gives Rams great start back in Div One	7
1987	19/08: QPR vs. Derby (D 1-1) – Gee keeps up the good start – (W1, D1, L0)	7
1987	12/09: Norwich vs. Derby (W 1-2) – Davison, Gregory – Rams have 2 GIH on most	11
1987	12/09: Gary Micklewhite injury ends a run of 112 consecutive league apps	11
1987	10/10: Derby vs. Nottingham Forest (L 0-1) – Wilkinson – 5 without a win	13
1987	17/10: Charlton vs. Derby (W 0-1) – Cross – (W3, D4, L4)	11
1987	31/10: Derby vs. Coventry (W 2-0) – Garner 2 – (W4, D4, L5)	11
1987	November: Club hero Bobby Davison is surprisingly sold to Leeds for £350,000	
1987	14/11: Newcastle vs. Derby (D 0-0) – Peter Shilton's 800th football league game	13
1987	22/11: Derby vs. Chelsea (W 2-0) – Cross, Gregory – Shilton's 1,000th club game	13
1987	28/11: Southampton vs. Derby (W 1-2) – Gee, Garner – (W6, D5, L5)	10
1987	05/12: Derby vs. Watford (D 1-1) – Wright – Rams 7 pts behind 4th-placed Forest	9
1987	Rams lose 8 league games on spin, equalling club record; 6 of these are 2-1 defeats	18
1988	February: Derby sign former Rangers winger Ted McMinn from Sevilla for £300,000	18

Year	Event	Pos
1988	10/02: Derby vs. Man Utd (L 1-2) – McMinn scores a wonder goal on home debut	18
1988	27/02: Derby vs. West Ham (W 1-0) – Callaghan – (W7, D7, L13) – 3 pts above 19th	18
1988	16/03: Derby vs. Liverpool (D 1-1) – Forsyth secures draw with runaway leaders	17
1988	March: Derby sign veteran striker Frank Stapleton (32) from Ajax	17
1988	19/03: Coventry vs. Derby (W 0-3) – Forsyth, Gee, Williams – (W8, D10, L13)	16
1988	19/03: Following clash between Peter Shilton's head and Dave Bennett's leg, John Gregory had to keep goal for Derby; poor Dave Bennett's leg came off the worst	16
1988	26/03: Arsenal vs. Derby (D 0-0) – 7 w/o defeat for Rams; 5 points above 19th	16
1988	02/04: Manchester United vs. Derby (L 4-1) – Cross – Rams 3 pts above trap-door	17
1988	04/04: Derby vs. Newcastle (W 2-1) – Gee, Micklewhite – 5 point cushion	15
1988	30/04: Watford vs. Derby (D 1-1) – Callaghan – Peter Shilton breaks Terry Paine's record of 824 league appearances	15
1988	Derby finish 15th (15:21), on 43 pts, 8 pts above drop-zone, but 1 pt above play-off!	15
1988	Phil Gee and John Gregory are top scorers with only 6 goals apiece (all league)	
1988	Michael Forsyth is Derby's Player of the Year	

Quirk Alert: Odd Saturday's

Season 1987/88 was a major oddity as Division One was in the process of being reduced from 22 teams to 20 over the course of two seasons. This meant that season 1987/88 saw an odd number of teams in the English First Division for the first (and only) time – 21 in this particular case – which meant that each weekend, one team didn't have a game! Unfortunately for Derby, this first occurred on the second Saturday of the season; thankfully they already had 4 points out of 6, so things could have been worse. However, participation in the early rounds of the League Cup meant that by mid-September, Derby were already TWO games behind most of the other First Division teams!

Peter Shilton and Mark Wright, both England internationals, arrived at Derby from Southampton in the summer of 1987.
PHOTOS: Andy Ellis

Quirk Alert: Kicking the Bucket

When Derby beat Newcastle 2-1 on 4 April 1988, in a vital First Division game, Newcastle's line-up included a young Paul Gascoigne. Gazza already had a big reputation, but canny Arthur Cox – the man who signed Gascoigne as an apprentice at Newcastle – knew how to snuff him out. He therefore instructed Geraint Williams to "play inside Gazza's shorts", and the young man therefore didn't get a kick – well, not until he aimed one at Williams, anyway – for which he received an inevitable red card.

This delighted a crowd which had spent most of the game winding Gazza up, and as he stormed off the pitch, face and legs glowing bright red, he booted a bucket of water in the direction of the Derby dug out. At which point, the crowd reacted with a pantomime-like "Oooooh!" which somehow managed to make Gazza even more apoplectic!

Year	Event	Pos
Season 1988/89 (Division One)		
1988	Summer: Derby sign Paul Goddard from Newcastle for £425,000 and Trevor Hebberd from Oxford United for £250,000	
1988	27/08: Derby vs. Middlesbrough (W 1-0) – Goddard scores on league debut	6
1988	10/09: Derby vs. Newcastle (W 2-0) – Goddard and Hebberd score – (W2, D0, L1)	7
1988	17/09: Nottingham Forest vs. Derby (D 1-1) – Hebberd with late equaliser	7
1988	22/10: Derby vs. Charlton (D 0-0) – five games without a win – (W2, D3, L3)	15
1988	Derby sign Dean Saunders for a club-record £1 million from Oxford United	15
1988	29/10: Derby vs. Wimbledon (W 4-1) – Saunders 2, Sage, Micklewhite	13
1988	05/11: Tottenham vs. Derby (W 1-3) – McMinn 2, Saunders – Rams 4 pts off 2nd	6
1988	12/11: Derby vs. Manchester United (D 2-2) – Saunders, Hebberd	8
1988	19/11: Aston Villa vs. Derby (W 1-2) – Saunders, Goddard – (W5, D4, L3)	6
1988	26/11: Derby vs. Arsenal (W 2-1) – Callaghan and Gee despatch eventual Champs	7
1988	03/12: Sheffield Wed vs. Derby (D1-1) – Callaghan – 7 without defeat	5
1988	17/12: Coventry vs. Derby (W 0-2) – Saunders, McMinn – Rams above LIV with GIH	4
1988 1989	Derby frustrate, losing 4 home games on spin by 1 goal (Luton, Liverpool, Millwall, West Ham) but winning 3 away; 2 home wins would have put the Rams 2nd	
1989	04/02: Derby vs. Southampton (W 3-1) – Hebberd, Goddard, Saunders	7
1989	25/02: Derby vs. Everton (W 3-2) – Goddard 2 (one, a classy chip), Saunders	6
1989	15/04: Man Utd vs. Derby (W 0-2) – M'White, Goddard – Hillsborough disaster	8
1989	22/04: Derby vs. Sheffield Wednesday (W 1-0) – Saunders – (W15, D7, L11)	6
1989	13/05: Arsenal vs. Derby (W 1-2) – Saunders brace puts Arsenal title in jeopardy	5
1989	Derby finish season 5th (5:20), on 58 points, 18 points behind Champions, Arsenal	5
1989	Derby should have qualified for the UEFA Cup, but English clubs were still banned following Heysel – otherwise it would have been Div Three to Europe in 3 years!	
1989	Dean Saunders is Derby's leading scorer with 14 league goals (15 in all comps)	
1989	Mark Wright is Derby's Player of the Season	

Quirk Alert: Fever Pitch
Derby's 1988/89 double over Arsenal very nearly de-railed the Gunners' title bid, especially the 2-1 victory at Highbury on 13 May 1989. The result certainly meant that Arsenal had to travel to Anfield for the final game of the season requiring a win by two goals. The game against Derby therefore finds its way into Nick Hornby's book Fever Pitch, as it does also in the subsequent film adaptation, starring Colin Firth.

Year	Event	Pos
Season 1989/90 (Division One)		
1989	Having finished 5th, Derby were perfectly placed to push on; alas, Robert Maxwell's days were numbered – and so were Derby's as a top flight club	
1989	26/08: Derby vs. Manchester United (W 2-0) – Goddard, Saunders	6

Year	Event	Pos
1989	30/08: Forest vs. Derby (L 2-1); 09/09: Derby vs. Liverpool (L 0-3)	14
1989	16/09: QPR vs. Derby (W 0-1) – Saunders – (W2, D2, L2)	9
1989	23/09: Derby vs. Southampton (L 0-1); Aston Villa vs. Derby (L 1-0)	16
1989	04/10: L Cup 2nd Rd: Derby vs. Cambridge (W 5-0) – Saunders 3, Goddard, McMinn	16
1989	14/10: Derby vs. Crystal Palace (W 3-1) – Goddard 2, Saunders – (W3, D2, L4)	11
1989	25/10: L Cup 3rd Rd: Derby vs. Sheff Wed (W 2-1) – Saunders 2 (90, 92)	15
1989	04/11: Luton Town vs. Derby (L 1-0) – Rams now only 3 points off the bottom	17
1989	11/11: Derby vs. Man C (W 6-0) – Saunders 2, Wright, Hebberd, Goddard, M'white	12
1989	18/11: Derby vs. Sheffield Wednesday (W 2-0) – Goddard, Saunders	12
1989	22/11: League Cup 4th Rd: Derby vs. West Brom (W 2-1) – McMinn 2	12
1989	25/11: Tottenham vs. Derby (W 1-2) – Saunders, Goddard (bad McMinn injury)	9
1989	02/12: Derby vs. Charlton (W 2-0) – Saunders Micklewhite – (W7, D3, L6)	6
1989	Derby sell Paul Goddard to Millwall for £800,000, a club record fee received; at this point, Goddard & Saunders were terrorising defences with 23 goals between them	
1989	30/12: Derby vs. Coventry (W 4-1) – Hebberd 2, Pickering, Craig Ramage (19)	9

The 1990s

Year	Event	Pos
1990	13/01: Manchester United vs. Derby (W 1-2) – Wright, Pickering – Rams complete the double over Man Utd, also winning back-to-back games at Old Trafford	7
1990	Derby sign Mick Harford from Luton Town for £450,000	7
1990	20/01: Derby vs. Nottingham Forest (L 0-2) – Forest were only point above Derby	9
1990	24/01: League Cup Quarter-Final Replay: Derby vs. West Ham (D 0-0)	10
1990	31/01: League Cup Quarter-Final, 2nd Replay: West Ham vs. Derby (L 2-1) - Saunders	10
1990	10/02: Derby vs. QPR (W 2-0) – Gee, Saunders – (W10, D5, L9)	7
1990	24/02: Derby vs. Tottenham (W 2-1) – Saunders, Harford – (W11, D5, L9)	7
1990	24/02: Rams have 2 games in hand which would take them up to 3rd if won; alas, injuries take their toll, Derby only win twice more and the season peters out...	7
1990	Derby finish season 16th (16:20) on 46 points, three points clear of relegation	16
1990	Dean Saunders is Derby's leading scorer with 11 league goals (21 in all comps)	
1990	Mark Wright is Derby's Player of the Year for the second successive season	
1990	06/06: England vs. Holland – Peter Shilton passes Roy McFarland for most England caps (29) whilst at Derby County; he eventually wins 34 while at Derby	
1990	06/06: ENG vs. EGY – Mark Wright first Ram to score for Eng since Jack Lee in 1950	
1990	Peter Shilton also captains England against Egypt and Italy during Italia '90	

Quirk Alert: Land of the Giants

When 6ft 7in striker Kevin Francis made his debut for Derby, as a substitute in the 1-1 FA Cup 3rd round draw with Port Vale, he became Derby's tallest-ever player. That's a full two inches taller than the seemingly beanpolesque Ian Ormondroyd, who joined the club two seasons later! As for Kevin Francis, he scored his only goal for the club in the replay against Port Vale – an embarrassing 2-3 home defeat.

Year	Event	Pos
Season 1990/91 (Division One)		
1990	15/09: Derby vs. Aston Villa (L 0-2) – Rams are bottom – (W0, D2, L3)	20
1990	06/10: Derby vs. Liverpool (L 0-2) – 5 defeats on the spin – (W0, D2, L6)	20
1990	20/10: Derby vs. Man City (D 1-1) – Saunders has 4 of a meagre 5 Derby goals	19
1990	27/10: Southampton vs. Derby (W 0-1) – Harford – a win at the 10th attempt	19
1990	31/10: League Cup 3rd Rd: Derby vs. Sunderland (W 6-0) – Harford 3, Ramage 2	19
1990	03/11: Derby vs. Luton (W 2-1) – Saunders, Callaghan – (W2, D3, L6)	19
1990	10/11: Derby vs. Manchester United (D 0-0) – four without defeat	19
1990	24/11: Derby vs. Nottingham Forest (W 2-1) – Ramage, Saunders	17
1990	24/11: Geraint Williams hits 100 consecutive appearances; then injured for 2 mths	
1990	01/12: Sunderland vs. Derby (W 1-2) – Saunders, Harford – (W4, D4, L7)	14
1990	Optimism after a run of W4, D2, L1...but the Rams don't win again until May!	
1990	12/12: League Cup 4th Rd Replay: Sheffield Wed vs. Derby (L 2-1) – Micklewhite	14
1990	15/12: Derby vs. Chelsea (L 4-6) – Saunders 2, Hebberd, Micklewhite	15
1990	29/12: Everton vs. Derby (L 2-0) – Rams drop back into the bottom three	18
1991	01/01: Injury brings an end to Michael Forsyth's consecutive appearances (124)	18
1991	02/02: Aston Villa vs. Derby (L 3-2) – Harford, Sage – Rams hit bottom spot again	20
1991	02/03: Derby vs. Sunderland (D 3-3) – Saunders 3 – Rams 8 points from safety	20
1991	23/03: Derby vs. Liverpool (L 1-7) – Saunders – Rams joint-record home defeat	20
1991	16/04: Man City vs. Derby (L 2-1) – Harford – Rams relegated with 4 games to go	20
1991	23/04: Derby vs. Leeds (L 0-1) – 20 games w/o win (D5, L15), another Rams record	20
1991	04/05: Derby vs. Southampton (W 6-2) – Paul Williams 3, Saunders 2, Phillips	20
1991	Derby finish season 20th (20:20), 17 points adrift of safety	20
1991	Dean Saunders is Derby's top scorer with 17 goals (21 in all competitions)	
1991	Dean Saunders is Derby's Player of the Season	
1991	21/05: Mark Wright captains England against Russia at Wembley	

Stats Blast: Deano the Robot
Dean Saunders was an ever-present for Derby from his first game against
Wimbledon on 29 October 1988 to his final game against Luton on 11
May 1991 – clocking up 130 consecutive appearances of which 106 were
league matches. During this time, he scored 52 goals for Derby.

Dean Saunders was outstanding at Derby, and joined Liverpool
for a British transfer record of £2.9m in July 1991. PHOTO: Andy Ellis

Stats Alert: Derby the Disastrous
Throughout season 1990/91, Derby were unable to buy any new players or afford another player
on loan. With injuries also biting hard, it is not really surprising that the club set an unwanted
record of 20 games without a win between December and April, while on 23 March, the Rams
equalled the club's worst-ever home defeat when they lost to Liverpool 1-7.

Quirk Alert: Harford the Hatter
Derby's last game of the season was away at Luton Town, with the Rams already relegated, but with Sunderland and Luton neck-and-neck above them on 34 points apiece. Cue Mick Harford. The big striker was destined to re-join Luton four months later, and his own-goal in the Luton vs. Derby game helped the home side to a 2-0 victory and First Division safety – amid rumours that the own goal was deliberate! Ironically, Sunderland were Harford's home-town club and he actually joined them three years later.

Quirk Alert: Ramsline Halt
In 1990, a single-platform railway station was built at the back of the Ley Stand to serve the Baseball Ground, and was known as Ramsline Halt. The station was funded by the Football Trust and was intended for Football Specials only, in a bid to help avoid trouble in the city centre. The station cost £26,000 to build – but only four trains ever stopped there! The station name board is now at the National Football Museum!

Year	Event	Pos
Season 1991/92 (Division Two)		
1991	July: Dean Saunders is sold to Liverpool for a British transfer record of £2.9m	
1991	July: Mark Wright is sold to Liverpool for £2.5m – a national transfer record for a defender; alas, these huge funds had to be used to pay off Robert Maxwell...	
1991	Derby sign centre-backs Andy Comyn and Simon Coleman from Aston Villa and Middlesbrough respectively for modest fees – very shrewd business indeed	
1991	01/09: Charlton vs. Derby (W 0-2) – P Williams, Harford – (W2, D1, L1)	5
1991	September: Mick Harford is sold back to Luton Town for £325,000	
1991	18/09: Oxford United vs. Derby (L 2-0) – 4 without a win – (W2, D3, L3)	15
1991	Derby secure loan signings of Bobby Davison (Leeds) and Ian Ormondroyd (A Villa)	15
1991	21/09: Derby vs. Brighton (W 3-1) – Davison, Patterson, P Williams	11
1991	28/09: Newcastle United vs. Derby (D 2-2) – Davison, Ormondroyd	13
1991	28/09: Bobby Davison becomes 10th Derby player to score 100 goals for the club	13
1991	05/10: Derby vs. Bristol City (W 4-1) – Davison 2, Micklewhite, Aizlewood (og)	8
1991	12/10: Swindon Town vs. Derby (W 1-2) – P Williams, Gee	6
1991	19/10: Derby vs. Portsmouth (W 2-0) – McMinn, P Williams	6
1991	26/10: Millwall vs. Derby (W 1-2) – Davison, Orm'royd – 5 wins in 6; 4 pts off top	6
1991	November: Lionel Pickering becomes majority shareholder of Derby County	6
1991	09/11: Wolves vs. Derby (W 2-3) – Davison, Ormondroyd, Bennett (og)	6
1991	16/11: Derby vs. Ipswich (W 1-0) – Davison – Rams 3 pts behind leaders, Cambridge	3
1991	23/11: Bristol R vs. Derby (W 2-3) – Patterson, P Williams, Davison – 3 pts off top	3
1991	23/11: Game marks Davison's last and 106th goal for Rams as he returns to Leeds	3
1991	07/12: Derby vs. Watford (W 2-1) – Ormondroyd 2 – Rams are 2 points off the top	4
1992	18/01: Derby vs. Sunderland (L 1-2) – G Williams – 5 without a win	11
1992	Derby sign Marco Gabbiadini from Crystal Palace for a club record-equalling £1m	11
1992	01/02: Portsmouth vs. Derby (W 0-1) – Gabbiadini scores on his debut	11
1992	Derby sign Paul Simpson from Oxford United for £500,000	10
1992	22/02: Leicester vs. Derby (W 1-2) – Ormondroyd, Simpson (also scores on debut)	9
1992	29/02: Derby vs. Watford (W 3-1) – P. Williams 3 – Rams 8 & 11 pts off 2nd & 1st	6

Year	Event	Pos
1992	March: Derby sign Paul Kitson from Leicester for a club record £1.3m	7
1992	Phil Gee and Ian Ormondroyd move to Leicester for £800,000 as part of the deal	7
1992	11/03: Derby vs. Port Vale (W 3-1) – G Williams, Simpson, Gabbiadini – 7 pts off 2nd	4
1992	March: Derby sign Tommy Johnson from Notts County for a club record £1.375m	4
1992	21/03: Derby vs. Wolves (L 1-2) – Kitson – 2 defeats on spin – now 9 points off 2nd	9
1992	25/03: Derby vs. Plymouth (W 2-0) – Johnson, McMinn – 6 points off 2nd	5
1992	28/03: Ipswich vs. Derby (L 2-1) – Simpson – Rams 8 pts off 2nd; Ipswich go top	8
1992	Derby's new strike-force of Johnson, Kitson, Gabbiadini and Simpson clicks; they terrorise defences, scoring 28 goals in last 13 league games, winning 6 of last 7	
1992	04/04: Barnsley vs. Derby (W 0-3) – Simpson, Forsyth, P Williams – 7 pts off 2nd	5
1992	07/04: Grimsby vs. Derby (W 0-1) – Gabbiadini – Rams 4 pts behind 2nd (Cambridge)	4
1992	11/04: Derby vs. Oxford (D 2-2) – Simpson, P Williams – Rams only 3 pts off 2nd	5
1992	15/04: Brighton vs. Derby (W 1-2) – Gabbiadini 2 – Rams 2 points off 2nd (Leicester)	4
1992	20/04: Derby vs. Newcastle (W 4-1) – Ramage 2, P Williams, Kitson – 2 pts off 2nd	3
1992	25/04: Bristol City vs. Derby (W 1-2) – Gabbiadini, Micklewhite – still 2 pts off 2nd	3
1992	25/04: New club record of 12 away wins in a season set, having won last 5 on spin	3
1992	02/05: Derby vs. Swindon (W 2-1) – Kitson, Johnson – promotion missed by mins!	3
1992	Derby finish season 3rd (3:24), on 78 points, two points behind Middlesbrough	3
1992	10/05: Play-Off 1st Leg: Blackburn vs. Derby (L 4-2) – Gabbiadini, Johnson	
1992	13/05: Play-Off 2nd Leg: Derby vs. Blackburn (W 2-1) – Comyn, McMinn – [agg: 4-5]	
1992	Paul Williams is Derby's top scorer with 13 league goals (16 in all competitions)	
1992	Ted McMinn is Derby's Player of the Season	

Quirk Alert: Coming or Going?

Ian Ormondroyd was initially signed on loan from Aston Villa in September and alongside fellow-loanee, Bobby Davison, both players hit a rich vein of scoring form to haul Derby up from 15th to 3rd between September and November. Ormondroyd was then signed permanently in December, and went on to complete 31 appearances for Derby during which time he scored 9 goals, 2 of which were scored against Leicester City. The latter fact probably influenced Leicester's signing of Ormondroyd in early March 1992, when he and Phil Gee went to Leicester in exchange for England Under-21 international striker, Paul Kitson. All of which meant that Ian Ormondroyd was loaned, signed and sold by Derby within five months!

Naturally, both Ormondroyd and Gee came back to haunt Derby over the next two years!

Quirk Alert: Not the Foggiest

One of Ian Ormondroyd's 9 goals for Derby came in an FA Cup 3rd round replay at the Baseball Ground on 25 January, which Derby won 2-0. He was lucky to get that goal, though, as an earlier replay had been abandoned at the Baseball Ground because of fog, with only 20 minutes to go. Derby were also winning 2-0 on that occasion – a bitter-sweet one for Mark Patterson, who scored a cracking goal, but then suffered a serious knee injury. Insult was then added to the injury when his goal was officially wiped out due to the fixture abandonment.

Coincidentally, this was the SECOND game at the Baseball Ground abandoned due to fog, that season, with Derby's home game with Plymouth Argyle having suffered the same fate!

Quirk Alert: What If 1?

When Derby signed Paul Kitson and Tommy Johnson in March 1992, the duo joined Paul Williams, Craig Ramage and Jason Kavanagh as Derby's FIVE current England Under-21 internationals. Recent signings Marco Gabbiadini and Paul Simpson had also both played for the England Under-21 side, boosting an already-strong team. The potential in Derby's side at this stage was therefore enormous, but alas, the side was put together one game too late...

Quirk Alert: What If 2?

With ten minutes of the 1991/92 season remaining, Derby had achieved the highly unlikely, and climbed into a promotion place for the first time that season. Leicester were on their way to a 1-2 home defeat by Newcastle, and Derby were beating Swindon Town 2-1. The key team now was Middlesbrough – and with ten minutes to go, they were losing 1-0 at Wolves, and were down to ten men. Cue Steve Bull, clean through on goal to wrap it all up.

Of course, he missed, and Middlesbrough then equalised to draw level on points with Derby, but with an inferior goal difference. Inevitably, they went on to score a late winner through Paul Wilkinson, and Derby were pipped at the post! Annoyingly, Steve Bull had also scored the winner at Derby on 21 March. Against the run of play! Thanks Steve!

Quirk Alert: What If 3?

Nevertheless, Derby were nailed-on favourites to go up through the play-offs. They were the form side, having won 6 of their last 7 games, although the other – a 2-2 home draw with Oxford – now took on new significance! Conversely, they were playing Blackburn Rovers who, having been 15 points ahead of Derby in February, and still leading the division in late March, had then suffered 6 straight league defeats and only just rallied to scrape into 6th place. True to form, Derby raced into a 0-2 lead at Ewood Park, but let Blackburn back in with two late first-half goals. That lifted Kenny Dalglish's men, and they ran out 4-2 winners. Derby threw everything at Blackburn in the return leg, but could only win 2-1, thus losing 4-5 on aggregate.

Paul Simpson.   Marco Gabbiadini .   Paul Kitson.   Tommy Johnson.

Signed within six weeks of each other in early 1992, Derby's dynamic new strike-force should have graced the inaugural Premier League. Alas, Derby missed out by the finest of margins. PHOTOS: Andy Ellis

Year	Event	Pos
Season 1992/93 (Division 1)		
1992	Summer: Derby sign Mark Pembridge from Luton Town for £1.2m	
1992	Summer: Derby sign Darren Wassall from Nottingham Forest for £600,000	
1992	FA Premier League is formed, Division Two re-named Division 1, optimism high...	12
1992	15/08: Peterborough vs. Derby (L 1-0)	15
1992	22/08: Derby vs. Newcastle (L 1-2) – Pembridge	20
1992	26/08: Leicester vs Derby (L 3-2) – Simpson 2 – Phil Gee brace for Leicester	21
1992	06/09: Derby vs. Bristol City (L 3-4) – Simpson 3 – Rams now bottom of Division 1	24
1992	Craig Short bought from Notts Co for club record £2.65m; record fee outside Prem	24
1992	20/09: West Ham vs. Derby (D 1-1) – Miklosko (og) – no win after 7 (W0, D3, L4)	24
1992	Derby buy Martin Kuhl from Portsmouth for £650,000	24
1992	26/09: Derby vs. Southend (W 2-0) – Gabbiadini, Simpson – first win at 8th attempt	22
1992	03/10: Cambridge vs. Derby (W 1-3) – Simpson 2, Gabbiadini – 2 wins on spin	16
1992	06/10: L Cup 2nd Rd: Derby vs. Southend (W 7-0) – Rams League Cup record win	16
1992	06/10: Goalscorers are Kitson 2, Gabbiadini 2, Martin (og), Simpson and Johnson	16
1992	17/10: Luton vs. Derby (W 1-3) – Kitson 2, Johnson – (W3, D3, L5)	15
1992	24/10: Derby vs. Charlton (W 4-3) – Gabbiadini, Minto (og), Pembridge, Simpson	14
1992	31/10: Wolves vs. Derby (W 0-2) – Kitson, Short – 3 wins on the spin	10
1992	28/10: L Cup 3rd Rd: Derby vs. Arsenal (D 1-1) - Simpson; Derby lose replay 2-1	14
1992	03/11: Notts County vs. Derby (W 0-2) – 6th win in 7 – (W6, D3, L5)	8
1992	11/11: Anglo-Italian Cup: Derby vs. Pisa (W 3-0) – Johnson, Forsyth, Pembridge	13
1992	24/11: Anglo-Italian Cup: Cosenza vs. Derby (W 0-3) – Comyn, Kitson, Gabbiadini	12
1992	28/11: Derby vs. Tranmere (L 1-2) – one win in last four – (W7, D3, L8)	13
1992	06/12: Swindon vs. Derby (W 2-4) – Johnson, Pembridge, Kuhl, McMinn	11
1992	08/12: Anglo-Italian Cup: Derby vs. Cremonese (L 1-3) – Kitson	11
1992	12/12: Derby vs. Birmingham City (W 3-1) – Johnson, Kitson, Williams	9
1992	16/12: Anglo-I Cup: Reggiana vs. Derby (W 0-3) – Kit, Pem, Gab – Rams into Semis	9
1992	20/12: Grimsby Town vs. Derby (W 0-2) – Johnson, Kitson – Rams 4 pts off 3rd	7
1992	20/12: A new club record is set of 7 consecutive away wins	7
1992	H: Pl9, W3, D0, L6, F15, A16, Pts9, Pos23; A: Pl12, W7, D3, L2, F22, A11, Pts24, Pos1	
1993	23/01: FA Cup 4th Rd: Luton vs. Derby (W 1-5) – Pembridge 3, Short, Gabbiadini	10
1993	27/01: Anglo-Italian Cup SF 1st Leg: Brentford vs. Derby (W 3-4) – Pat 2, Gab, Kit	12
1993	31/01: Newcastle vs. Derby (D 1-1) – Johnson – 5 w/o win – 13 points off 3rd	12
1993	03/02: Anglo-Italian Cup Semi-Final 2nd Leg: Derby vs. Brentford (L 1-2) – Gabbiadini – [agg: 5-5]; Derby go through to the Anglo-Italian Cup Final on away goals	12
1993	06/02: Derby vs. Peterborough (L 2-3) – Kitson 2 – 6 w/o win – (W10, D5, L12)	16
1993	13/02: FA Cup 5th Rd: Derby vs. Bolton Wanderers (W 3-1) – Short 2, Williams	11
1993	20/02: Derby vs. Watford (L 1-2) – a record 10th home defeat in a season	14
1993	08/03: FA Cup QF: Derby vs. Sheffield Wed (D 3-3) – Nicholson, Gabbiadini, Kitson	10
1993	10/03: Derby vs. Bristol R (W 3-1) – Short, Williams, Gabbiadini – 4th win in 6	8
1993	17/03: FA Cup Quarter-Final Replay: Sheffield Wednesday vs Derby (L 1-0)	10
1993	27/03: Anglo-Italian Cup Final (Wembley): Derby vs. Cremonese (L 1-3) – Gab'dini	11
1993	Derby finish season 8th (8:24) on 66 points, 10 points off a play-off place	8
1993	Derby play a record 64 games during season 1992/93	

Year	Event	Pos
1993	Paul Kitson is Derby's top scorer with 17 league goals (24 in all competitions)	
1993	Marco Gabbiadini is Derby's Player of the Season	

Stats Blast: What odds a 4-5 defeat?
Derby lost four of their first five league games of the 1992/93 season, losing 0-1, 1-2, 2-3, and 3-4, in that order! Thankfully, they didn't continue the sequence after that!

Stats Blast: What odds 7 straight away wins?
Between 03/10/1992 and 20/12/1992, Derby set a new club record of seven consecutive away wins. Frustratingly, throughout the same period, they lost at home to Millwall (1-2), Sunderland (0-1) and Tranmere (1-2), while after the 7th consecutive away win at Grimsby on 20th December, they lost the NEXT THREE at home as well – to Portsmouth (2-4), West Ham (0-2) and Peterborough (2-3).

Quirk Alert: Derby Cabbies
Season 1992/93 was Gary Micklewhite's last at Derby, having played 278 times for the Rams between 1985 and 1993. A superb servant of both Derby County and QPR, Gary missed out on the football riches that were just around the corner. As a result he had a variety of jobs after football retirement, including as a London black cab driver – a profession that Mel Sage also went into following his retirement, in his home town of Gillingham.

Year	Event	Pos
Season 1993/94 (Division 1)		
1993	Summer: Derby sign Gary Charles from Nottingham Forest for £750,000	
1993	14/08: Derby vs. Sunderland (W 5-0) – Pembridge 2, Gabbiadini, Kitson, Short	1
1993	18/08: Nottingham Forest vs. Derby (D 1-1) – Forsyth	2
1993	11/09: Derby vs. Peterborough (W 2-0) – Gabbiadini, Johnson – (W3, D1, L2)	6
1993	25/09: Notts County vs. Derby (L 4-1) – Gabbiadini – (W3, D2, L3)	11
1993	02/10: After 9.5 years as manager, Arthur Cox resigns due to severe back pain; he is still the longest-serving Rams manager since George Jobey (1925-1941)	12
1993	02/10: Roy McFarland takes over as manager with Derby in 12th position	12
1993	03/10: Derby vs. West Brom (W 5-3) – Simpson 2, Kitson, Pembridge, Short	7
1993	09/10: Derby vs. Luton (W 2-1) – Kitson, Johnson – strong at home this season	6
1993	30/10: Bolton vs. Derby (W 0-2) – Pembridge, Simpson – Rams finally win away	6
1993	02/11: Charlton (1st) vs. Derby (W 1-2) – Simpson, Pembridge – Rams 3 pts off top	4
1993	07/11: Away form sorted, Derby lose 0-4 at home to mid-table Wolves	5
1993	27/11: Derby vs. Southend (L 1-3) – Simpson – Rams now 7th; Southend up to 3rd!	7
1993	18/12: Sunderland vs. Derby (L 1-0) – Rams now 8 points off 2nd	10
1993	28/12: Derby vs. Leicester (W 3-2) – Pembridge, Gabbiadini, Johnson	9
1994	03/01: Derby vs. Tranmere (W 4-0) – Gabbiadini 3, Williams – Rams 6 pts off 2nd	9
1994	15/01: Derby vs. Portsmouth (W 1-0) – Johnson – Rams only 4 pts off top spot	6
1994	Derby sign veteran midfielder Gordon Cowans from Aston Villa	
1994	05/02: Crystal Palace vs. Derby (D 1-1) – Charles – 10 pts behind leaders, Palace	7

Year	Event	Pos
1994	19/02: Watford vs. Derby (W 3-4) – Kitson, Johnson, Gabbiadini, (og) – 3 pts off 2nd	5
1994	16/03: Peterborough vs. Derby (D 2-2) – Johnson, Nicholson – no win in 6	6
1994	02/04: Derby vs. Barnsley (W 2-0) – Johnson, Harkes – Rams 8 pts off 2nd (Forest)	5
1994	05/04: Leicester (3rd) vs. Derby (6th) (D 3-3) – Kitson 2, Willis (og) – (W17, D9, L13)	6
1994	09/04: Derby vs. Stoke (W 4-2) – Simpson, Pembridge, Kitson, Butler (og)	6
1994	16/04: Derby vs. Charlton (W 2-0) – Johnson, Kitson – Rams 5 pts off 2nd (Forest)	4
1994	20/04: Derby vs. Notts County (D 1-1) – Dijkstra (og) – Rams 6 pts off 2nd (Forest)	4
1994	27/04: Derby vs. Nottingham Forest (L 0-2) – auto-promotion now gone	6
1994	30/04: Derby vs. Oxford (W 2-1) – Pembridge, Johnson – Rams can still be caught	5
1994	08/05: Southend vs. Derby (L 4-3) – Simpson 2, Johnson – but Notts Co also lose	6
1994	Derby finish season 6th (6:24), on 71 points, and face Millwall (3rd) in the play-offs	6
1994	15/05: Play-Off Semi-Final, 1st Leg: Derby vs. Millwall (W 2-0) – Cowans, Johnson	
1994	18/05: Play-Off SF 2nd Leg: Millwall vs. Derby (W 1-3) – Gabbiadini, Johnson, Van den Hauwe og [agg: 1-5]; Derby also survive two Millwall pitch invasions with some players being kicked and punched	
1994	30/05: Play-Off Final: Leicester City vs. Derby (L 2-1) – Johnson – complete travesty!	
1994	Marco Gabbiadini, Tommy Johnson and Paul Kitson are joint top scorers in the league (all 13); Tommy Johnson 19 goals in all competitions	
1994	Martin Taylor is Derby's Player of the Season	

Stats Blast: Captain John Harkes
Derby signed USA captain John Harkes in the summer of 1993. A year later, he became Derby's first representative at a World Cup from a country other than the five nations of the British Isles – this when he played in the USA's 1-1 draw with Switzerland in the opening Group A game in Pontiac, Detroit. There have been many others since then!

Stats Blast: 2-4-6-8, Here's a Stat to Appreciate
Four of the top eight Division 1 clubs at the end of season 1993/94, came from the East Midlands, with Forest 2nd, Leicester 4th, Derby 6th and Notts County 8th (well, Notts were 7th actually on goals scored, even though they had an inferior Goal Difference to Wolves who finished 8th).

Quirk Alert: Travesty
Derby County dominated the 1994 Division One Play-Off final at Wembley. They took the lead through Tommy Johnson, and the result appeared a mere formality. However, Leicester hung in there and equalised under controversial circumstances four minutes before half-time – with Derby goalkeeper Martin Taylor pretty much assaulted by Iwan Roberts leaving Steve Walsh to head goalwards in slow motion…where Paul Williams just watched it go past him, assuming the ref had blown for a foul. He hadn't (it was Roger Milford). And worse was to come. First, Simon Grayson inexplicably avoided being sent off for a professional foul on Tommy Johnson when clean through on 60 minutes (Milford again). Nevertheless, Derby continued to dominate, but five minutes from time a fine header from ex-Ram Ian Ormondroyd was brilliantly saved by Taylor only for Steve Walsh to bundle in the winner. Inevitably, the cross for the goal had been supplied by Simon Grayson!

Year	Event	Pos
Season 1994/95 (Division 1)		
1994	31/08: Derby vs. Middlesbrough (L 0-1) – Rams are bottom after 4 games (D1, L3)	24
1994	September: Derby sell Paul Kitson to Newcastle United for £2.25m	
1994	25/09: Derby vs. Stoke (W 3-0) – Hodge, Gabbiadini, Charles – 4th win in 5	6
1994	02/11: Derby vs. Reading (L 1-2) – Gabbiadini – 6th game without a win	19
1994	27/11: Wolves vs. Derby (W 0-2) – Johnson, Stallard – 3rd win in 4	11
1994	December: Derby sign Paul Trollope from Torquay United for £100,000	
1995	02/01: Derby vs. West Brom (D 1-1) – Trollope – 4th draw in 6 – (W8, D9, L8)	16
1995	Derby sell Tommy Johnson and Gary Charles to Aston Villa for £2.9m	
1995	14/01: Charlton vs. Derby (W 3-4) – Gabbiadini 2, Short, Stallard	13
1995	22/01: Derby vs. Portsmouth (W 3-0) – Simpson 3 – Rams 5 pts off 5th with GIH	8
1995	21/02: Port Vale vs. Derby (L 1-0) – 3 defeats on the bounce – 13 points off 5th	14
1995	Derby sign centre half Dean Yates from Notts County for £350,000	
1995	Derby also sign Lee Mills from Wolves and Russell Hoult on loan from Leicester	
1995	26/02: Derby vs. Bolton (W 2-1) – Yates, Mills (a screamer on debut)	12
1995	07/03: Grimsby vs. Derby (W 0-1) – Pembridge – (W12, D10, L11)	11
1995	11/03: Derby vs. Millwall (W 3-2) – Pembridge, Trollope, Gabbiadini	10
1995	15/03: Derby vs. Burnley (W 4-0) – Mills, Trollope, Simpson, Gabbiadini	8
1995	18/03: Middlesbrough vs. Derby (W 2-4) – Mills 2, Pembridge, Gabbiadini	8
1995	22/03: Derby vs. Swindon (W 3-1) – Simpson, Pembridge, Mills – 6 wins in 7	7
1995	01/04: Derby vs. Bristol C (W 3-1) – Gabbiadini, Williams, Wrack – 4 pts off 5th	8
1995	15/04: Burnley vs. Derby (L 3-1) – Trollope – no win in 3 – 5 points off play-offs	8
1995	17/04: Derby vs. Tranmere (W 5-0) – Pembridge 2, Mills, Williams, Gabbiadini	7
1995	Derby finish season 9th (9:24), on 66 points, 10 points short of a play-off place	9
1995	Marco Gabbiadini is top scorer with 11 league goals (13 in all competitions)	
1995	Craig Short is Derby's Player of the Season	

RAMS CHRONOLOGY: Jim's Premier Rams

The 1990s

Year	Event	Pos
Season 1995/96 (Division 1)		
1995	Roy McFarland's contract is not renewed; Jim Smith is appointed Derby County manager, and Jim appoints former player, Steve McClaren as his assistant.	
1995	Derby swap Lee Mills and £475,000 for Port Vale's Robin van der Laan	
1995	Harsh on Mills as he made a big impact at end of previous season in just 15 games; however, van der Laan is installed as Derby's captain and proves a shrewd buy	
1995	Derby also sign Sean Flynn, Gary Rowett, Darryl Powell and Ron Willems	
1995	30/08: Wolves vs. Derby (L 3-0) – yet another bad start (W0, D2, L2)	23
1995	02/09: Luton vs. Derby (W 1-2) – Sturridge 2 – a sign of things to come	16
1995	01/10: Derby vs. Millwall (D 2-2) – Willems, van der Laan – (W2, D4, L4)	20
1995	28/10: Derby vs. Oldham (W 2-1) – van der Laan, Simpson – 5 games w/o defeat	14
1995	Derby sign Croatian international Igor Stimac from Hadjuk Split for £1.57m	13

Year	Event	Pos
1995	04/11: Tranmere R vs. Derby (L 5-1) – Stimac gets Derby's consolation goal	17
1995	11/11: Derby vs. West Brom (W 3-0) – Gabbiadini 2, Sturridge – (W5, D6, L5)	14
1995	18/11: Derby vs. Charlton (W 2-0) – Willems, Gabbiadini – (W6, D6, L5)	10
1995	21/11: Birmingham vs. Derby (W 1-4) – Sturridge, Willems, Gabbiadini, D Powell	8
1995	02/12: Derby vs. Sheffield United (W 4-2) – Willems 2, Sturridge, Gabbiadini	7
1995	09/12: Derby vs. Barnsley (W 4-1) – Carsley, Gabbiadini, Sturridge, Willems	2
1995	16/12: Millwall vs. Derby (W 0-1) – Sturridge – Rams now 1 pt behind Sunderland	2
1995	23/12: Derby vs. Sunderland (W 3-1) – Gabbiadini, Willems, Sturridge – RAMS LEAPFROG SUNDERLAND TO GO TOP OF DIVISION 1 – (W11, D7, L5)	1
1995	26/12: Huddersfield vs. Derby (W 0-1) – Willems – RAMS GO 4 POINTS CLEAR	1
1996	01/01: Derby vs. Norwich (W 2-1) – Willems, Gabbiadini – RAMS 7 POINTS CLEAR	1
1996	13/01: Derby vs. Reading (W 3-0) – Sturridge 2, Flynn – RAMS NOW 8 PTS CLEAR	1
1996	Derby have won an incredible 7 league games on spin, and 10 in 11 (31 pts/33)	1
1996	10/02: Derby vs. Wolves (D 0-0) – 3 draws on bounce; Derby's lead cut to 3 points	1
1996	Derby sign left-back Chris Powell from Southend United for £750,000	
1996	02/03: Derby vs. Huddersfield (W 3-2) – Simpson 2, van der Laan – Rams 9 pts clear	1
1996	05/03: Watford vs. Derby (D 0-0) – 20 games unbeaten (W13, D7, L0)	1
1996	The 20 game unbeaten run is a record for Derby within a single season	
1996	09/03: Sunderland vs. Derby (L 3-0) – Sunderland close to within 4 pts of Rams	1
1996	Derby sign centre-forward Ashley Ward from Norwich City for £1.19m	
1996	23/03: Norwich vs. Derby (L 1-0) – Rams overtaken by Sunderland, while a rampant Crystal Pal are only 3 pts behind, having come from even farther back than Rams	2
1996	30/03: Derby vs. Stoke (W 3-1) – Sturridge 2, D Powell – top three all win	2
1996	02/04: Ipswich vs. Derby (L 1-0) – fortunately, Sunderland and Palace only draw	2
1996	06/04: Derby vs. Oldham (W 1-0) – Simpson – Palace lose – Rams 5 pts clear of 3rd	2
1996	08/04: Derby vs. Tranmere (W 6-2) – Simpson 3, D Powell, Yates, Sturridge	2
1996	14/04: Charlton vs. Derby (D 0-0) – Palace win and close gap to 3 pts; 3 to play	2
1996	20/04: Derby vs. Birmingham (D 1-1) – Simpson – S'land 81, Derby 76, Palace 75	2
1996	28/04: Derby vs. Crystal Pal (W 2-1) – Sturridge, Van der Laan	2
1996	DERBY ARE PROMOTED TO THE PREMIER LEAGUE FOR THE FIRST TIME	2
1996	Derby finish season 2nd (2:24), on 79 points, 4 pts behind S'land, 4 ahead of Palace	2
1996	Dean Sturridge is Derby's top scorer with 20 goals, all in the league	
1996	Dean Yates is Derby's Player of the Season	

Quirk Alert: Double Drubbing

When Derby lost 5-1 at Tranmere on the 4 November 1995, they were 17th and Crystal Palace 19th. You would have got slim odds on both teams finishing in the top three at that stage. After that, Derby won an incredible 10 out of the next 11 league games to sweep them not only to the top of the table, but at one stage, 9 points clear. The Rams also went 20 league games without defeat after the Tranmere watershed – which was brought full circle on 8 April 1996, when Derby returned the favour with a 6-2 drubbing at the Baseball Ground. Typical of British football humour, the Tranmere fans were seen celebrating after the game, amid claims that they had "won on away goals"!

Interestingly, in that "oh-so close" season of 1991/92, Derby lost both games to Tranmere, including a 4-3 defeat at Prenton Park (having led 1-3). Just two points from those two games would have seen the Rams reach the Premier League for its inaugural season! The interim four years between failure and success saw a massive turnover of players and cash, with only Paul Simpson and Marco Gabbiadini surviving from the class of 1991/92 to eventually taste the success of promotion with the Rams.

Quirk Alert: Double Dutch
When Derby drew 2-2 at home to Millwall on 1 October 1995, their scorers were Dutchmen Robin van der Laan and Ron Willems (both pictured below) – definitely a first for the club!

PHOTOS: Andy Ellis

Igor Stimac.   Ron Willems.   Robin van der Laan.   Dean Sturridge.

Stats Blast: 47 Years Since '48
When Derby won 4-1 away at Birmingham City on the 21st November, incredibly this was the first time that the Rams had won at St Andrew's since 30 October 1948 – when a single goal scored by Billy Steel separated the sides! The latter was Derby's 15th game of the 1948/49 season, and they were top of the original First Division – in other words, top of Tier 1!

Year	Event	Pos
Season 1996/97 (Premier League)		
1996	June: Derby sign Croatian international Aljosa Asanovic from Hadjuk Split for £950K	
1996	June: Derby sign Danish international Jacob Laursen from Silkeborg IF for £500K	
1996	August: Derby sign Christian Dailly from Dundee United for £500,000	
1996	17/08: Derby vs. Leeds (D 3-3) – Sturridge 2, Simpson – much in the last 5 minutes!	7
1996	21/08: Tottenham vs. Derby (D 1-1) – very late equaliser from Dailly	13
1996	04/09: Derby vs. Manchester United (D 1-1) – rockets from Laursen and Beckham	16
1996	09/09: Blackburn vs. Derby (W 1-2) – Willems, Flynn – (W1, D3, L1)	12
1996	14/09: Derby vs. Sunderland (W 1-0) – Asanovic (pen) – Rams 3 points off top	9
1996	14/09: 23rd home league game without defeat, equalling record set in 1929/1930	9
1996	21/09: Sheffield Wednesday vs. Derby (D 0-0) – Rams have lost only 1 of first 7	9
1996	28/09: Derby vs. Wimbledon (L 0-2) – record over	11
1996	October: Derby sign Paul McGrath from Aston Villa for £106,000	

Year	Event	Pos
1996	19/10: Nottingham Forest vs. Derby (D 1-1) – Dailly – 3 without a win	12
1996	27/10: Liverpool vs. Derby (L 2-1) – Ward – (W2, D5, L4)	16
1996	02/11: Derby vs. Leicester (W 2-0) – Ward, Whitlow (og) – (W3, D5, L4)	11
1996	17/11: Derby vs. Middlesbrough (W 2-1) – Asanovic, Ward – (W4, D5, L4)	10
1996	30/11: Derby vs. Coventry (W 2-1) – Asanovic, Ward – (W5, D6, L4)	9
1996	07/12: Arsenal vs. Derby (D 2-2) – Sturridge (a Worldie), D Powell	11
1997	21/01: FA Cup 3rd Rd: Gillingham vs. Derby (W 0-2) – van der Laan, Willems	15
1997	25/01: FA Cup 4th Rd: Derby vs. A Villa (W 3-1) – Sturridge, van der Laan, Willems	15
1997	01/02: Derby vs. Liverpool (L 0-1) – 9 league games w/o win (D4, L5)	16
1997	15/02: Derby vs. West Ham (W 1-0) – Asanovic (pen) – (W6, D10, L9)	13
1997	26/02: FA Cup 5th Rd: Derby vs. Coventry City (W 3-2) – Sturridge, v d Laan, Ward	13
1997	01/03: Derby vs. Chelsea (W 3-2) – (og), Asanovic, Ward – Rams 7 pts clear of drop	12
1997	05/03: Middlesbrough vs. Derby (L 6-1) – Simpson – Rams still 7 points clear	14
1997	08/03: FA Cup Quarter-Final: Derby vs. Middlesbrough (L 0-2)	14
1997	22/03: Derby vs. Tottenham (W 4-2) – van der Laan, Trollope, Sturridge, Ward	14
1997	26/03: Derby sign goalkeeper Mart Poom from Portsmouth for £595,000	14
1997	26/03: Derby sign Paulo Wanchope and Mauricio Solis from Herediano for £600K	14
1997	05/04: Manchester United vs. Derby (W 2-3) – Ward, Wanchope, Sturridge	12
1997	12/04: Derby vs. Aston Villa (W 2-1) – Rowett, van der Laan – Rams 8 pts clear	11
1997	23/04: Nottm F vs. Derby (D 0-0) – Rams virtually safe; Forest (20th) virtually down	11
1997	03/05: Coventry vs. Derby (W 1-2) – Rowett, Sturridge – (W11, D13, L13)	10
1997	11/05: Derby vs. Arsenal (L 1-3) – Ward – last first-team game at Baseball Ground	12
1997	Derby finish season 12th (12:20), with 46 points, 6 points clear of relegation	12
1997	Dean Sturridge is Derby's top scorer with 11 league goals (14 in all competitions)	
1997	Chris Powell is Derby's Player of the Season	

On securing promotion to the Premier League, canny Jim Smith (pictured far left with Steve McClaren) wasted no time on securing the signings of Aljosa Asanovic (centre left) and Jacob Laursen (centre right). A month later after Euro '96, and the value of these relatively unknown players had at least doubled! Paulo Wanchope was signed later in March 1997 – and promptly scored one of Derby's most famous goals on his debut at Old Trafford in a 2-3 win for the Rams. PHOTOS: Andy Ellis

Year	Event	Pos
Season 1997/98 (Premier League)		
1997	May: Derby sign Stefano Eranio from AC Milan on a free transfer	
1997	18/07: Queen Elizabeth II opens Pride Park Stadium in front of 30,000 spectators	
1997	01/08: Derby sign Francesco Baiano from Sampdoria for £650,000	
1997	04/08: Derby vs. Sampdoria (L 0-1) – first competitive game at Pride Park	
1997	06/08: Derby sign striker Deon Burton from Portsmouth for £1.06m	
1997	14/08: Derby vs. Wimbledon – match abandoned when the floodlights go out in 56th minute with Derby leading 2-1 – cue the Pride-based gags	16
1997	30/08: Derby vs. Barnsley (W 1-0) – Eranio – first league win at Pride Park	16
1997	13/09: Derby vs. Everton (W 3-1) – Hunt, C Powell, Sturridge – (W2, D0, L2)	10
1997	24/09: Sheffield Wed vs. Derby (W 2-5) – Baiano 2, Laursen, Wanchope, Burton	12
1997	24/09: Derby's first win at Hillsborough, including FA Cup Semi-Finals, since 1936	12
1997	27/09: Derby vs. Southampton (W 4-0) – Eranio, Wanchope, Baiano , Carsley	8
1997	06/10: Leicester City vs. Derby (W 1-2) – Baiano 2 – (W5, D0, L3) – and 2 GIH	6
1997	18/10: Derby vs. Man Utd (D 2-2) – Baiano, Wanchope – (W5, D1, L3)	7
1997	22/10: Derby vs. Wimbledon (D 1-1) – Baiano scores for the 6th game on the trot	6
1997	01/11: Derby vs. Arsenal (W 3-0) – Wanchope 2, Sturridge sink eventual Champs	6
1997	08/11: Leeds vs. Derby (L 4-3) – Sturridge 2, Asanovic – Rams 0-3 up and temp 4th	8
1997	22/11: Derby vs. Coventry City (W 3-1) – Baiano, Eranio, Wanchope – (W7, D2, L5)	5
1997	26/12: Derby vs. Newcastle (W 1-0) – Eranio – 5 without defeat (W2, D3)	7
1998	11/01: Derby vs. Blackburn (W 3-1) – Sturridge 2, Wanchope – (W10, D5, L7)	6
1998	31/01: Derby vs. Spurs (W 2-1) – Sturridge, Wanchope – home record is W9, D3, L0	6
1998	07/02: Derby vs. Aston Villa (L 0-1) – first home defeat of season	6
1998	14/02: Everton vs. Derby (W 1-2) – Stimac, Wanchope – 4 pts off 2nd (Liverpool)	6
1998	28/02: Derby vs. Sheffield Wed (W 3-0) – Wanchope 2, Rowett – 3 points off 2nd	6
1998	11/04: West Ham vs. Derby (D 0-0) – 4 games without a win	9
1998	13/04: Derby vs. Bolton (W 4-0) – Burton 2, Wanchope, Baiano	7
1998	10/05: Derby vs. Liverpool (W 1-0) – Wanchope	9
1998	Derby finish season in 9th (9:20), on 55 points, 2 points/places off a UEFA Cup place	9
1998	Paulo Wanchope is top scorer with 13 league goals (17 in all competitions)	
1998	Francesco Baiano is Derby's Player of the Season	
1998	A record five Derby players represent their countries in 1998 World Cup: D Burton, D Powell (Jamaica), C Dailly (Scotland), J Laursen (Denmark), I Stimac (Croatia)	

Pride Park Stadium became home to Derby County for the start of the 1997/98 season – but had an inauspicious start to Premier League life on 14 August 1997! PHOTO: Author

Quirk Alert: Philip's Quip

Due to demand from corporate clients for executive boxes, the two remaining "open" corners of Pride Park Stadium were still under construction when the stadium was opened by Queen Elizabeth II in the summer of 1997. This led Prince Philip, Duke of Edinburgh to jokingly ask Taylor Woodrow contract manager Ross Walters, "Haven't you been paid yet?" This occasion was also the first time that the Queen had opened a football stadium.

Quirk Alert: Crafty Joe

Ashley Ward had the distinction of being the last Derby County first-team player to score at the Baseball Ground in the 1-3 defeat to Arsenal at the end of the 1996/97 season. He also scored the first league goal at Pride Park Stadium on 14 August 1997 against Wimbledon – only to have that honour chalked out when the floodlights went out in the 56th minute! With Derby leading 2-1, referee Uriah Rennie abandoned the match following a delay of more than half an hour – with chief-prompter Joe Kinnear (Wimbledon's manager) getting what he wanted. The irony was that the lights came back on a few minutes later, and stayed on – but it was too late! Meanwhile, Joe and his players were already back on the team coach!

Stats Blast: Owls Woe

When Derby won 5-2 at Hillsborough on 24 September 1997, it was the first time that Derby had beaten Sheffield Wednesday on their home patch in 61 years – the last win having been on 12 September 1936 when Jack Bowers was on the scoresheet in a 3-2 win. Of course, they didn't fare much better in FA Cup Semi-Finals there either! Conversely, the Rams also won on their next three visits to Hillsborough, too!

Quirk Alert: Vertigo

Check out the Premier League on 6 October 1997. Note that as well as being 6th, the Rams had two games in hand on most teams – one of which should have been the 3 points against Wimbledon when the floodlights went out! Derby would later reach 5th on 22 November 1997.

Pos	Team	Pld	W	D	L	GF	GA	GD	Pts
1	Arsenal	10	6	4	0	27	10	17	22
2	Manchester Utd	10	6	3	1	14	4	10	21
3	Blackburn Rovers	10	5	4	1	20	9	11	19
4	Leicester City	10	5	3	2	14	8	6	18
5	Chelsea	9	5	1	3	24	14	10	16
6	**Derby County**	8	5	0	3	16	8	8	15
7	Liverpool	9	4	3	2	16	10	6	15
8	Newcastle United	7	5	0	2	7	5	2	15
9	Leeds United	10	4	2	4	11	11	0	14
10	Aston Villa	10	4	1	5	11	15	-4	13

Quirk Alert: Rams for the Champions League?

When Derby County beat Everton 1-2 at Goodison Park on 14 February 1998, the Rams were still 6th and only two points behind eventual Champions,

Premier League Table: 14/02/1998

Pos	Team	Pld	W	D	L	GF	GA	GD	Pts
1	Manchester Utd	25	15	5	5	52	19	33	50
2	Liverpool	26	13	7	6	44	25	19	46
3	Chelsea	25	14	3	8	52	27	25	45
4	Blackburn Rovers	25	12	9	4	44	27	17	45
5	Arsenal	24	12	8	4	44	26	18	44
6	**Derby County**	26	12	6	8	41	32	9	42

Arsenal. They were also only 4 points behind second-placed Liverpool. The Rams were – at this pretty advanced stage of the season – genuine Champions League contenders!

Two weeks later, having lost 2-0 at Manchester United and beaten Sheffield Wednesday 3-0 at Pride Park, the Rams were even closer (see right). Alas, Derby only won two more games after this point and finished 9th on 55 points.

Premier League Table: 28/02/1998

Pos	Team	Pld	W	D	L	GF	GA	GD	Pts
1	Manchester Utd	28	18	5	5	57	19	38	59
2	Blackburn Rovers	27	13	9	5	49	33	16	48
3	Arsenal	25	13	8	4	45	26	19	47
4	Liverpool	28	13	8	7	46	28	18	47
5	Chelsea	27	14	3	10	52	30	22	45
6	**Derby County**	**28**	**13**	**6**	**9**	**44**	**34**	**10**	**45**

Year	Event	Pos
Season 1998/99 (Premier League)		
1998	Derby sign Horacio Carbonari from Rosario Central for a club record £2.8m	
1998	Derby sell Christian Dailly to Blackburn for £5.35m, a record transfer fee received by Derby; the Rams had only paid Dundee Utd £500,000 for him two years earlier	
1998	19/09: Derby vs. Leicester (W 2-0) – Schnoor, Wanchope – (W3, D3, L0)	2
1998	26/09: Aston Villa (1st) vs. Derby (2nd) (L 1-0) – Rams remain in 2nd place	2
1998	17/10: Newcastle vs. Derby (L 2-1) – Burton – 3 defeats on spin – (W3, D3, L3)	10
1998	24/10: Derby vs. Manchester United (D 1-1) – Burton – 4 without a win	10
1998	07/11: Liverpool vs. Derby (W 1-2) – Harper, Wanchope – (W4, D5, L3)	5
1998	16/11: Nottingham Forest vs. Derby (D 2-2) – Dorigo, Carbonari	8
1998	26/12: Everton vs. Derby (D 0-0) – four draws on the bounce – (W5, D10, L4)	11
1999	02/01: FA Cup 3rd Rd: Plymouth vs. Derby (W 0-3) – Burton 2, Eranio	11
1999	23/01: FA Cup 4th Rd: Swansea City vs. Derby (W 0-1) – Harper	10
1999	30/01: Sheffield Wednesday vs. Derby (W 0-1) – Prior – (W8, D10, L5)	8
1999	07/02: Derby vs. Everton (W 2-1) – Burton 2 – (W9, D10, L6)	6
1999	09/02: Pride Park hosts international football for first time; England U-21's play France U-21; attendance of 32,865 is a record for an England U-21 international	6
1999	24/02: FA Cup 5th Rd Replay: Derby vs. Huddersfield T (W 3-1) – Baiano 2, Dorigo	7
1999	06/03: FA Cup QF: Arsenal vs. Derby (L 1-0) – late Kanu strike sinks Rams	9
1999	10/03: Derby vs. Aston Villa (W 2-1) – Baiano, Burton – (W10, D11, L7)	6
1999	13/03: Derby vs. Liverpool (W 3-2) – Wanchope 2, Baiano – rare double over Reds	6
1999	03/04: Derby vs. Newcastle (L 3-4) – Burton, Baiano, Wanchope – Rams drop to 7th	7
1999	10/04: Derby vs. Nottingham F (W 1-0) – Carbonari all-but sends Reds down	7
1999	05/05: Leicester vs. Derby (W 1-2) – Sturridge, Beck – first win in 4	9
1999	Derby finish season 8th (8:20), on 52 points, having won only 2 of last 9 games	8
1999	D Burton and P Wanchope top scorers with 9 league goals (Burton 12 in all comps)	
1999	Jacob Laursen is Derby's Player of the Season	

Quirk Alert: Heroes and Villains
Check out Derby's unbeaten start to the 1998/99 season. It all came to an end with the next game, though, as they lost 1-0 at Aston Villa to send the Villains 5 points clear.

Pos	Team	Pld	W	D	L	GF	GA	GD	Pts
1	Aston Villa	6	4	2	0	7	1	6	14
2	**Derby County**	**6**	**3**	**3**	**0**	**6**	**2**	**4**	**12**
3	Liverpool	6	3	2	1	12	7	5	11
4	Wimbledon	6	3	2	1	10	8	2	11

Year	Event	Pos
Season 1999/2000 (Premier League)		
1999	June: Derby sign Seth Johnson from Crewe for £3m, a Rams record transfer fee	
1999	July/August: Derby sell Wanchope (£3.5m) and Stimac (£600,000) to West Ham	
1999	21/08: Coventry vs. Derby (L 2-0) – no win in first 4 games – (W0, D1, L3)	19
1999	Derby sign Esteban Fuertes from Colón de Santa Fe for £2.3m – or do they???	19
1999	25/08: Sheffield Wednesday vs. Derby (W 0-2) – Delap, Sturridge – (W1, D1, L3)	18
1999	28/08: Derby vs. Everton (W 1-0) – Fuertes – Derby move up to 13th – or do they???	13
1999	18/09: Derby vs. Sunderland (L 0-5) – biggest Prem away win of season	15
1999	04/10: Southampton vs. Derby (D 3-3) – Delap, Laursen, Beck – (W2, D3, L5)	16
1999	Derby sign Lee Morris (19) from Sheff Utd for £3m, the 4th-most expensive teenager in British football history at time – and Derby's joint-record transfer fee paid	
1998	25/10: Newcastle vs. Derby (L 2-0) – Rams drop back to 19th – (W2, D3, L7)	19
1999	30/10: Derby vs. Chelsea (W 3-1) – Delap 2, Burton – (W3, D3, L7)	16
1999	Unkind quartet of fixtures against top 4: Liverpool (L 2-0), Man Utd (L 1-2), Arsenal (L 2-1), Leeds (L 0-1 – including shocking dive for penalty winner in injury time!)	18
1999	November: Derby sign Giorgi Kinkladze on loan from Ajax	
1999	Derby sign Craig Burley from Celtic for £3m, equalling record club transfer fee paid	
1999	Derby sign Branko Strupar from KRC Genk for £3m, also equalling the record	
1999	18/12: Leicester City vs. Derby (W 0-1) – D Powell – (W4, D3, L11)	18

The 2000s

Year	Event	Pos
2000	03/01: Derby vs. Watford (W 2-0) – Strupar 2 – (W5, D4, L12)	17
2000	03/01: Strupar's after 2 mins is first player in Britain to score in new millennium!	
2000	15/01: Middlesbrough vs. Derby (W 1-4) – Christie 2, Burton, Burley	16
2000	05/02: Sheffield Wed vs. Derby (D 3-3) – Strupar, Burley, Srnicek (og)	17
2000	04/03: Derby vs. Wimbledon (W 4-0) – Kinkladze, Christie, Burton, Sturridge	17
2000	11/03: Man Utd vs. Derby (L 3-1) – Strupar – largest attendance of season – 61,619	17
2000	18/03: Derby vs. Liverpool (L 0-2) – a record Pride Park attendance (33,378)	17
2000	02/04: Derby vs. Leicester (W 3-0) – Burley, Delap, Sturridge – Rams 5 pt cushion	17
2000	Derby sign Giorgi Kinkladze from Ajax for £3m – Rams' 5th £3m player in 9 months	
2000	21/04: Bradford City vs. Derby (D 4-4) – Burley 2, Delap, Strupar – 6 point cushion	16
2000	24/04: Derby vs. Southampton (W 2-0) – D Powell, Christie – (W9, D9, L17)	16
2000	Derby finish season 16th (16:20) on 38 points, 5 points clear of the drop-zone	16
2000	Rory Delap is Derby's top scorer with 8 league goals (8 goals in all competitions)	
2000	Mart Poom is Derby's Player of the Season	

Quirk Alert: Santa Fe Catastrophe

Derby's signing of Esteban Fuertes from Colón de Santa Fe was a complete farce. He played 10 times for Derby, scoring 2 goals. But on his return from a club training break in Portugal, he was refused entry back into the UK, as his passport – claiming Italian ancestry – had been forged! He never played for Derby again!

Year	Event	Pos
Season 2000/01 (Premier League)		
2000	July: Derby sign defender Danny Higginbotham from Manchester United for £2m	
2000	19/08: Derby vs. Southampton (D 2-2) – Strupar, Burton	8
2000	06/09: Derby vs. Middlesbrough (D 3-3) – Christie 2, Strupar – 4 in 4 for Strupar	17
2000	30/09: Aston Villa vs. Derby (L 4-1) – Riggott – Rams are bottom – (W0, D5, L3)	20
2000	11/11: Arsenal vs. Derby (D 0-0) – 13 games in and no win – (W0, D7, L6)	19
2000	Derby sign centre-half Taribo West on loan from AC Milan	19
2000	18/11: Derby vs. Bradford City (W 2-0) –Christie, Delap – a win at 14th attempt	19
2000	02/12: Derby vs. Ipswich (W 1-0) – Delap – (W2, D7, L7)	17
2000	23/12: Derby vs. Newcastle (W 2-0) – Carbonari, Burton – 3 wins in 4	16
2001	01/01: Derby vs. Everton (W 1-0) – Burton – (W5, D8, L9) – 3 point cushion	15
2001	03/03: Derby vs. Tottenham (W 2-1) – Strupar 2 – (W8, D10, L11) – 8 pt cushion	14
2001	18/03: Liverpool vs. Derby (D 1-1) – Burton – (W8, D11, L11) – 8 pts above 18th	15
2001	14/04: West Ham vs. Derby (L 3-1) – Gudjonsson – 3 defeats on spin – 5 pt cushion	17
2001	16/04: Derby vs. Leicester (W 2-0) – Boertien, Eranio – still 5 points clear of drop	16
2001	25/04: Deon Burton plays his 35th game for Jamaica whilst at Derby, becoming Derby's most capped international, passing Peter Shilton's 34 caps for England	17
2001	28/04: Derby vs. Arsenal (L 1-2) – Eranio – Rams 4 pts above 18th-placed Man City	17
2001	05/05: Manchester United vs. Derby (W 0-1) – Christie screamer – Rams are safe	16
2001	Derby finish season 17th (17:20) on 42 points, 8 points clear of relegation	17
2001	Malcolm Christie is Derby's leading scorer with 8 league goals (12 in all comps)	
2001	Chris Riggott is Derby's Player of the Season	
2001	25/05: England vs. Mexico (W 4-0) – Derby host first full England int'nal since 1911	

Quirk Alert: First of the Mohicans

On 25th May 2001, England beat Mexico 4-0 at Pride Park Stadium in an international friendly. It was also the debut for a certain England captain's famous Mohican!

Stats Blast: Go West

When Taribo West signed for Derby County in November 2000, the Rams had not won any of their first 13 league games and were rooted in the bottom three. West went on to play 18 league games for Derby who took a remarkable 31 points out of 54 from those 18 games.

Year	Event	Pos
Season 2001/02 (Premier League)		
2001	July: Derby sign Fabrizio Ravanelli from Lazio on a free transfer (but huge wage)	
2001	18/08: Derby vs. Blackburn R (W 2-1) – Ravanelli, Christie	4
2001	08/09: Derby vs. West Ham (D 0-0) – Rams are 10th after 4 games (W1, D2, L1)	10
2001	29/09: Derby vs. Arsenal (L 0-2) – 3 defeats on the spin – (W1, D2, L4)	19
2001	07/10: Derby sack Jim Smith and install assistant Colin Todd as new manager	19
2001	16/10: Derby sell Seth Johnson to Leeds for a record transfer fee received of £7m	18
2001	03/11: Middlesbrough vs. Derby (L 5-1) – Ravanelli – 10 w/o win and now bottom	20
2001	17/11: Derby vs. Southampton (W 1-0) – Mawene – (W2, D4, L6)	17
2001	22/12: Derby vs. Aston Villa (W 3-1) – Ravanelli, Carbone, Christie – (W4, D4, L10)	18
2001	29/12: Blackburn vs. Derby (W 0-1) – Christie – (W5, D4, L11) – level with 16th	18
2002	02/01: Derby vs. Fulham (L 0-1) – Rams three points adrift of 17th	18
2002	06/01: FA Cup 3rd Round: Derby vs. Bristol Rovers (L 1-3) – Ravanelli	18
2002	12/01: Aston Villa vs. Derby (L 2-1) – D Powell – Rams still 3 points adrift	19
2002	14/01: Derby sack Colin Todd; Billy McEwan becomes caretaker manager	19
2002	29/01: Charlton vs. Derby (L 1-0) – 4th defeat on spin – Rams 6 pts from safety	19
2002	30/01: Derby appoint John Gregory as their FOURTH manager of the season	19
2002	02/02: Derby vs. Tottenham (W 1-0) – Morris – Rams now only 3 pts from safety	19
2002	23/02: Leicester vs. Derby (W 0-3) – Kinkladze, Strupar, Morris – 4 points adrift	19
2002	03/03: Derby vs. Man U (D 2-2) – Christie 2 – denied hat-trick by poor decision	19
2002	16/03: Bolton vs. Derby (W 1-3) – Christie, Ravanelli, Higginbotham – 2 pts adrift	19
2002	23/03: Derby vs. Everton (L 3-4) – Strupar 2, Morris – crucial defeat – 3 pts adrift	19
2002	13/04: Derby vs. Newcastle (L 2-3) – Christie, Morris – more bad decisions	19
2002	20/04: Liverpool vs. Derby (L 2-0) – DERBY ARE RELEGATED TO DIVISION 1	19
2002	Derby finish season 19th (19:20) eventually 10 points from safety	19
2002	Ravanelli and Christie top scorers in league with 9 goals (Ravanelli 11 all comps)	
2002	Danny Higginbotham is Derby's Player of the Year	
2002	Derby use 34 players during season 2001/02, a new club record	

RAMS CHRONOLOGY: Yo-Yo Rams

The 2000s

Year	Event	Pos
Season 2002/03 (Division 1) – A Struggle		
2002	No signings during the summer, but equally, no key departures either	
2002	10/08: Derby vs. Reading (W 3-0) – Lee, Ravanelli, Christie	3
2002	17/08: Grimsby vs. Derby (W 1-2) – Bolder 2 – (W2, D0, L1)	6
2002	24/08: Derby vs. Wolves (L 1-4); 28/08: Rotherham vs. Derby (L 2-1)	13
2002	31/08: Derby vs. Stoke (W 2-0) – Christie 2 – (W3, D0, L3)	10
2002	07/09; Derby vs. Burnley (L 1-2); 14/09: Leicester vs. Derby (L 3-1)	15
2002	17/09: Crystal Palace vs. Derby (W 0-1) – Kinkladze – (W4, D0, L5)	9
2002	28/09: Ipswich vs. Derby (W 0-1) – Carbonari – (W5, D0, L6) – Rams 3 pts off 6th	9
2002	20/10: Derby vs. Nottingham Forest (D 0-0) – 3 draws on the bounce	12
2002	02/11: Sheffield Wed vs. Derby (W 1-3) – Morris 2, McLeod – Rams 4 pts off 6th	10

Year	Event	Pos
2002	18/11: Mart Poom moves to Sunderland on loan (permanent in Jan-03 for £3.2m)	14
2002	14/12: Derby vs. Brighton (W 1-0) – Higginbotham – (W10, D3, L10) – 6 pts off 6th	10
2002	26/12: Lee Holmes becomes Derby's youngest-ever player, aged 15 yrs, 268 days	15
2002	28/12: Reading vs. Derby (L 2-1) – 3 defeats in a week – (W10, D3, L13)	16
2003	04/01: Lee Holmes becomes youngest player of any club in full round of FA Cup	15
2003	18/01: Stoke vs. Derby (W 1-3) – Christie, Zavagno, Morris – still only 5 pts off 6th	15
2003	Malcolm Christie and Chris Riggott are sold to Middlebrough for £3m	
2003	Danny Higginbotham joins Southampton initially on loan (sold Feb for £1.5m)	
2003	01/02: Derby vs. Rotherham (W 3-0) – Kinkladze, Bolder, McLeod – Rams (W12, D5, L13) are only 4 points off a play-off spot and 16 above the drop-zone...	14
2003	19/03: Nottingham Forest vs. Derby (L 3-0) – 8 without a win (D2, L6)	20
2003	21/03: John Gregory is suspended for alleged "gross misconduct", later unproven	20
2003	31/03: George Burley takes over as interim manager	20
2003	19/04: Derby vs. Coventry (W 1-0) – Ravanelli – 3 wins in 4 – Rams 12 pts clear	18
2003	Derby finish season 18th (18:24) on 52 points, 6 points above the drop-zone	18
2003	M Christie and L Morris are top scorers in league with 8 goals (both 9 in all comps)	
2003	Giorgi Kinkladze is Derby's Player of the Season	
2003	Derby use 36 players during season, a new record, beating the previous season	

PHOTOS: Author

END OF AN ERA: Left: This sculpture by Denis O'Connor commemorates the former Baseball Ground, which used to stand on this site until its demolition in 2003. The Baseball Ground was the home of Derby County from 1895 until 1997, and was graced by most of the greats of British football throughout its 102-year history. Centre: The former ticket office from the Baseball Ground which was preserved and built into the western frontage of Pride Park Stadium. Right: Also on the former site of the Baseball Ground are around 150 new homes – many of them sited on this appropriately-named street.

Year	Event	Pos
Season 2003/04 (Division 1) – Another Struggle		
2003	Derby sign Ian Taylor and Michael Johnson on free's from Villa and Birmingham	
2003	09/08: Derby vs. Stoke (L 0-3) – Tom Huddlestone makes Derby debut, aged 16	22
2003	30/08: Derby vs. West Brom (L 0-1) – (W0, D1, L4) – Rams are bottom	24
2003	17/09: Derby vs. Watford (W 3-2) – Taylor, Svensson, Junior – (W2, D1, L4)	18
2003	20/09: Derby vs. Sunderland (D 1-1) – Taylor; Poom heads brilliant IT equaliser!	20
2003	27/09: Nottingham Forest vs. Derby (D 1-1) – Junior – Junior serious knee injury	21
2003	30/09: Bradford City vs. Derby (W 1-2) – Morris 2 – five without defeat	16

Year	Event	Pos
2003	October: Lionel Pickering removed as chairman; Rams in artificial receivership; Sleightholme, Keith and Harding (The Three Amigos) buy the club for £1 each	
2003	Pride Park sold to Panama-based ABC Corp with Rams paying c.£1m annual rent	
2003	The Baseball Ground is demolished and new houses built on the land	
2003	08/11: Derby vs. Ipswich (D 2-2) – Kennedy, Dichio – 8 games without a win	22
2003	28/12: Derby vs. Norwich (L 0-4) – Rams now 4 points from safety	22
2004	10/01: Stoke vs. Derby (L 2-1) – Morris – 5 more w/o win (D2, L3) – still 4 pts adrift	22
2004	Derby sign Leon Osman on loan from Everton – a key signing	22
2004	28/01: Derby vs. Sheffield United (W 2-0) – Tudgay, McLeod – (W7, D9, L12)	21
2004	21/02: Derby vs. Crystal Pal (W 2-1) – Manel, Osman – Rams 3 pts above Forest	21
2004	28/02: Coventry vs. Derby (L 2-0) – Derby and Forest swap places	22
2004	Derby sign Paul Peschisolido from Sheffield United on a free transfer	22
2004	13/03: Derby vs. Rotherham (W 1-0) – Peschisolido – Rams still 2 pts adrift	22
2004	20/03: Derby vs. Nottingham F (W 4-2) – Taylor, Peschisolido 2, Tudgay	22
2004	12/04: Derby vs. Bradford C (W 3-2) – Osman, Taylor, Combe (og) – 4 to play	22
2004	17/04: Derby vs. Preston (W 5-1) – Manel 2, Tudgay 2, Junior – 2 pts above 22nd	19
2004	01/05: Derby vs. Millwall (W 2-0) – Bolder, Reich – Rams are safe	20
2004	Derby finish season 20th (20:24) with 52 points, one point above the drop-zone	20
2004	Ian Taylor is Derby's top scorer with 11 league goals (12 in all competitions)	
2004	Youl Mawene is Derby's Player of the Season	
2004	Derby use 36 players in a season for 2nd year running, equalling the club record	
Season 2004/05 (Championship) – Strong		
2004	July: Derby sign Iñigo Idiakez and Tommy Smith on free's from Rayo Vallecano and Sunderland, and Morten Bisgaard from F.C. Copenhagen for £1m	
2004	07/08: Leeds vs. Derby (L 1-0); 11/08: Derby vs. Leicester (L 1-2) – bad start	23
2004	14/08: Derby vs. Ipswich (W 3-2) – Reich 2, Idiakez – (W1, D0, L2)	19
2004	21/08: QPR vs. Derby (W 0-2) – Smith, Tudgay – Rams move up to 9th	9
2004	28/08; Derby vs. Crewe (L 2-4); 30/08: Stoke vs. Derby (L 1-0) – (W2, D0, L4)	15
2004	18/09: Cardiff vs. Derby (W 0-2) – Reich, Taylor – (W4, D0, L4)	11
2004	24/09: Derby sign striker Grzegorz Rasiak on a free from Dyskobolia Grodzisk	14
2004	19/10: Wolves vs. Derby (L 2-0) – 6 games without a win – (W4, D4, L6)	16
2004	03/11: Derby vs. Brighton (W 3-0) – Rasiak 2, Smith – 3rd win on the spin	8
2004	13/11: Gillingham vs. Derby (W 0-2) – Rasiak, Taylor – (W8, D5, L6)	7
2004	20/11; Derby vs. Sheffield United (L 0-1); 27/11: Preston vs. Derby (L 3-0)	10
2004	11/12: Derby vs. Nottingham F (W 3-0) – Rasiak 2, Smith – (W9, D6, L8)	10
2004	18/12: Plymouth vs. Derby (W 0-2) – Coughlin (og), Peschisolido – 2 pts off 6th	8
2004	26/12: Wigan Athletic vs. Derby (W 1-2) – Rasiak and Smith sink leaders	7
2004	28/12; Derby vs. Millwall (L 0-3); 01/01: Derby vs. Cardiff (L 0-1)	9
2005	Tottenham sign Tom Huddlestone for £2.5m but loan him back for rest of season	
2005	16/01: Derby vs. Sunderland (L 0-2) – 3rd home loss on the bounce	9
2005	23/01: West Ham vs. Derby (W 1-2) – Rasiak 2 – 3rd away win on the spin	8
2005	26/01: Derby vs. Leeds (W 2-0) – Smith, Bolder – (W14, D6, L11)	5
2005	05/02: Brighton vs. Derby (W 2-3) – Tudgay 2, Bisgaard – Rams 6 pts behind 2nd	5
2005	08/02: Lewin Nyatanga becomes youngest-ever Welsh U-21 player, 16 yrs 174 days	5
2005	19/02: Rotherham vs. Derby (W 1-3) – Rasiak, Tudgay, Idiakez – (W16, D6, L11)	4

Year	Event	Pos
2005	26/02: Nottingham Forest vs. Derby (D 2-2) – Rasiak 2 – Rams 10 pts behind 2nd	4
2005	16/03: Derby vs. QPR (D 0-0) – 9 without defeat (W5, D4), but now 14 pts off 2nd	4
2005	02/04: Ipswich (1st) vs. Derby (5th) (L 3-2) – Tudgay, Idiakez – Rams drop to 6th	6
2005	09/04: Derby vs. Stoke (W 3-1) – Rasiak, Bisgaard, Idiakez – (W19, D10, L12)	5
2005	15/04: Sheff U vs. Derby (W 0-1) – Bisgaard – equal club rec 12 away wins/season	5
2005	23/04: Derby vs. Gillingham (W 2-0) – Bisgaard, Peschisolido – 4 straight wins	5
2005	30/04: Coventry vs. Derby (L 6-2) – lucky Rams stay 5th as chasers also lose	5
2005	08/05: Derby vs. Preston (W 3-1) – Idiakez, Smith, Peschisolido – W22, D10, L14)	4
2005	Derby finish season in 4th place on 76 points and will face in the play-offs the team they've just beaten – without the key injured duo of Rasiak and Idiakez	4
2005	Play-Off Semi-Final 1st Leg: Preston vs. Derby (L 2-0)	
2005	Play-Off Semi-Final 2nd Leg: Derby vs. Preston (D 0-0) – play-off heartbreak – again!	
2005	Grzegorz Rasiak is Derby's top scorer with 16 league goals (17 in all competitions)	
2005	Iñigo Idiakez is Derby's Player of the Season	

Quirk Alert: Three in One

For the 2004/05 season, the second tier of English football became re-branded as The Championship – which is what the first tier had also been known as (as well as League Division One) prior to the introduction of the Premier League for season 1992/93. Meanwhile, the third tier, and what had traditionally been known as the Third Division was now League One – not to be confused with League Division One (1888-1992) or League Division 1 (1992-2004)!

Quirk Alert: Déjà-vu!

During season 2004/05, Derby County equalled their 1991/92 season record of 12 away wins in the league – but also frustratingly lost 6 matches at home (they lost 8 at home in 91/92). The outcome in the play-offs was also the same!

Year	Event	Pos
Season 2005/06 (Championship) – Struggle		
2005	07/06: George Burley resigns as Derby manager citing board interference	
2005	24/06: Derby appoint Phil Brown as their new manager	
2005	Derby re-sign Seth Johnson from Leeds on a free transfer (£7m profit)	
2005	20/08: Derby vs. Cardiff City (W 2-1) – Bisgaard, Idiakez – (W2, D2, L0)	3
2005	31/08: Derby sell Grzegorz Rasiak to Tottenham for £2.98m	10
2005	18/09: Derby vs. Southampton (D 2-2) – Idiakez, Davies – (W2, D6, L1)	9
2005	01/10: Derby vs. Leicester (D 1-1) – El Hamdaoui – 8 without a win (W2, D7, L3)	16
2005	18/11: Derby vs. Wolves (L 0-3) – 6 more without a win – (W3, D9, L7)	20
2005	03/12: Derby vs. Norwich (W 2-0) – Andrew Davies 2 – (W5, D10, L7)	14
2006	02/01: Millwall vs. Derby (L 2-1) – S Johnson – 6 more w/o win – (W5, D14, L9)	18
2006	14/01: Derby vs. Crewe (W 5-1) – Peschisolido, M Johnson, Smith 2, Idiakez	16
2006	21/01: Coventry vs. Derby (L 6-1) – Peschisolido – Rams 6 pts above drop-zone	18
2006	Derby sign Darren Moore from West Bromwich Albion for £300,000	
2006	28/01: FA Cup 4th Rd: Colchester United vs. Derby (L 3-1) – Smith	19
2006	30/01: Phil Brown is sacked and Terry Westley appointed caretaker manager	19

Year	Event	Pos
2006	01/02: Derby vs. Sheffield United (L 0-1) – Rams 3 points above 22nd (Brighton)	19
2006	11/03: Derby vs. Burnley (W 3-0) – Smith, Idiakez, Moore – 9 point cushion	19
2006	Peter Gadsby takes over from The Three Amigos and secures ownership of Pride Park; prison sentences await some of previous regime for false accounting & fraud	
2006	Derby finish season 20th (20:24) with 50 points, 8 points above the drop-zone	20
2006	Iñigo Idiakez is Derby's leading scorer with 11 league goals (11 in all competitions)	
2006	Tommy Smith is Derby's Player of the Season	
2006	Derby use 39 players during the 2005/06 season, a new club record	
2006	22 of the 39 players made their debuts for Derby – also a club record for a season	
2006	Derby also set a record for the number of league draws in a season (20)	
2006	01/05: Ted McMinn's testimonial (vs. Rangers) attracts a massive crowd (33,475)	
Season 2006/07 (Championship) – Promotion		
2006	02/06: Derby appoint Billy Davies as manager	
2006	22/07: Derby sign striker Steve Howard from Luton Town for £1m	
2006	31/08: Iñigo Idiakez & Tommy Smith join Southampton & Watford, respectively	19
2006	09/09: Derby vs. Sunderland (L 1-2) – Oakley – (W1, D1, L3)	23
2006	20/09: League Cup 2nd Rd: Doncaster vs. Derby (D 3-3 AET) – Rams lose 8-7 on pens	17
2006	23/09: Sheffield Wed vs. Derby (W 1-2) – Peschisolido, Howard (90) – (W3, D3, L3)	13
2006	30/09: Derby vs. Southend (W 3-0) – Lupoli 2, M Johnson – (W4, D3, L3)	9
2006	11/11: Coventry vs. Derby (W 1-2) – Stead, Howard – (W8, D4, L5) – 5 pts off 2nd	5
2006	15/11: Derby sign David Jones on loan from Man Utd (permanent for £1m Jan-07)	5
2006	25/11: Derby vs. Leicester City (W 1-0) – Stead – (W10, D4, L5) – 3 pts off top	4
2006	29/11: Derby vs. Ipswich T (W 2-1) – Howard, Lupoli – 6 wins on spin; 1 pt off top	4
2006	09/12: Leeds vs. Derby (W 0-1) – Barnes – Rams 3 points behind Birmingham	2
2006	16/12: Derby vs. Crystal Pal (W 1-0) – Jones – 9 wins in 10 – 3 points off top	2
2006	26/12: Derby vs. Wolves (L 0-2) – Rams now 8 points behind leaders, Birmingham	3
2007	01/01: Preston vs. Derby (W 1-2) – Howard 2 – (W15, D5, L7) – 3 points off top	2
2007	06/01: FA Cup 3rd Rd: Derby vs. Wrexham (W 3-1) – Lupoli 3	2
2007	09/01-11/01: Derby sign Craig Fagan from Hull City for £750,000, Stephen Pearson from Celtic for £750,000 and Gary Teale from Wigan Athletic for £600,000	2
2007	13/01: Derby vs. Sheffield Wed (W 1-0) – Jones (90) – Rams level with Birmingham	2
2007	20/01: Southend vs. Derby (W 0-1) – Howard – RAMS GO 3 POINTS CLEAR AT TOP	1
2007	27/01: FA Cup 4th Rd: Derby vs. Bristol Rovers (W 1-0) – Peschisolido	1
2007	30/01: Derby vs. Burnley (W 1-0) – Howard – RAMS GO 6 POINTS CLEAR AT TOP	1
2007	03/02: Southampton vs. Derby (W 0-1) – Howard – 8 wins on spin, 6 in league	1
2007	10/02: Derby vs. Hull (D 2-2) – Teale, Moore – RAMS 7 POINTS CLEAR AT TOP	1
2007	17/02: FA Cup 5th Rd: Plymouth vs. Derby (L 2-0); Birmingham cut lead to 3 points	1
2007	24/02: Sunderland vs. Derby (L 2-1) – Rams knocked off top by West Brom	2
2007	02/03: Derby vs. Colchester (W 5-1) – Jones, Lupoli, Barnes, Howard, (og) – TOP	1
2007	06/03: Norwich vs. Derby (W 1-2) – Jones 2 (C Martin [18] scores for Norwich)	1
2007	09/03: Birmingham vs. Derby (L 1-0) – Birmingham leapfrog Rams into 1st place	2
2007	17/03: Derby vs. Cardiff C (W 3-1) – Howard 2, Barnes – Rams 3 pts clear at top	1
2007	31/03: Barnsley vs. Derby (W 1-2) – Jones, Oakley – Rams 3 pts ahead of Sun'land	1
2007	09/04: Derby vs. Coventry (D 1-1) – Rams overtaken by Sunderland, with 4 to go	2
2007	14/04: Ipswich vs. Derby (L 2-1); 29/04: Crystal P vs. Derby (L 2-0) – all going wrong	3

Year	Event	Pos
2007	06/05: Derby vs. Leeds (W 2-0) – Currie, Mears – Leeds are relegated to the 3rd tier for the first time in their history; Rams fans are suitably sympathetic...	3
2007	Derby finish season 3rd (3:24) on 84 points, 2 pts behind 2nd-placed Birmingham	3
2007	12/05: Play-Off Semi-Final 1st Leg: Southampton vs. Derby (W 1-2) – Howard 2	
2007	15/05: Play-Off Semi-Final 2nd Leg: Derby vs. Southampton (L 2-3) – Moore, (og)	
2007	15/05: Ex-Derby striker Rasiak scores in 89th minute to force extra time	
2007	15/05: Derby win 4-3 on penalties when ex-Ram, Idiakez, misses his penalty	
2007	28/05: Play-Off Final: Derby vs. West Brom (W 1-0) – Pearson	
2007	DERBY ARE PROMOTED TO THE PREMIER LEAGUE FOR THE SECOND TIME	
2007	Steve Howard is Derby's top scorer with 19 goals	
2007	Steve Howard is also Derby's Player of the Season	

Quirk Alert: Rasiak and Idiakez Reprise
When Derby County narrowly missed promotion two years earlier by losing to Preston in the play-offs, the main reason they lost was because their two star players, Grzegorz Rasiak and Iñigo Idiakez were both injured. It was therefore brutally ironic that Rasiak should score that 89th minute goal that took the 2006/07 Play-Off Semi-Final into extra-time. However, just when Derby fans were starting to think about Gypsy's Curses again, poor Iñigo went and missed his crucial penalty kick! Oh, and George Burley was Southampton's manager, too!

Year	Event	Pos
Season 2007/08 (Premier League) – Relegation		
2007	In: R Earnshaw (Norwich, £3.5m), T Mears (West Ham, £1m), C Davis (Sheffield United, £3m), A Todd (Blackburn Rovers, £750,000)	
2007	11/08: Derby vs. Portsmouth (D 2-2) – Oakley, Todd – not a bad start	7
2007	18/08: Tottenham vs. Derby (L 4-0) – sign of things to come – (W0, D1, L2)	19
2007	31/08: Derby sign Kenny Miller from Celtic for £3m with Rams bottom of Prem	20
2007	01/09: Liverpool vs. Derby (L 6-0) – 4 defeats on spin – (W0, D1, L4)	20
2007	17/09: Derby vs. Newcastle – Miller – win actually takes Rams off bottom	19
2007	22/09: Arsenal vs. Derby (L 5-0) – (W1, D1, L5) – Goal Difference is already -16	20
2007	29/09: Derby (20th) vs. Bolton (19th) (D 1-1) – Miller – a rare point	20
2007	20/10: Fulham vs. Derby (D 0-0) – an even rarer away point, and off bottom	19
2007	10/11: Derby vs. West Ham (L 0-5) – GD is now -26, but Rams still only 2 pts off 17th	20
2007	26/11: Billy Davies leaves Derby by "mutual consent"; Paul Jewell is replacement	20
2007	15/12: Derby vs. Middlesbrough (L 0-1) – 7 straight defeats, Rams 8 points adrift of 17th, but still 32,676 at Pride Park	20
2007	23/12: Newcastle vs. Derby (D 2-2) – Barnes, Miller – Rams 7 pts adrift of 17th	20
2007	26/12: Derby vs. Liverpool (L 1-2) – McEveley – Gerrard winner in injury time	20
2008	04/01: Derby sign Emmanuel Villa from UAG for £2m	
2008	09/01: Derby sign Robbie Savage from Blackburn Rovers for £1.5m	
2008	30/01: Derby vs. Man City (D 1-1) – a good point, but Rams 12 pts from safety	20
2008	02/02: Birmingham vs. Derby (D 1-1) – Villa – Rams are now 13 points from safety	20
2008	Derby only gain 2 more points, losing 11 of their last 13 games, including 6-0, 6-1 and 6-2 defeats to Aston Villa, Chelsea and Arsenal, respectively	20

Year	Event	Pos
2008	Derby finish season bottom with record-low of 11 points, 25 points from safety!	20
2008	Kenny Miller is Derby's top scorer with 6 goals	
2008	Derby's Player of the Year goes to the fans; despite a disastrous season, all home gates exceeded 30,000, while the Rams took many thousands to each away game	

Quirk Alert: Out of the Blocks

On 11 August 2007, Derby County actually scored the first goal of the new Premiership season (from 3 o'clock kick-off time), when Matt Oakley scored against Portsmouth at Pride Park Stadium after only five minutes. Things went downhill from that moment, culminating in the worst-ever season in Derby's 134-year history. However, for 16 minutes, the Rams were actually top of the Premier League until Newcastle took a 0-2 lead at Bolton.

Stats Blast: 'Ad by Adebayor

Emmanuel Adebayor scored hat-tricks in both league games against Derby – which Arsenal won 5-0 at home and 2-6 away – to become the first player in Premier League history to score a hat-trick against the same team twice in one season.

Stats Blast: Things Could Only Get Better...

When Paul Jewell took over as Derby County manager on 28 November 2007, he eventually acquired yet another unwanted record – the longest run without a win on taking over at a new club – an impressive 28 games in Mr Jewell's case.

Stats Blast: Unwanted Rams Records – Season 2007-08

- Most league defeats in a season – 29 in 38 matches.
- Fewest league goals scored in a season – 20 in 38 matches.
- Fewest points in a league season (2 or 3 for a win) – 11 (from a possible 114).
- Longest-ever Premier League winless run (32 matches).
- First club in Premier League history to be relegated in March.
- Derby's record Premier League defeat – 0-6 (twice; away v. Liverpool, 01/09/2007 and home v. Aston Villa 12/04/2008).
- Second-most Rams league goals conceded in a season – 89 in 38 matches (in season 1936/37, Derby conceded 90 goals in 42 matches – although they did score 96 that season, too!)
- Equalled Loughborough's 108-year record, set during the 1899/1900 season in the Second Division, of going through an entire season and only winning 1 league game.
- And therefore joint-owning the status of being the worst football club in a single season in football league history.

Stats Blast: Could Have Been Better Than Villa

To be fair to Paul Jewell, performances improved under him, but results did not. Under Jewell, Derby also picked up a habit of conceding in the 90th minute – as they did in his first game at Sunderland, losing 1-0 to an Anthony Stokes heartbreaker. Derby also conceded late winners or equalisers in seven games between late December 2007 and late January 2008, dropping seven *points from games they had been winning or drawing as the clock hit 90 minutes; those 7 points would have made matters a little more respectable, and would actually have given Derby more Premiership points (18) than Aston Villa got during season 2015/16 (17)!*

Stats Blast: Best In The Land

Finally, some cheer. For despite all of that rubbish, Derby County's average league attendance that season was 32,432. Pride Park's capacity is around 33,500, so this must truly make Derby County fans the best (or the daftest) in the land!

RAMS CHRONOLOGY: Championship Rams

The 2000s

Year	Event	Pos
Season 2008/09 (Championship)		
2008	Out: R Earnshaw (Forest, £2.65m), C Fagan (Hull, £750,000), D Jones (Wolves, £1.2m), K Miller (Rangers, £2m), D Moore (Barnsley, free); Released: Edworthy, Feilhaber, Hinchliffe, Holmes, M. Johnson, Lewis, Stubbs	
2008	In: M Albrechtsen (West Brom, Free), N Barazite (Loan, Arsenal), K Commons (Nottm F, Free), P Connolly (Plymouth, Free), S Davies (Tranmere, £275,000), N Ellington (Watford, loan), L Dickinson (Stockport, £750,000), R Hulse (Sheffield Utd, £1.75m), P Green (Doncaster, Free), P Kazmierczak (Loan, Porto), A Pereplotkins (Loan, Skonto FC Rīga), A Prijović (Loan, Parma), J Stewart (Watford, Free)	
2008	09/08: Derby vs. Doncaster (L 0-1) – attendance is 33,010	18
2008	12/08: League Cup 1st Rd: Derby vs. Lincoln City (W 3-1) – Ellington 3	20
2008	26/08: League Cup 2nd Rd: Preston vs. Derby (W 0-1) – Green	20
2008	30/08: Barnsley vs. Derby (L 2-0) – Rams bottom after four games (W0, D1, L3)	24
2008	13/09: Derby vs. Sheffield Utd (W 2-1) – Green, Hulse – 1st league win in a year!	20
2008	27/09: QPR vs. Derby (W 0-2) – Albrechtsen, Villa – 4 without defeat – (W2, D3, L3)	17
2008	04/10: Norwich vs. Derby (W 1-2) – Hulse, Ellington – 6 w/o defeat – W3, D4, L3)	15
2008	18/10: Derby vs. Plymouth A (W 2-1) – Hulse, Green – 7 without defeat	9
2008	28/10: Derby vs. Norwich (W 3-1) – Green, Hulse, Kazmierczak – (W5, D5, L4)	10
2008	02/11: Derby vs. Forest (D 1-1) – Villa – ref is Stuart Attwell – see Quirk Alert	9
2008	04/11: League Cup 3rd Rd: Brighton vs. Derby (W 1-4) – Villa 3, Ellington	
2008	11/11: League Cup 4th Rd: Derby vs. Leeds (W 2-1) – Villa, Ellington	13
2008	15/11: Derby vs. Sheffield Wed (W 3-0) – Commons, Addison, Stewart	12
2008	Promising season so far: 4 points off the play-offs and in the QF of the League Cup	
2008	02/12: League Cup Quarter-Final : Stoke vs. Derby (W 0-1) – Ellington (90)	
2008	28/12: Derby vs. Ipswich (L 0-1) – Rams drop to 18th after a run of W1, D2, L6	18
2008	29/12: Paul Jewell resigns as Derby County manager	18
2008	03/01: FA Cup 3rd Rd: Forest Green vs. Derby (W 3-4) – Hulse, A'sen, Green, Davies	18
2009	06/01: Derby appoint Nigel Clough as their new manager	18
2009	07/01: League Cup Semi-Final, 1st Leg: Derby vs. Man Utd (W 1-0) – Commons	18
2009	17/01: Derby vs. QPR (L 0-2) – Rams two points above the drop-zone	20
2009	20/01: League Cup SF, 2nd Leg: Man Utd vs. Derby (L 4-2) – Barnes 2 – [agg: 4-3]	

Year	Event	Pos
2009	23/01: FA Cup 4th Rd: Derby vs. Nottingham Forest (D 1-1) – Hulse	
2009	27/01: Birmingham vs. Derby (L 1-0) – Rams drop into bottom three	22
2009	03/02: Derby sign Chris Porter from Motherwell for £400,000	
2009	04/02: FA Cup 4th Rd Replay: Nottm F vs. Derby (W 2-3) – Hulse, Green, Commons	
2009	07/02: Plymouth vs. Derby (W 0-3) – Teale, Hulse 2 – (W9, D8, L13) – 5 pts clear	16
2009	15/02: FA Cup 5th Rd: Derby vs. Man Utd (L 1-4) – Addison	
2009	18/02: Derby vs. Blackpool (W 4-1) – Commons 2, Green, Barazite – 6 pts clear	16
2009	21/02: Nottingham Forest vs. Derby (W 1-3) – Nyatanga, Hulse, Davies – gap 8 pts	15
2009	Season peters out after this with the Rams never in serious danger	
2009	13/04: Derby vs. Wolves (1st) (L 2-3) – highest Champ att'nce of season (33,079)	
2009	Derby finish season 18th (18:24) on 54 points, 8 points clear of the drop-zone	18
2009	Rob Hulse is Derby's top scorer with 15 league goals (18 in all competitions)	
2009	Rob Hulse is also Derby's Player of the Season	

Stats Blast: The Longest Year
When Derby County drew 1-1 at home to Bristol City on 16 August 2008, it stretched their winless league run to 34 games – making it yet another unwanted record as this broke the English league record for number of league games without a win. The record was stretched to 36 games with two more league defeats, but the run was finally ended against Sheffield United on 13 September 2008, almost exactly one year since Derby beat Newcastle United 1-0 in the Premier League on 17th September 2007.

Quirk Alert: Forest Fables
When Derby County played Nottingham Forest on 2 November 2008, Emanuel Villa scored at both ends. Meanwhile, in the FA Cup replay on 4 February, Derby were actually 2-0 down to Forest before a brilliant comeback saw them rattle in goals from Hulse, Green and Commons to secure an unlikely win and the F&C Performance of The Week award. The win was also Derby's first at the City Ground since October 1971, when Derby had been managed by Nigel Clough's father, Brian.

Quirk Alert: Rearrange: Know You're Don't Doing What You
In the home league match against Forest, the score was 1-1 going into the 90th minute, when Miles Addison headed Derby 2-1 in front – except referee Stuart Attwell belatedly awarded Derby a penalty instead – which Nacer Barazite then missed. Not to worry. Over comes the corner, and Miles Addison heads home again, so all's well that ends well. Oh hang on, despite replays showing that no foul was committed, Mr Attwell decides to disallow the goal...

Stats Blast: 7 Games Beats 38
When Derby County went on an unbeaten league run of four wins and three draws between 13 September and 18 October 2008, they amassed four more points in just 7 games than they had in the entire previous season!

Stats Blast: 2 Wins Beats 1
When Derby County beat Manchester United in the first leg of the League Cup semi-final on 7 January 2009, it bizarrely meant that they had beaten more Premier League teams in the 2008/09 Championship season (having already beaten Stoke in the Quarters), than they had in 38 attempts the previous year whilst actually IN the Premier League!

Year	Event	Pos
Season 2009/10 (Championship)		
2009	Out: L Dickinson (Brighton, £300,000), T Mears (Burnley, £500,000), L Nyatanga (Bristol City, £500,000), E Villa (Cruz Azul, £1.7m); Released/Free: M Albrechtsen, R Carroll, C Davis, M Sterjovski, A Todd	
2009	In: S Barker (Blackpool, £900,000), J Buxton (Burton, Free), L Croft (Norwich, Free), S Deeney (Burton, Free), D Moxey (Exeter, £300,000), B Pringle (Ilkeston, Free)	
2009	08/08: Derby vs. Peterborough (W 2-1) – Addison, Teale – attendance: 33,010	2
2009	22/08: Derby vs. Plymouth (W 2-1) – Buxton, Addison – (W2, D1, L1)	10
2009	29/09: Cardiff vs. Derby (L 6-1) – Chopra scores 4 as Rams lose 5th game in 6	20
2009	October: Derby's injury list rises from 11 to 16 throughout the month	
2009	31/10: Ipswich vs. Derby (L 1-0) – 3 more defeats on the bounce – (W4, D2, L9)	20
2009	12/12: Watford vs. Derby (W 0-1) – Porter – 4 without defeat – (W7, D4, L10)	17
2009	28/12: Newcastle vs. Derby (D 0-0) – credible draw at runaway league leaders	18

The 2010s

Year	Event	Pos
2010	09/01: Derby vs. Scunthorpe (L 1-4) – Rams are 5 points above 22nd	18
2010	16/01: Peterborough vs. Derby (W 0-3) – Davies, DJ Campbell 2 – (W8, D5, L13)	18
2010	30/01: Derby vs. Nottingham Forest (W 1-0) – Hulse – attendance: 32,674	18
2010	09/02: Derby vs. Newcastle (W 3-0) – Hulse, Commons, Barker – (W10, D6, L14)	15
2010	16/02: Derby vs. Preston (W 5-3) – Jones (og), Commons, Hulse 2, Barker	12
2010	13/03: Doncaster vs. Derby (L 2-1) – Hulse – 4 defeats in 5 – (W12, D6, L18)	18
2010	Concerned by lack of US investment, Peter Gadsby launches unsuccessful takeover	
2010	03/04: Coventry vs. Derby (W 0-1) – Barker – 5 without defeat – (W14, D9, L18)	15
2010	Derby finish season 14th (14:24) with 56 points, 9 points clear of relegation	14
2010	Rob Hulse is Derby's top scorer with 12 goals, all in the league	
2010	Shaun Barker is Derby's Player of the Season	
2010	Derby County Reserves win the Central League Division One Central Section	

Quirk Alert: The Heart of the Issue
Derby's 2009/10 season was hit by a crippling injury list. At one time in October, an incredible 16 players were out injured for Derby's match away at Ipswich. One of those players, Mark O'Brien, had to undergo heart surgery to correct a valve problem, while it was later revealed that when Jay McEveley had surgery on his broken cheekbone, his heart actually stopped for two minutes during the operation. Meanwhile, reserve keeper Saul Deeney was ruled out for six weeks after he slipped and twisted his ankle during an unplanned fire drill at the hotel Derby were staying at after their defeat away to Swansea in November!

Quirk Alert: World Cup Derby

There were plans afoot during 2009/10 for Derby to be a host city for England's 2018 World Cup bid, with Derby City Council looking to raise £26m through an extra levy on local businesses to help fund the expansion of Pride Park to 45,000 from its 33,500 capacity. Local businesses were not impressed, but in the end, Derby was not chosen as a host city, and in any case, England didn't have a prayer of landing the World Cup, anyway...

Quirk Alert: Infamous January

January 2010 saw an infamous outburst from Robbie Savage against BBC Radio Derby in response to suggestions that some players were unhappy with Nigel Clough's backroom staff. Meanwhile, the month also saw an infamous melee at Pride Park during the local Derby against Nottingham Forest, with most of the two clubs' players and staff involved, and which ended with Billy Davies bizarrely claiming to have been "assaulted" by Nigel Clough.

Quirk Alert: Robbie Shilton

Typical of Derby's injury-hit season was the 4-1 defeat at Reading on 10 March. Stephen Bywater went off in the 13th minute with a back injury, to be replaced by debutant Saul Deeney. But poor Saul had a debut to forget when he brought down Jay Tabb after 41 minutes, thus conceding a penalty and earning a red card. With no other goalkeeper to call on, Robbie Savage donned the gloves, and went on to make a few decent saves, too – although Nigel Clough later joked that Savage was the obvious choice for going in goal as he "hadn't had a kick all game in midfield!"

Quirk Alert: Crockby County

Derby completed the 2009/10 season by beating Cardiff 2-0 – but with 14 players out injured!

Year	Event	Pos
Season 2010/11 (Championship)		
2010	Out: P Connolly, L Hendrie, J McEveley, L Price, G Teale	
2010	In: J Bailey and J Brayford (Crewe, £800,000), T Cywka, D Martin, G Roberts	
2010	07/08: Leeds vs. Derby (W 1-2) – Hulse, Commons	9
2010	Coventry vs. Derby (L 2-1) – Moxey – injury-hit Rams play left-back Moxey up front	14
2010	28/08: Derby vs. QPR (D 2-2) – Commons, Bailey – QPR score twice in injury time	15
2010	31/08: Derby sell Rob Hulse to QPR for £750,000	15
2010	Derby sign Alberto Bueno and Shefki Kuqi on season-long & 3-month loans	
2010	14/09: Hull vs Derby (L 2-0) – 4 defeats in 5 – Rams drop into bottom three	22
2010	25/09: Derby vs. Crystal Pal (W 5-0) – Bueno 2, Commons, Green, Kuqi	19
2010	28/09: Derby vs. Middlesbrough (W 3-1) – Barker, Commons 2 – (W3, D2, L4)	15
2010	16/10: Derby vs. Preston (W 3-0) – Moxey, Bueno, Savage – (W4, D3, L4)	13
2010	30/10: Derby vs. Watford (W 4-1) – Brayford, Cywka 2, Kuqi – (W6, D3, L5)	7
2010	09/11: Ipswich vs. Derby (W 0-2) – Commons 2 – Rams now five points off second	4
2010	20/11: Derby vs. Scunthorpe (W 3-2) – Cywka, Commons, Moore – (W9, D3, L6)	4
2010	27/11: Burnley vs. Derby (L 2-1) – Moore – two late Burnley goals rob Rams of 3rd	4
2010	29/12: Nottingham F vs. Derby (L 5-2) – Moore, Commons – 5 defeats on spin	12
2011	20/01: Derby sign Ben Davies from Notts County for £350,000	

Year	Event	Pos
2011	28/01: Derby sell Kris Commons to Celtic for £300,000	
2011	31/01: Derby sell Dean Moxey to Crystal Palace for £400,000	
2011	01/02: Derby vs. Ipswich (L 1-2) – Bueno – 3 defeats on the spin – (W10, D4, L14)	16
2011	12/02: Derby vs. Leicester (L 0-2) – 4th defeat in 5 – Rams 7 points above 22nd	17
2011	22/02: Derby vs. Hull (L 0-1) – 9 without a win – Rams now only 5 pts above 22nd	
2011	26/02: Sheffield United vs. Derby (W 0-1) – Robinson – now 8 points above 22nd	18
2011	After only 4 wins in 2011, Derby finish 19th on 49 points, 9 pts clear of relegation	19
2011	Kris Commons is Derby's top scorer with 13 goals, all in the league	
2011	John Brayford is Derby's Player of the Season	
2011	Derby County Reserves retain the Central League Div One Central Section title	

Quirk Alert: Hospital Bed Shortage

Despite getting good results during October 2010, Derby were without five central defenders (Addison, Anderson, Buxton, Hanson and Leacock), forcing right back John Brayford to deputise at centre half and midfielder Paul Green to move to right back.

Stats Blast: Home Rule

Derby's 3–2 win over Scunthorpe United on 20 November 2010 was the Rams' sixth consecutive home win, with 20 goals scored in the process. This set a record at Pride Park, while it was also the club's best run of home form in over 15 years.

Stats Blast: Francis & Co 49ers

Derby County took only 49 points from a possible 138 during season 2010/11, their lowest ever total from a 46-game programme with 3 points for a win. It was also Derby's lowest points total in the second tier since 1984, when they took just 42 points from 42 fixtures – and were relegated to the Third Division! However, a remarkable 18 of those 49 points gained during 2010/11 came from loanee goalkeeper Frank Fielding's first eight games!

Year	Event	Pos
Season 2011/12 (Championship)		
2011	Out: C Porter, B Pringle, R Savage, L Varney (Portsmouth, £750,000)	
2011	In: C Bryson (Kilmarnock, £350,000), F Fielding (Blackburn, £400,000), A Legzdins, Burton, Free), K Kilbane (Hull, Loan), C Maguire (Aberdeen, £400,000), J Shackell (Barnsley, £1m), T Robinson (Millwall, £250,000), N Tyson (Nottm Forest, Free), J Ward (Sheffield Utd, £250,000)	
2011	06/08: Derby vs. Birmingham (W 2-1) – Shackell, S Davies	4
2011	13/08: Watford vs. Derby (W 0-1) – S Davies – Rams are 3rd in early table	3
2011	17/08: Blackpool vs. Derby (W 0-1) – Bryson – Rams still 3rd despite 100% record	3
2011	Derby's best start since 1948 and first time with first 3 including 2 away games	
2011	20/08: Derby vs. Doncaster (W 3-0) – Kilbane, S Davies, B Davies – (W4, D0, L0)	2
2011	Four wins out of four is Derby's best start to a season since 1905/06	
2011	27/08: Derby vs. Burnley (L 1-2); 10/09: Coventry vs. Derby (L 2-0) – (W4, D0, L2)	5
2011	17/09: Nottingham Forest vs. Derby (W 1-2) – Ward, Hendrick – 2 points off top	4

Year	Event	Pos
2011	24/09: Derby vs. Millwall (W 3-0) – Bryson, Hendrick, S Davies – (W6, D0, L2)	3
2011	27/09: Derby vs Barnsley (D 1-1) – S Davies – Rams miss the chance to go top	2
2011	15/10: Derby vs. Southampton (D 1-1) – S Davies fractures eye-socket	4
2011	21/10: M'brough vs Derby (L 2-0) – M Bennett becomes Derby's youngest player	4
2011	29/10: Derby vs. Portsmouth (W 3-1) – Bryson, Maguire, Ward – (W7, D3, L4)	5
2011	November: Rams lose all 5 league games amid another terrible injury crisis	16
2011	02/12: Crystal Palace vs. Derby (D 1-1) – Derby's 5,000th league point	15
2011	26/12: Derby vs. Leeds (W 1-0) – Ward – (W9, D4, L10) – Rams are 5 pts off 6th	14
2011	31/12: Derby vs. West Ham (W 2-1) – Ball, Green – Rams still 5 pts off 6th	11
2012	02/01: Hull C vs. Derby (W 0-1) – Robinson – Rams only team to take 9 festive pts	9
2012	14/01: Derby vs. Coventry (W 1-0) – Ball – 4 wins on trot – 2 points off play-offs	8
2012	23/02: Derby vs. Leicester (L 0-1) – 6 without a win – (W12, D6, L14)	15
2012	06/03: Derby vs. Blackpool (W 2-1) – a brace from a recovered Steven Davies	14
2012	13/03: Derby vs. Nottingham Forest (W 1-0) – Buxton (95) – captain Shaun Barker suffers a horrific knee dislocation – Rams first league double over Forest in 40 yrs	13
2012	17/03: Doncaster vs. Derby (W 1-2) – Robinson, Roberts – Rams 7 pts off play-offs	11
2012	24/03: Derby vs. Crystal P (W 3-2) – S Davies, Hendrick, Robinson – 5 pts off 6th	12
2012	09/04: Leeds vs. Derby (W 0-2) – Bryson, S Davies – Rams still 5 pts off play-offs	11
2012	09/04: Derby's 7th consecutive win vs. Leeds and 3rd consecutive league double	11
2012	Derby finish season 12th (12:24) on 64 points, 11 points short of the play-offs	12
2012	Steven Davies is top scorer in league with 12 goals (Theo Robinson 12 in all comps)	
2012	Craig Bryson is Derby's Player of the Season	

Stats Blast: Fielding for England

When Frank Fielding was called up into the England squad for European Championship qualifiers in September 2011, he became the first Derby player in 11 years to be selected for England, since Seth Johnson's appearance against Italy in 2000.

Quirk Alert: Parallel Worlds

When Derby played Nottingham Forest at the City Ground on 17th September 2011, Frank Fielding was sent off after just 66 seconds after allegedly fouling Ishmail Miller. Forest scored the resulting penalty, but Derby famously went on to win with ten men, thanks to goals from Jamie Ward and Jeff Hendrick. However, unbeknown to most, this game had remarkable parallels with Derbyshire and England Test cricketers of the 1970s. Think about it: Miller was the victim of some dodgy Fielding, before Ward and Hendrick strikes turned the game on its head! Almost Taylor-made, wasn't it?

Stats Blast: Derby Counteeny

When Mason Bennett made his first appearance for the Rams against Middlesbrough on 22nd October 2011, he became Derby's youngest ever player, at 15 years and 99 days old, beating Lee Holmes' record by 169 days. Meanwhile, Will Hughes made his debut for Derby against Peterborough on 5 November 2011, aged 16, joining four other Derby teenagers on the pitch: Callum Ball (19), Mason Bennett (15), Jeff Hendrick (19) and Mark O'Brien (18).

Stats Blast: Festive Nine

When Derby beat Hull 1-0 on 2nd January 2012 at the KC Stadium, the Rams were the only club in English football to take all 9 points over the festive period

Year	Event	Pos
Season 2012/13 (Championship)		
2012	Out: M Addison (Bournemouth, undisc), S Davies (Bristol City, £750,000), C Maguire (Sheff Wed, £200,000), J Shackell (Burnley, £1.1m); Free/Loan: R Atkins, J Bailey, C Ball, L Croft, P Green, T Naylor	
2012	In: P Coutts (Preston, £150,000), R Keogh (Coventry, £1m), C Sammon (Wigan, £1.2m); Undisclosed: K Freeman (Nottm For), V Gjokaj (Luzern), M Jacobs (Northampton), J O'Connor (Doncaster)	
2012	14/08: League Cup 1st Rd: Derby vs. Scunthorpe (D 5-5) [L 6-7 on penalties]	
2012	01/09: Derby vs. Watford (W 5-1) – Keogh, Hendrick, Sammon, Hughes, Ward	14
2012	18/09: Derby vs. Charlton (W 3-2) – Ward 2, Bryson – (W2, D2, L2)	9
2012	30/09: Nottingham Forest vs. Derby (W 0-1) – Bryson – (W3, D2, L3)	12
2012	23/10: Ipswich vs. Derby (W 1-2) – Robinson, Tyson – 5 without defeat	12
2012	03/11: Derby vs. Blackpool (W 4-1) – Robinson 2, Brayford, Sammon	11
2012	06/11: Derby vs. Barnsley (W 2-0) – O'Connor, Tyson – 1 point off the play-offs	9
2012	13/11: Will Hughes aged 17 years and 210 days, becomes England Under-21's second youngest-ever player (after Theo Walcott) – vs. N Ireland Under-21	9
2012	Nov: Arsenal, Liverpool, Man City and even Barcelona all linked with Will Hughes	
2012	24/11: Derby vs. Birmingham (W 3-2) – Sammon 2, Tyson – 3 points off play-offs	12
2012	01/12: Leicester vs. Derby (L 4-1) – Robinson – (W7, D6, L7)	16
2012	08/12: Derby vs. Leeds (W 3-1) – Sammon, Buxton, B Davies – (W8, D6, L7)	10
2012	15/12: Bristol City vs. Derby (W 0-2) – Hendrick, Bryson – 3 points off play-offs	10
2013	01/01: Derby vs. M'brough (W 3-1) – Jacobs, Hendrick, Sammon – 3 pts off p-offs	10
2013	05/01: FA Cup 3rd Rd: Derby vs. Tranmere (W 5-0) – Davies, Sammon, Brayford, Hendrick, Bennett – Bennett is youngest goalscorer in Derby County's history	10
2013	19/01: Derby vs. Forest (D 1-1) – Ward – highest Champ atten'ce/season (33,010)	13
2013	02/02: Derby vs. Huddersfield (W 3-0) – Bryson, Ward, Keogh – 6 points off p-offs	9
2013	22/02: Derby sign Chris Martin on loan from Norwich City	10
2013	09/03: Birmingham vs. Derby (L 3-1) – eight without a win – (W11, D12, L14)	15
2013	29/03: Derby vs. Bristol C (W 3-0) – Hendrick, Ward, B Davies – (W13, D12, L14)	12
2013	01/04: Leeds vs. Derby (W 1-2) – Coutts, Buxton – 6 pts off play-offs, 7 off drop	8
2013	16/04: Derby vs. Barnsley (D 1-1) – Brayford (90) – no win in 3; 4 pts above drop	15
2013	20/04: Derby vs. Peterborough (W 3-1) – Bryson, Martin, Keogh – (W15, D13, L16)	11
2013	Derby finish season 10th (10:24) on 61 points – 7 pts from the p-offs, 7 from drop	10
2013	Jamie Ward is Derby's top scorer with 12 league goals from only 24 games	
2013	Richard Keogh is Derby's Player of the Season	

Stats Blast: Paying the Penalty

During Derby's home game with Ipswich, Jamie Ward missed a penalty, Derby's fourth consecutive penalty miss and their third in three consecutive games!

Quirk Alert: High Fives

Derby's first competitive game of the season was an extraordinary affair against Scunthorpe United in the First Round of the League Cup. Derby coasted to a 3-0 half-time lead through Keogh, Buxton and Robinson, and when Scunthorpe pulled one back in the 52nd minute, Derby promptly made it 4-1 after 53 minutes with Jake Buxton's second of the night. At 4-2, Theo Robinson missed a 72nd minute penalty for Derby, Scunthorpe then made it 4-3 and then Nathan Tyson restored Derby's two-goal lead in the 83rd minute. Going into injury time, Derby led 5-3 – but then conceded twice. With no further goals in extra-time, the game went to a penalty shoot-out, which Scunthorpe won 7-6.

Stats Blast: Three's-Up!

In the second half of the Derby vs. Scunthorpe game, goals were scored after 53, 63, 73, 83 and 93 minutes!

Year	Event	Pos
Season 2013/14 (Championship)		
2013	Out: J Brayford (Cardiff, £1.5m), F Fielding (Bristol City, £200,000), T Robinson (Doncaster, £150,000); Out (Free/Loan): C Ball, C Doyle, T Naylor, J O'Connor, G Roberts, N Tyson	
2013	In: J Eustace (Watford, Free), C Forsyth (Watford, £150,000), L Grant (Burnley, Free), C Martin (Norwich, Free), J Russell (Dundee United, £750,000)	
2013	10/08: Brighton vs. Derby (W 1-2) – Martin 2 – (W1, D1, L0)	5
2013	17/08: Derby vs. Leicester (L 0-1) – Rams drop down to 10th after 3 games	10
2013	24/08: Yeovil vs. Derby (W 0-3) – Russell, Bryson, Martin – (W2, D1, L1)	8
2013	27/08: L Cup 2nd Rd: Derby vs. Brentford (W 5-0) – Martin 2, Sammon 2, Hughes	8
2013	31/08: Derby vs. Burnley (L 0-3) – Rams still haven't won at home in the league	14
2013	14/09: Millwall vs. Derby (W 1-5) – Buxton, Bryson 3, Bennett – (W3, D1, L2)	7
2013	14/09: Derby win their first 3 away league games for the first time in 101 years	7
2013	21/09: Derby vs. Reading (L 1-3) – Hughes – (W3, D2, L3)	11
2013	24/09: League Cup 3rd Rd: Leicester vs. Derby (L 2-1) – Martin	12
2013	28/09: Nottingham Forest vs. Derby (L 1-0) – Rams now 7 points off the play-offs	14
2013	28/09: Derby sack Nigel Clough – ironically at a time when he has put together Derby's best side in years, with a genuine shot at promotion	14
2013	01/10: Derby appoint Steve McClaren as their new manager	14
2013	01/10: Derby vs. Ipswich (D 4-4) – Whitbread, Bryson 2, Ward – from 1-4 down	14
2013	05/10: Derby vs. Leeds (W 3-1) – Martin, Russell, Hughes – (W4, D3, L4)	10
2013	05/10: Derby's 10th straight win over Leeds – a truly remarkable statistic	10
2013	14/10: Derby sign Simon Dawkins from Tottenham on loan	10
2013	19/10: Watford vs. Derby (W 2-3) – Ward 2, Sammon – (W5, D3, L4)	8
2013	22/10: Derby sign Andre Wisdom from Liverpool on a season-long loan	8
2013	09/11: Derby vs. Sheffield Wed (W 3-0) – Buxton, Hughes, Martin – (W6, D4, L5)	9
2013	23/11: Bournemouth vs. Derby (W 0-1) – Ward – Rams are 1 pt off 6th, 10 off 2nd	7
2013	01/12: Wigan Athletic vs. Derby (W 1-3) – Bryson, Dawkins, Martin	5
2013	04/12: Derby vs. Middlesbrough (W 2-1) – Martin, Sammon – (W9, D4, L5)	4
2013	07/12: Derby vs. Blackpool (W 5-1) – Martin 3, Bryson, Keogh – 5 wins on spin	4

Year	Event	Pos
2013	14/12: Charlton vs. Derby (W 0-2) – Ward, Bryson – Rams only 3 points off 2nd	4
2013	21/12: Derby vs. D'caster (W 3-1) – Ward, Daw, Bry – 7 wins on spin – 3 pts off top	4
2013	29/12: Barnsley vs. Derby (W 1-2) – Martin 2 – 4 pts behind leaders Leicester	2
2013	29/12: Derby win 10 of McClaren's first 13 games, taking 32 points from 39; Derby have also scored 48 goals, 9 more than next best (Leicester) and 13 more than 3rd	2
2014	01/01: Derby vs. Wigan (L 0-1) – Rams drop to 4th, now 3 pts behind 2nd (Burnley)	4
2014	03/01: Derby sign Simon Dawkins from Tottenham Hotspur on a permanent deal	4
2014	03/01: Derby sign Patrick Bamford from Chelsea on loan until end of season	4
2014	10/01: Leicester vs. Derby (L 4-1) – Rams still 4th, but now 10 pts behind Leicester	4
2014	18/01: Derby vs. Brighton (W 1-0) – Bamford – still 4th, but 5 pts behind 2nd (QPR)	4
2014	28/01: Derby vs. Yeovil (W 3-2) – Bamford, Bryson, Martin – 4 points behind 2nd	4
2014	30/01: Derby sign George Thorne on loan from West Brom until end of season	4
2014	01/02: Birmingham vs. Derby (D 3-3) – Bamford, Martin, Forsyth – (W15, D7, L7)	4
2014	10/02: Derby vs. QPR (W 1-0) – Eustace – Rams now one point behind BUR, QPR	4
2014	18/02: Sheffield Wed vs. Derby (W 0-1) – Bamford – (W17, D7, L7)	3
2014	22/02: Derby vs. Bournemouth (W 1-0) – Martin – Rams 2 points behind Burnley	3
2014	01/03: Burnley (2nd, 63 pts) vs. Derby (3rd, 61 pts) (L 2-0) – crucial defeat	3
2014	15/03: Reading vs. Derby (D 0-0) – 4 w/o win or goal – Leicester/Burnley have gone	3
2014	22/03: Derby vs. Nottingham Forest (W 5-0) – Bryson 3, Hendrick, Russell	3
2014	25/03: Ipswich vs. Derby (L 2-1) – Bamford – Rams lose to injury-time winner	4
2014	29/03: Derby vs. Charlton (W 3-0) – Russell, Bamford Martin – Rams 10 pts off 2nd	4
2014	08/04: Blackpool vs. Derby (W 1-3) – Martin, Bamford, Bryson – (W21, D9, L11)	3
2014	12/04: Derby vs. H'field (W 3-1) – Russell, og, Martin – 8 pts behind BUR, 4 to go	3
2014	18/04: Doncaster vs. Derby (W 0-2) – Thorne, Martin – still 8 points behind	3
2014	21/04: Derby vs. Barnsley (W 2-1) – Hendrick, Russell – Burnley win/promoted	3
2014	26/04: Derby vs. Watford (W 4-2) – Hendrick 2, Forsyth, Martin – (W25, D9, L11)	3
2014	08/05: Play-Off Semi-F 1st Leg: Brighton vs. Derby (W 1-2) – Martin, Kuszczak (og)	
2014	11/05: P-Off SF 2nd: Derby vs. Brighton (W 4-1) – Hughes, Martin, Thorne, Hendrick	
2014	24/05: Play-Off Final Derby vs. QPR (L 0-1) – Zamora (90) – QPR's only shot/target	
2014	Chris Martin is Derby's top scorer with 22 league goals (25 in all competitions)	
2014	Craig Bryson is Derby's Player of the Season for the second time	

Stats Blast: Tame Lions

When Derby won 1-5 at Millwall on 14 September, this was the first time that Derby had won their opening three away league games since 1912. Craig Bryson scored his first career hat-trick in the game and became the first Derby player to score a league hat-trick since Paul Simpson in April 1996. Bryson would go on to grab a second hat-trick later in the season in the 5-0 win over Nottingham Forest. He thus became only the third Ram to grab a hat-trick against Forest, following Steve Bloomer (3 times) and Alf Bentley – all over a century before!

Quirk Alert: Mr MacMotivator

When Derby played Ipswich at home on Tuesday 1 October, Darren Wassall was put in temporary charge, even though Steve McClaren had been appointed manager earlier that day. After a disas-

trous first half, Derby trailed 1-4 – at which point McClaren went into the dressing room and delivered a "rousing speech". Derby then fought back to draw the game 4-4, with Craig Bryson's equaliser coming in the 88th minute.

Stats Blast: Derby vs. Leeds – Remarkable Statistics

Steve McClaren's first full game in charge of Derby was the 3-1 victory at home to Leeds United on 5 October 2013. Incredibly, this was Derby's TENTH league win on the bounce against Leeds. That statistic would be amazing under any circumstances, for it is highly unusual for even the very top teams in English football to record ten straight wins against the same opposition. What is more remarkable, though, is that Derby had a truly TERRIBLE record against Leeds before they won the first of those ten games – a 0-1 success on 9 December 2006. Even today (Jan-18), they have still won only 37 games against Leeds in almost a century, drawing 27 and losing 54. But before that victory on 9 December 2006, Derby had only won ONE of their previous TWENTY games against Leeds, and only THREE of the previous THIRTY FIVE games. In fact, Derby's record against Leeds from October 1953 to October 2004 (over 51 years) was as follows: Won 7, Drawn 21, Lost 39. Truly awful!

Hurt Alert: Fine Margins

On 1 March 2014, 3rd-placed Derby travelled to 2nd-placed Burnley with just two points between them. Derby fell behind to ex-Rams midfielder David Jones' strike in the 29th minute. There then occurred one of those moments in a club's history when their entire future is potentially changed. Bobby Madley had already booked Chris Martin in the 20th minute for a nothing challenge. Then, two minutes before half time, Martin turned in the box, was CLEARLY caught by a Burnley defender and went down. The loose ball fell to Craig Forsyth who swept the ball into the net. Cue Madley, who promptly issued Martin with a second yellow for diving and sent him off. He then disallowed Forsyth's goal, claiming he'd already blown for the "dive". Burnley won 2-0.

Now 5 points behind Burnley, Derby never made up the difference, despite finishing with 85 points – 6 more than 2nd-placed Hull the season before. However, the Rams swept aside Brighton in the Play-Off Semis and dominated the Final against QPR – before Bobby Zamora scored in the 90th minute with QPR's only shot on target. The same QPR who had flagrantly breached the Financial Fair-Play rules by a HUGE margin the very same year, and even more astonishingly, were later to get away with it, too. Football can be a very cruel game.

Year	Event	Pos
Season 2014/15 (Championship)		
2014	Out (Loan): M Bennett, K Freeman, T Naylor, M O'Brien, C Sammon	
2014	In: L Best (Blackburn, Loan), Iván Calero (Atlético Madrid, Free), C Christie (Coventry, undisclosed), O Mascarell (Real Madrid, Loan), J Mitchell (Newcastle, Free), G Thorne (West Brom, £2.6m), Z Whitbread (Leicester, Free)	
2014	22/07: Four days after signing from West Brom for £2.6m, key midfielder George Thorne suffers a cruciate knee ligament injury and is out for the entire season	
2014	09/08: Derby vs. Rotherham (W 1-0) – Hendrick – attendance: 30,105	7
2014	11/08: League Cup 1st Rd: Carlisle vs. Derby (W 0-2) – Hendrick, Martin	7

Year	Event	Pos
2014	23/08: Derby vs. Fulham (W 5-1) – Ward, Bryson, Martin 2, Dawkins – (W2, D1, L1)	7
2014	25/08: Derby sign Ryan Shotton from Stoke City on loan	7
2014	26/08: League Cup 2nd Rd: Derby vs. Charlton (W 1-0) – Calero	7
2014	29/08: Derby sign Jordan Ibe from Liverpool on loan for the season	7
2014	30/08; Derby vs. Ipswich (D 1-1); 14/09: Nottingham Forest vs. Derby (D 1-1)	10
2014	17/09: Blackburn vs. Derby (W 2-3) – Ward 2, Hughes – (W3, D3, L1)	7
2014	23/09: League Cup 3rd Rd: Derby vs. Reading (W 2-0) – Russell, Pearce og	9
2014	27/09: Bolton vs. Derby (W 0-2) – Martin 2 – (W4, D4, L1) – Rams 4 pts off top	6
2014	30/09: Derby vs. Bournemouth (W 2-0) – Hughes, Martin – Rams 1 point off top	4
2014	18/10: Reading vs. Derby (W 0-3) – Martin 2, Ibe – Rams still 1 point off top	2
2014	21/10: Blackpool vs. Derby (W 0-1) – Martin – RAMS GO TOP OF CHAMPIONSHIP	1
2014	28/10: L Cup 4th Rd: Fulham vs. Derby (W 2-5) – Martin, Russell, Dawkins 2, H'drick	1
2014	25/10; 01/11: Derby vs. Wigan (L 1-2); Brentford vs. Derby (L 2-1)	5
2014	04/11: Derby vs. Huddersfield (W 3-2) – Ibe, Russell, Dawkins – 1 point off top	4
2014	08/11: Derby vs. Wolves (W 5-0) – Shotton, Hendrick 2, Russell 2 – RAMS TOP	1
2014	22/11: Watford vs. Derby (W 1-2) – Ibe, Bryson – RAMS GO THREE POINTS CLEAR	1
2014	29/11: Leeds vs. Derby (L 2-0) – Rams still top but lead is cut to one point	1
2014	06/12: Derby vs. Brighton (W 3-0) – Martin 2, Russell – RAMS STILL POINT CLEAR	1
2014	13/12: Middlesbrough vs. Derby (L 2-0) – Rams overtaken by B'mouth and Boro	3
2014	16/12: League Cup Quarter-Final: Derby vs. Chelsea (L 1-3) – Bryson	3
2014	26/12: Birmingham vs. Derby (W 0-4) – Ibe, Martin, Forsyth, Russell	3
2014	30/12: Derby vs. Leeds (W 2-0) – Mowatt og, Buxton – 3 points off top (B'mouth)	3
2015	02/01: Derby sign Darren Bent on loan from Aston Villa	3
2015	10/01: Ipswich (2nd) vs. Derby (3rd) (W 0-1) – Martin – Rams level with B'mouth	2
2015	17/01: Derby vs. Nottingham F (L 1-2) – injury time sickener – Rams 3 pts off top	3
2015	24/01: FA Cup 4th Rd: Derby vs. Chesterfield (W 2-0) – Bent, Hughes	5
2015	27/01: Derby vs. Blackburn (W 2-0) – Bent 2 – Rams level with Bournemouth again	2
2015	31/01: Cardiff vs. Derby (W 0-2) – Malone og, Martin – still level with Bournemouth	2
2015	02/02: Derby sign Tom Ince and Jesse Lingaard on loan from Hull and Man Utd	2
2015	07/02: Derby vs. Bolton (W 4-1) – Ince 2, Hendrick 2 – Rams still level with leaders	2
2015	10/02: Bournemouth vs. Derby (D 2-2) – Ince, Bent – both teams are overtaken by Middlesbrough; worse still, Chris Martin tears hamstring	3
2015	14/02: FA Cup 5th Rd: Derby vs. Reading (L 1-2) – Bent	3
2015	17/02: Rotherham vs. Derby (D 3-3) – Ince 2, Bent – (W17, D8, L6) – still joint-top	2
2015	21/02: Derby vs. Sheff Wed (W 3-2) – Buxton 2, Bent – Rams go 2 pts clear at top	1
2015	24/02: Derby vs. Charlton (W 2-0) – Hendrick, Lingard – Rams 5 pts clear of 3rd	1
2015	28/02; Fulham vs. Derby (L 2-0); 03/03: Brighton vs. Derby (L 2-0)	2
2015	07/03: Derby vs. Birmingham (D 2-2) – Blues score twice in injury time	2
2015	07/03: Champ table, all Pl 36: BOU, DER, WAT, MID, NOR – 66, 66, 66, 66, 65	2
2015	14/03: Norwich vs Derby (D 1-1) – Ruddy (og) – (W19, D10, L8)	4
2015	17/03; Derby vs. Middlesbrough (L 0-1) ; 20/03: Wolves vs. Derby (L 2-0)	5
2015	03/04: Derby (5th) vs. Watford (2nd) – (D 2-2) – Bent, Ince – Rams 6 points off 2nd	6
2015	11/04: Derby vs. Brentford (D 1-1) – Bent (90) – Rams 7 pts off 2nd (Norwich)	5
2015	14/04: Derby vs. Blackpool (W 4-0) – Bryson, Ince, Bent 2 – Rams 5 pts above 7th	5
2015	18/04: Huddersfield vs. Derby (D 4-4) – Ince 2, Dawkins, Lingard – 3 pts above 7th	5

Year	Event	Pos
2015	25/04: Millwall vs. Derby (D 3-3) – Ince, Martin, Hendrick – Rams 2 pts above 7th	6
2015	Tom Ince is Championship Player of the Month for April, scoring 5 goals in 6 games	6
2015	Rams need 1 point from final game vs. Reading who haven't won in 9 games	6
2015	02/05: Derby vs. Reading – (L 0-3) – Derby are passed by Brentford and Wolves	8
2015	Derby finish season 8th (8:24) on 77 points, one point shy of the play-offs	8
2015	Chris Martin is Derby's top league scorer with 18 goals (21 in all competitions)	
2015	Will Hughes is Derby's Player of the Season	
2015	25/05: Steve McClaren is sacked as Derby County manager	

Stats Blast: An Unwanted Record

Derby County finished season 2014/15 in 8th place on 77 points, the largest points total ever for an eighth-placed team in the second tier of English football. They also won 10 games more than they lost. In other years (i.e. season 2012-13), Leicester City finished two places higher in 6th position on 68 points, having only won 3 more games than they had lost. As for 8th place, the nearest challenger to Derby is Huddersfield (74 points) from season 1999-2000, while in season 2005/06, Coventry finished 8th on just 63 points, as did Huddersfield during 1995/96!

Year	Event	Pos
Season 2015/16 (Championship)		
2015	01/06: Paul Clement is appointed as Derby County manager	
2015	Out: S Barker, S Dawkins, J Eustace, T Naylor, M O'Brien, J Ward, Z Whitbread; Out on loan: R Albentosa, C Baird, M Bennett, F Rawson, K Roos, C Sammon, R Shotton, K Thomas, S Warnock	
2015	In: C Baird (West Brom, Free), D Bent (Aston Villa, Free), S Carson (Wigan, undisclosed), A Pearce (Reading, Free), A Weimann (Aston Villa, £2.75m), T Ince (Hull, £4.75m), J Shackell (Burnley £3m)	
2015	08/08: Bolton vs. Derby (D 0-0) – Bryson and Hughes suffer long-term injuries	15
2015	29/08: Derby vs. Leeds (L 1-2) – Rams have no win in 5 – (W0, D4, L1)	19
2015	01/09: Derby sign Jacob Butterfield from Huddersfield Town for £4m	19
2015	01/09: Derby sign Bradley Johnson from Norwich City for a club record £6m	19
2015	26/09: MK Dons vs. Derby (W 1-3) – Johnson, Bent, Ince – 3 wins in 4	8
2015	03/10: Derby vs. Brentford (W 2-0) – Martin, Ince – Rams 5 points off top	7
2015	18/10: Derby vs. Wolves (W 4-2) – Martin 2, Johnson, Russell – one point off 2nd	6
2015	24/10: Huddersfield vs. Derby (W 1-2) – Martin, Thorne – 8 unbeaten (W6, D2)	5
2015	31/10: Derby vs. Rotherham (W 3-0) – Weimann, Butterfield, Keogh – 3 pts off top	5
2015	03/11: Derby vs. QPR (W 1-0) – Weimann – 10 unbeaten (W8, D2); 1 pt off top	5
2015	21/11: Derby vs. Cardiff (W 2-0) – Thorne, Weimann – 2 pts behind leaders Hull	4
2015	27/11: Hull vs. Derby (W 0-2) – Butterfield 2 – RAMS GO TOP OF CHAMPIONSHIP	1
2015	06/12: Sheff Wed vs. Derby (D 0-0); 12/12: Derby vs. Brighton (D 2-2)	4
2015	15/12: Derby vs. Bristol City (W 4-0) – Ince 3, Russell – Rams are 2 points off top	3
2015	19/12: Ipswich vs. Derby (W 0-1) – Ince – Rams 2 points behind Middlesbrough	2
2015	26/12: Derby vs. Fulham (W 2-0) – Ream og, Butterfield – RAMS GO TOP AGAIN	1
2015	29/12: Leeds vs. Derby (D 2-2); 02/01: Middlesbrough vs. Derby (L 2-0)	2
2016	04-06/01: Derby sign A Camara/N Blackman from Angers/Reading for £1.25/£2.5m	2

Year	Event	Pos
2016	16/01: Derby vs. Birmingham (L 0-3) – Rams now 6 points behind Middlesbrough	3
2016	25/01: Burnley vs. Derby (L 4-1) – Butterfield – Rams now 7 pts off leaders, Hull	5
2016	26/01: Derby sign Marcus Olsson from Blackburn Rovers (fee undisclosed)	5
2016	06/02: Fulham vs. Derby (D 1-1) – Bryson – no win in 7 – (W13, D12, L5)	5
2016	08/02: Paul Clement is sacked as Derby County manager	5
2016	08/02: Academy Manager, Darren Wassall, is appointed as caretaker manger	5
2016	13/02: Derby vs. MK Dons (L 0-1) – Rams are now 6 points off 2nd place	6
2016	20/02: Brentford vs. Derby (W 1-3) – Hendrick, Christie, Martin – 5 points off 2nd	5
2016	24/02: Derby vs. Blackburn (W 1-0) – Butterfield – still 5 points off 2nd	5
2016	12/03: Rotherham vs. Derby (D 3-3) – Ince 2, Martin – auto-promotion gone	5
2016	19/03: Derby vs. Nottingham Forest (W 1-0) – Olsson – (W17, D13, L8)	5
2016	02/04: Cardiff vs. Derby (L 2-1) – Martin – Cardiff now 2 points behind Rams	6
2016	05/04: Derby vs. Hull (W 4-0) – Johnson 2, Martin, Bryson – 4-point cushion	6
2016	09/04: Derby vs. Bolton (W 4-1) – Russell 2, Ince, Butterfield – 7-point cushion	5
2016	19/04: Bristol City vs. Derby (W 2-3) – Russell, Bryson, Ince – four wins on spin	5
2016	19/04: Derby qualify for the play-offs with three games to spare	5
2016	07/05: Derby vs. Ipswich (L 0-1) – George Thorne suffers double leg break	5
2016	Derby finish season 5th (5:24) with 78 points, 11 points adrift of auto-promotion	5
2016	14/05: Play-Off Semi-Final, 1st Leg: Derby vs. Hull (L 0-3)	
2016	17/05: Play-Off SF, 2nd Leg: Hull vs. Derby (W 0-2) – Russell, Rob'son og – [agg: 3-2]	
2016	Chris Martin is Derby's top scorer for 3rd year running with 13 goals (all league)	
2016	Richard Keogh is Derby's Player of the Season for the second time	
Season 2016/17 (Championship)		
2016	27/05: Nigel Pearson is appointed as Derby County manager	
2016	Out: I Calero, C Sammon, R Shotton, K Thomas, S Warnock, R Albentosa, J Buxton	
2016	16/08: Preston vs. Derby (W 0-1) – Forsyth – (W1, D1, L1)	14
2016	19/08: League Cup 2nd Rd: Derby vs. Carlisle (D 1-1) – Derby win 14-13 on pens	16
2016	27/08: Derby sign Matěj Vydra from Watford for £8m – a new Derby record	18
2016	31/08: Jeff Hendrick is sold to Burnley for an outgoing Derby record of £10.5m	18
2016	31/08: Derby sign Ikechi Anya from Watford for an undisclosed fee	18
2016	13/09: Derby vs. Ipswich (L 0-1) – 3rd defeat on spin – (W1, D2, L4) – and only 1 goal	20
2016	24/09: Derby vs. Blackburn (L 1-2) – Vydra – 3rd home league defeat on spin	22
2016	26/09: Nigel Pearson is sacked and Chris Powell takes over as Caretaker Manager	22
2016	27/09: Cardiff vs. Derby (W 0-2) – Ince, Blackman – (W2, D3, L5)	20
2016	12/10: Steve McClaren is appointed Derby County manager for the second time	20
2016	15/10: Derby vs. Leeds (W 1-0) – Russell – Mac starts with win over Leeds again	19
2016	19/11: Derby vs. Rotherham (W 3-0) – Ince 2, Bent – 3rd win on the spin	12
2016	11/12: Derby vs. Nottm For (W 3-0) – (og), Ince, Hughes – 6th win on spin	5
2016	14/12: QPR vs. Derby (W 0-1) – Ince – 7 wins on spin – (W10, D5, L6) – 10 pts off 2nd	5
2017	07/01: FA Cup 3rd Rd: West Brom vs. Derby (W 1-2) – Bent, Ince – Prem scalp	7
2017	13/01: Leeds vs. Derby (L 1-0) – 2 league defeats on the bounce – 12 pts off 2nd	7
2017	31/01: Ipswich vs. Derby (W 0-3) – Bryson, Ince, Bent – (W13, D7, L8)	6
2017	10/03: Brighton vs. Derby (L 3-0) – 1 win in 9 (W1, D3, L5); overall (W14, D10, L13)	10
2017	12/03: Steve McClaren is sacked as Derby manager for the second time	10

Year	Event	Pos
2017	14/03: Gary Rowett is appointed as Derby County manager	10
2017	18/03: Nottm Forest vs. Derby (D2-2) – Vydra, Nugent – Forest equalize in 95th min	10
2017	04/04: Derby vs. Fulham (W 4-2) – Nugent 3, Russell – 2nd win on bounce	9
2017	08/04: Birmingham vs. Derby (W 1-2) – Kuszczak og, Ince – 3rd win on spin	8
2017	Derby finish season 9th (9:24) with 67 points, 13 points shy of the play-offs	9
2017	Tom Ince is Derby's top scorer with 14 goals (15 in all competitions)	
2017	Scott Carson is Derby's Player of the Season	
Season 2017/18 (Championship)		
2017	Out: W Hughes (Watford, £8m), T Ince (Huddersfield, £11m) a new club record	
2017	In: C Davies (Hull City, undisclosed), T Huddlestone (Hull City, £2m), J Ledley (Free Agent); A Wisdom (Liverpool, £3m),	
2017	15/08: Derby sign Tom Lawrence from Leicester City for £7m	14
2017	19/08: Bolton W vs. Derby (W 1-2) – Nugent 2 – (W2, D1, L1)	8
2017	31/08: Derby sign Sam Winnall on loan from Sheff Wed until eo season; Jacob Butterfield goes in opposite direction; Craig Bryson is loaned to Cardiff until eos	12
2017	08/09: Derby vs. Hull (W 5-0) – Vydra 2, Davies, Johnson 2 – (W3, D1, L2)	4
2017	16/09: Bristol C vs. Derby (L 4-1) – Vydra – (W3, D1, L3)	15
2017	15/10: Derby vs. Nottm F (W 2-0) – Vydra, Nugent – 4 w/o defeat	13
2017	21/10: Derby vs. Sheff W (W 2-0) – Vydra, Johnson – (W5, D4, L3)	8
2017	28/10: Norwich vs. Derby (W 1-2) – Nugent, Winnall – 3 wins on spin	7
2017	31/10: Leeds vs. Derby (W 1-2) – Winnall 2 – (W7, D4, L3) – 7 w/o defeat	5
2017	Gary Rowett is named Championship Manager of the Month with 4 wins out of 4	5
2017	25/11: Middlesbrough vs. Derby (W 0-3) – Vydra 3 – (W9, D5, L4)	6
2017	09/12: Barnsley vs, Derby (W 0-3) – Lawrence, Vydra, Weimann	4
2017	16/12: Derby vs. A Villa (W 2-0) – Weimann, Russell – 3 wins on spin	4
2017	23/12: Derby vs. Millwall (W 3-0) – Nugent 2, Vydra – 4 wins on spin	3
2017	30/12: Ipswich vs. Derby (W 1-2) – Winnall 2 – (W14, D6, L5)	2
2018	05/01: FA CUP 3rd Rd: Man U vs. Derby (L 2-0) – Rams lose to two late goals	2
2018	13/01: Birmingham vs. Derby (W 0-3) – Russell, Vydra, Weimann	2
2018	16/01: Derby sign Cameron Jerome from Norwich City for £1.5m	2
2018	19/01: Derby (2nd) vs. Bristol C (5th) (D 0-0) – 9 w/o defeat in league	2
2018	Here the story ends – for now. As of 24 January 2018, Derby County are 2nd in the Championship table, Gary Rowett is reigning Championship Manager of the Month following a December run of 5 wins and a draw (scoring 11 goals conceding only 1), and Matej Vydra is currently the Championship's leading scorer with 15 goals. Am I being fatalistic by worrying about the usual February collapse...″	2

Quirk Alert: The X Tractor

Since returning to the Championship in 2008, Derby County have played Ipswich Town in the league 20 times, and have an extraordinarily bad home record as follows: W0, D3, L7. Thankfully, their away record is slightly better: W6, D0, L4.

TO NO AVAIL: RAMS AT THE TOP (2014-2015)

A. Tuesday 21 October, 2014

#	Team	Pl	W	D	L	GF	GA	Pts
1	Derby County	13	7	5	1	23	10	26
2	Watford	13	7	4	2	25	14	25
3	Middlesbrough	13	7	2	4	18	11	23
4	Wolves	13	6	5	2	19	14	23
5	Norwich City	13	6	4	3	22	12	22
6	Nottingham F	13	5	7	1	22	13	22

B. Saturday 8 November, 2014

#	Team	Pl	W	D	L	GF	GA	Pts
1	Derby County	17	9	5	3	33	16	32
2	Bournemouth	17	9	4	4	33	16	31
3	Middlesbrough	17	9	4	4	26	12	31
4	Ipswich Town	17	8	6	3	25	17	30
5	Watford	17	8	5	4	30	19	29
6	Brentford	17	8	4	5	24	23	28

C. Saturday 22 November, 2014D.

#	Team	Pl	W	D	L	GF	GA	Pts
1	Derby County	18	10	5	3	35	17	35
2	Bournemouth	18	9	5	4	35	18	32
3	Middlesbrough	18	9	5	4	27	13	32
4	Ipswich Town	18	8	7	3	27	19	31
5	Brentford	18	9	4	5	26	24	31
6	Blackburn Rov	18	8	6	4	29	25	30

D. Saturday 6 December, 2014

#	Team	Pl	W	D	L	GF	GA	Pts
1	Derby County	20	11	5	4	38	19	38
2	Ipswich Town	20	10	7	3	32	20	37
3	Bournemouth	20	10	6	4	39	21	36
4	Middlesbrough	20	10	6	4	33	15	36
5	Brentford	20	10	4	6	31	26	34
6	Watford	20	9	5	6	36	22	32

E. Wednesday 24 February, 2015

#	Team	Pl	W	D	L	GF	GA	Pts
1	Derby County	33	19	8	6	66	33	65
2	Middlesbrough	33	18	9	6	50	22	63
3	Ipswich Town	33	17	9	7	54	34	60
4	Bournemouth	33	17	8	8	67	37	59
5	Norwich City	33	17	8	8	64	37	59
6	Watford	33	18	5	10	66	40	59
7	Brentford	33	18	4	11	53	43	58
8	Wolves	33	15	9	9	46	40	54

F. FINAL TABLE: Saturday 2 May, 2015

#	Team	Pl	W	D	L	GF	GA	Pts
1	Bournemouth	46	26	12	8	98	45	90
2	Watford	46	27	8	11	91	50	89
3	Norwich City	46	25	11	10	88	48	86
4	Middlesbrough	46	25	10	11	68	37	85
5	Brentford	46	23	9	14	78	59	78
6	Ipswich Town	46	22	12	12	72	54	78
7	Wolves	46	22	12	12	70	56	78
8	Derby County	46	21	14	11	85	56	77

G. Friday 27 November, 2015

#	Team	Pl	W	D	L	GF	GA	Pts
1	Derby County	18	10	6	2	26	11	36
2	Hull City	18	10	5	3	27	11	35
3	Brighton	17	9	8	0	22	13	35
4	Middlesbrough	17	10	3	4	25	12	33
5	Burnley	17	9	6	2	24	15	33
6	Brimingham City	17	8	4	5	24	18	28

H. Saturday 26 December, 2015

#	Team	Pl	W	D	L	GF	GA	Pts
1	Derby County	23	13	8	2	35	13	47
2	Middlesbrough	22	14	4	4	33	12	46
3	Hull City	23	13	5	5	34	16	44
4	Brighton	23	11	11	1	31	23	44
5	Burnley	23	10	8	5	30	23	38
6	Ipswich Town	23	10	7	6	33	30	37

DERBY COUNTY: Honours Matrix

Decade	European Winners	European Runners-Up	European Semi-Finalists	Tier 1 Champions	Tier 1 Runners-Up	Tier 1, 3rd Place	Tier 1, 4th Place	Tier 1, 5th Place	Tier 1, 6th Place	FA Cup Winners	FA Cup Runners-Up	FA Cup Semi-Finalists	FA Charity Shield Winners	League Cup Winners	League Cup Runners-Up	League Cup Semi-Finalists	Tier 2 Champions	Tier 2 Runners-Up	Tier 3 Champions	Tier 3 Runners-Up	Honours Total
1880s																					0
1890s					1	2			1		2	2									8
1900s									2		1	3									6
1910s																	2				2
1920s							1		1			1						1			4
1930s					2		2		3			1									8
1940s						1	1			1		1									4
1950s																			1	1	2
1960s																1	1				2
1970s			1	2		1	2					1	1								8
1980s								1									1				2
1990s		1																1			2
2000s																1					1
2010s																					0
Total	0	1	1	2	3	4	6	1	7	1	3	9	1	0	0	2	4	2	1	1	49

Left: Having won the 1971/72 League Championship whilst out in Majorca, Derby County's players returned to celebrate winning three trophies (League Championship, Texaco Cup and Central League) with their fans at the Baseball Ground. Centre: This time, it is season 1974/75 and the League Championship trophy is paraded before Derby's final league game of the season against Carlisle United, and held here by Francis Lee and Roy McFarland. Right: Later that year, Derby won the Charity Shield beating West Ham United 2-0 at Wembley with goals from Kevin Hector and Roy McFarland. Here manager Dave Mackay poses with the two trophies. PHOTOS: Andy Ellis

DERBY COUNTY: Every Season at a Glance

Season	Div	Tier	Pl	W	D	L	F	A	GAvg	GD	Pts	Pos	#T	Champions	Pts
1888/89	N/A	1	22	7	2	13	41	61	0.672	-20	16	10	12	Preston NE	40
1889/90	N/A	1	22	9	3	10	43	55	0.782	-12	21	7	12	Preston NE	33
1890/91	N/A	1	22	7	1	14	47	81	0.580	-34	15	11	12	Everton	29
1891/92	N/A	1	26	10	4	12	46	52	0.885	-6	24	10	14	Sunderland	42
1892/93	One	1	30	9	9	12	52	64	0.813	-12	27	13	16	Sunderland	48
1893/94	One	1	30	16	4	10	73	62	1.177	+11	36	3	16	Aston Villa	44
1894/95	One	1	30	7	9	14	45	68	0.662	-23	23	14	16	Sunderland	47
1895/96	**One**	**1**	**30**	**17**	**7**	**6**	**68**	**35**	**1.943**	**+33**	**41**	**2**	**16**	**Aston Villa**	**45**
1896/97	One	1	30	16	4	10	70	50	1.400	+20	36	3	16	Aston Villa	47
1897/98	One	1	30	11	6	13	57	61	0.934	-4	28	10	16	Sheffield Utd	42
1898/99	One	1	34	12	11	11	62	57	1.088	+5	35	9	18	Aston Villa	45
1899/00	One	1	34	14	8	12	45	43	1.047	+2	36	6	18	Aston Villa	50
1900/01	One	1	34	12	7	15	55	42	1.310	+13	31	12	18	Liverpool	45
1901/02	One	1	34	13	9	12	39	41	0.951	-2	35	6	18	Sunderland	44
1902/03	One	1	34	16	3	15	50	47	1.064	+3	35	9	18	Sheffield Wed	42
1903/04	One	1	34	9	10	15	58	60	0.967	-2	28	14	18	Sheffield Wed	47
1904/05	One	1	34	12	8	14	37	48	0.771	-11	32	11	18	Newcastle Utd	48
1905/06	One	1	38	14	7	17	39	58	0.672	-19	35	15	20	Liverpool	51
1906/07	One	1	38	9	9	20	41	59	0.695	-18	27	19	20	Newcastle Utd	51
1907/08	Two	2	38	21	4	13	77	45	1.711	+32	46	6	20	Bradford City	54
1908/09	Two	2	38	16	11	11	55	41	1.341	+14	43	5	20	Bolton W	52
1909/10	Two	2	38	22	9	7	72	47	1.532	+25	53	4	20	Manchester C	54
1910/11	Two	2	38	17	8	13	73	52	1.404	+21	42	6	20	West Brom	53
1911/12	**Two**	**2**	**38**	**23**	**8**	**7**	**74**	**28**	**2.643**	**+46**	**54**	**1**	**20**	**Derby County**	**54**
1912/13	One	1	38	17	8	13	69	66	1.045	+3	42	7	20	Sunderland	54
1913/14	One	1	38	8	11	19	55	71	0.775	-16	27	20	20	Blackburn R	51
1914/15	**Two**	**2**	**38**	**23**	**7**	**8**	**71**	**33**	**2.152**	**+38**	**53**	**1**	**20**	**Derby County**	**53**
1919/20	One	1	42	13	12	17	47	57	0.825	-10	38	18	22	West Brom	60
1920/21	One	1	42	5	16	21	32	58	0.552	-26	26	21	22	Burnley	59
1921/22	Two	2	42	15	9	18	60	64	0.938	-4	39	12	22	Nottingham F	56
1922/23	Two	2	42	14	11	17	46	50	0.920	-4	39	14	22	Notts County	53
1923/24	Two	2	42	21	9	12	75	42	1.786	+33	51	3	22	Leeds United	54
1924/25	Two	2	42	22	11	9	71	36	1.972	+35	55	3	22	Leicester City	59
1925/26	**Two**	**2**	**42**	**25**	**7**	**10**	**77**	**42**	**1.833**	**+35**	**57**	**2**	**22**	**Sheffield Wed**	**60**
1926/27	One	1	42	17	7	18	86	73	1.178	+13	41	12	22	Newcastle Utd	56
1927/28	One	1	42	17	10	15	96	83	1.157	+13	44	4	22	Everton	53
1928/29	One	1	42	18	10	14	86	71	1.211	+15	46	6	22	Sheffield Wed	52
1929/30	**One**	**1**	**42**	**21**	**8**	**13**	**90**	**82**	**1.098**	**+8**	**50**	**2**	**22**	**Sheffield Wed**	**60**
1930/31	One	1	42	18	10	14	94	79	1.190	+15	46	6	22	Arsenal	66
1931/32	One	1	42	14	10	18	71	75	0.947	-4	38	15	22	Everton	56
1932/33	One	1	42	15	14	13	76	69	1.101	+7	44	7	22	Arsenal	58
1933/34	One	1	42	17	11	14	68	43	1.259	+14	45	4	22	Arsenal	59

Season	Div	Tier	Pl	W	D	L	F	A	GAvg	GD	Pts	Pos	#T	Champions	Pts
1934/35	One	1	42	18	9	15	81	66	1.227	+15	45	6	22	Arsenal	58
1935/36	One	1	42	18	12	12	61	52	1.173	+9	48	2	22	Sunderland	56
1936/37	One	1	42	21	7	14	96	90	1.067	+6	49	4	22	Manchester C	57
1937/38	One	1	42	15	10	17	66	87	0.759	-21	40	13	22	Arsenal	52
1938/39	One	1	42	19	8	15	66	55	1.200	+11	46	6	22	Everton	59
1946/47	One	1	42	18	5	19	73	79	0.925	-6	41	14	22	Liverpool	57
1947/48	One	1	42	19	12	11	77	57	1.351	+20	50	4	22	Arsenal	59
1948/49	One	1	42	22	9	11	74	55	1.345	+19	53	3	22	Portsmouth	58
1949/50	One	1	42	17	10	15	69	61	1.131	+8	44	11	22	Portsmouth	53
1950/51	One	1	42	16	8	18	81	75	1.080	+6	40	11	22	Tottenham H	60
1951/52	One	1	42	15	7	20	63	80	0.788	-17	37	17	22	Manchester U	57
1952/53	One	1	42	11	10	21	59	74	0.797	-15	32	22	22	Arsenal	54
1953/54	Two	2	42	12	11	19	64	82	0.780	-18	35	18	22	Leicester City	56
1954/55	Two	2	42	7	9	26	53	82	0.646	-29	23	22	22	Birmingham C	54
1955/56	3North	3	46	28	7	11	110	55	2.000	+55	63	2	24	Grimsby Town	68
1956/57	3North	3	46	26	11	9	111	53	2.094	+58	63	1	24	Derby County	63
1957/58	Two	2	42	14	8	20	60	81	0.741	-21	36	16	22	West Ham Utd	57
1958/59	Two	2	42	20	8	14	74	71	1.042	+3	48	7	22	Sheffield Wed	62
1959/60	Two	2	42	14	7	21	61	77	0.792	-16	35	18	22	Aston Villa	59
1960/61	Two	2	42	15	10	17	80	80	1.000	0	40	12	22	Ipswich Town	59
1961/62	Two	2	42	14	11	17	68	75	0.907	-7	39	16	22	Liverpool	62
1962/63	Two	2	42	12	12	18	61	72	0.847	-11	36	18	22	Stoke City	53
1963/64	Two	2	42	14	11	17	56	67	0.836	-11	39	13	22	Leeds United	63
1964/65	Two	2	42	16	11	15	84	79	1.063	+5	43	9	22	Newcastle Utd	57
1965/66	Two	2	42	16	11	15	71	68	1.044	+3	43	8	22	Manchester C	59
1966/67	Two	2	42	12	12	18	68	72	0.944	-4	36	17	22	Coventry City	59
1967/68	Two	2	42	13	10	19	71	78	0.910	-7	36	18	22	Ipswich Town	59
1968/69	Two	2	42	26	11	5	65	32	2.031	+33	63	1	22	Derby County	63
1969/70	One	1	42	22	9	11	64	37	1.730	+27	53	4	22	Everton	66
1970/71	One	1	42	16	10	16	56	54	1.037	+2	42	9	22	Arsenal	65
1971/72	One	1	42	24	10	8	69	33	2.091	+36	58	1	22	Derby County	58
1972/73	One	1	42	19	8	15	56	54	1.037	+2	46	7	22	Liverpool	60
1973/74	One	1	42	17	14	11	52	42	1.238	+10	48	3	22	Leeds United	62
1974/75	One	1	42	21	11	10	67	49	1.367	+18	53	1	22	Derby County	53
1975/76	One	1	42	21	11	10	75	58	1.293	+17	53	4	22	Liverpool	60
1976/77	One	1	42	9	19	14	50	55	0.909	-5	37	15	22	Liverpool	57
1977/78	One	1	42	14	13	15	54	59	0.915	-5	41	12	22	Nottingham F	64
1978/79	One	1	42	10	11	21	44	71	0.620	-27	31	19	22	Liverpool	68
1979/80	One	1	42	11	8	23	47	67	0.701	-20	30	21	22	Liverpool	60
1980/81	Two	2	42	15	15	12	57	52	1.096	+5	45	6	22	West Ham Utd	66
Three points for a win introduced from herein															
1981/82	Two	2	42	12	12	18	53	68	0.779	-15	48	16	22	Luton Town	88
1982/83	Two	2	42	10	19	13	49	58	0.845	-9	49	13	22	Queens Park R	85
1983/84	Two	2	42	11	9	22	36	72	0.500	-36	42	20	22	Chelsea	88
1984/85	Three	3	46	19	13	14	65	54	1.204	+11	70	7	24	Bradford City	94

Season	Div	Tier	Pl	W	D	L	F	A	GAvg	GD	Pts	Pos	#T	Champions	Pts
1985/86	Three	3	46	23	15	8	80	41	1.951	+39	84	3	24	Reading	94
1986/87	Two	2	42	25	9	8	64	38	1.684	+26	84	1	22	Derby County	84
1987/88	One	1	40	10	13	17	35	45	0.778	-10	43	15	21	Liverpool	90
1988/89	One	1	38	17	7	14	40	38	1.053	+2	58	5	20	Arsenal	76
1989/90	One	1	38	13	7	18	43	40	1.075	+3	46	16	20	Liverpool	79
1990/91	One	1	38	5	9	24	37	75	0.493	-38	24	20	20	Arsenal	83
1991/92	Two	2	46	23	9	14	69	51	1.353	+18	78	3	24	Ipswich Town	84
1992/93	1	2	46	19	9	18	68	57	1.193	+11	66	8	24	Newcastle Utd	96
1993/94	1	2	46	20	11	15	73	68	1.074	+5	71	6	24	Crystal Palace	90
1994/95	1	2	46	18	12	16	66	51	1.294	+15	66	9	24	Middlesbrough	82
1995/96	1	2	46	21	16	9	71	51	1.392	+20	79	2	24	Sunderland	83
1996/97	Prem	1	38	11	13	14	45	58	0.776	-13	46	12	20	Manchester U	75
1997/98	Prem	1	38	16	7	15	52	49	1.061	+3	55	9	20	Arsenal	78
1998/99	Prem	1	38	13	13	12	40	45	0.889	-5	52	8	20	Manchester U	79
1999/00	Prem	1	38	9	11	18	44	57	0.772	-13	38	16	20	Manchester U	91
2000/01	Prem	1	38	10	12	16	37	59	0.627	-22	42	17	20	Manchester U	80
2001/02	Prem	1	38	8	6	24	33	63	0.524	-30	30	19	20	Arsenal	87
2002/03	1	2	46	15	7	24	55	74	0.743	-19	52	18	24	Portsmouth	98
2003/04	1	2	46	13	13	20	53	67	0.791	-14	52	20	24	Norwich City	94
2004/05	Champ	2	46	22	10	14	71	60	1.183	+11	76	4	24	Sunderland	94
2005/06	Champ	2	46	10	20	16	53	67	0.791	-14	50	20	24	Reading	106
2006/07	Champ	2	46	25	9	12	62	46	1.348	+16	84	3	24	Sunderland	88
2007/08	Prem	1	38	1	8	29	20	89	0.225	-69	11	20	20	Manchester U	87
2008/09	Champ	2	46	14	12	20	55	67	0.821	-12	54	18	24	Wolves	90
2009/10	Champ	2	46	15	11	20	53	63	0.841	-10	56	14	24	Newcastle Utd	102
2010/11	Champ	2	46	13	10	23	58	71	0.817	-13	49	19	24	Queens Park R	88
2011/12	Champ	2	46	18	10	18	50	58	0.862	-8	64	12	24	Reading	89
2012/13	Champ	2	46	16	13	17	65	62	1.048	+3	61	10	24	Cardiff City	87
2013/14	Champ	2	46	25	10	11	84	52	1.615	+32	85	3	24	Leicester City	102
2014/15	Champ	2	46	21	14	11	85	56	1.518	+29	77	8	24	Bournemouth	90
2015/16	Champ	2	46	21	15	10	66	43	1.535	+23	78	5	24	Burnley	93
2016/17	Champ	2	46	18	13	15	54	50	1.080	+4	67	9	24	Newcastle Utd	94
2017/18	Champ	2	46	20	15	11	70	48	1.458	+22	75	6	24	Wolves	99

Most Points from 42/46 Games (two points for a win) – Top Five Seasons:

Season	Div	Tier	Pl	W	D	L	F	A	GAvg	GD	Pts	Pos	#T	Champions	Pts
1968/69	Two	2	42	26	11	5	65	32	2.031	33	63	1	22	Derby County	63
1956/57	3North	3	46	26	11	9	111	53	2.094	58	63	1	24	Derby County	63
1955/56	3North	3	46	28	7	11	110	55	2.000	55	63	2	24	Grimsby Town	68
1971/72	One	1	42	24	10	8	69	33	2.091	36	58	1	22	Derby County	58
1925/26	Two	2	42	25	7	10	77	42	1.833	35	57	2	22	Sheffield Wed	60

Most Points from 42/46 Games (three points for a win) – Top Five Seasons:

Season	Div	Tier	Pl	W	D	L	F	A	GAvg	GD	Pts	Pos	#T	Champions	Pts
2013/14	Champ	2	46	25	10	11	84	52	1.615	32	85	3	24	Leicester City	102
1985/86	Three	3	46	23	15	8	80	41	1.951	39	84	3	24	Reading	94
1986/87	Two	2	42	25	9	8	64	38	1.684	26	84	1	22	Derby County	84
2006/07	Champ	2	46	25	9	12	62	46	1.348	16	84	3	24	Sunderland	88
1995/96	One	2	46	21	16	9	71	51	1.392	20	79	2	24	Sunderland	83

Most Points from Top Flight Games (two points for a win) – Top Five Seasons:

Season	Div	Tier	Pl	W	D	L	F	A	GAvg	GD	Pts	Pos	#T	Champions	Pts
1971/72	One	1	42	24	10	8	69	33	2.091	36	58	1	22	Derby County	58
1969/70	One	1	42	22	9	11	64	37	1.730	27	53	4	22	Everton	66
1974/75	One	1	42	21	11	10	67	49	1.367	18	53	1	22	Derby County	53
1948/49	One	1	42	22	9	11	74	55	1.345	19	53	3	22	Portsmouth	58
1975/76	One	1	42	21	11	10	75	58	1.293	17	53	4	22	Liverpool	60

Most Points from Top Flight Games (three points for a win) – Top Five Seasons:

Season	Div	Tier	Pl	W	D	L	F	A	GAvg	GD	Pts	Pos	#T	Champions	Pts
1988/89	One	1	38	17	7	14	40	38	1.053	2	58	5	20	Arsenal	76
1997/98	Prem	1	38	16	7	15	52	49	1.061	3	55	9	20	Arsenal	78
1998/99	Prem	1	38	13	13	12	40	45	0.889	-5	52	8	20	Manchester U	79
1989/90	One	1	38	13	7	18	43	40	1.075	3	46	16	20	Liverpool	79
1996/97	Prem	1	38	11	13	14	45	58	0.776	-13	46	12	20	Manchester U	75

Most Points from Top Flight Games (two and three points for a win) – Top Five Seasons:

Season	Div	Tier	Pl	W	D	L	F	A	GAvg	GD	Pts	Pos	#T	Champions	Pts
1971/72	One	1	42	24	10	8	69	33	2.091	36	58	1	22	Derby County	58
1988/89	One	1	38	17	7	14	40	38	1.053	2	58	5	20	Arsenal	76
1997/98	Prem	1	38	16	7	15	52	49	1.061	3	55	9	20	Arsenal	78
1969/70	One	1	42	22	9	11	64	37	1.730	27	53	4	22	Everton	66
1974/75	One	1	42	21	11	10	67	49	1.367	18	53	1	22	Derby County	53

Best Seasons for Goal Average – Top Five Seasons:

Season	Div	Tier	Pl	W	D	L	F	A	GAvg	GD	Pts	Pos	#T	Champions	Pts
1911/12	Two	2	38	23	8	7	74	28	2.643	46	54	1	20	Derby County	54
1914/15	Two	2	38	23	7	8	71	33	2.152	38	53	1	20	Derby County	53
1956/57	3North	3	46	26	11	9	111	53	2.094	58	63	1	24	Derby County	63
1971/72	One	1	42	24	10	8	69	33	2.091	36	58	1	22	Derby County	58
1968/69	Two	2	42	26	11	5	65	32	2.031	33	63	1	22	Derby County	63

Best Seasons for Goal Difference – Top Five Seasons:

Season	Div	Tier	Pl	W	D	L	F	A	GAvg	GD	Pts	Pos	#T	Champions	Pts
1956/57	3North	3	46	26	11	9	111	53	2.094	58	63	1	24	Derby County	63
1955/56	3North	3	46	28	7	11	110	55	2.000	55	63	2	24	Grimsby Town	68
1911/12	Two	2	38	23	8	7	74	28	2.643	46	54	1	20	Derby County	54
1985/86	Three	3	46	23	15	8	80	41	1.951	39	84	3	24	Reading	94
1914/15	Two	2	38	23	7	8	71	33	2.152	38	53	1	20	Derby County	53

Surname Synergy: Rams vs. England Rugby Union

The first table lists the Top Ten appearances and point scorers by English Rugby Union internationals, where their surnames correspond to a Derby County footballer, and is sorted on Rugby player appearances. The second table demonstrates an even closer match.

Table 1: England Rugby Union internationals by number of appearances (24/01/2018)

#	England Rugby*	Position	Years	App	Pts	Derby Footballer*	Position	Years	App	Gls
1	Jonny Wilkinson	Wing	1998-11	91	1,179	Marc B-Wilkinson	Midfielder	1997-00	1	0
2	Martin Johnson	Lock	1993-03	84	10	Seth Johnson	Midfielder	1999-07	146	6
3	Steve Thompson	Hooker	2002-11	73	20	George Thompson	Striker	1908-11	45	7
4	Mike Brown	Fullback	2007-	64	55	Gordon Brown	Striker	1957-60	61	22
5	Brian Moore	Hooker	1987-95	64	4	Darren Moore	Defender	2006-08	90	5
6	Will Greenwood	Centre	1997-04	57	155	Roy Greenwood	Striker	1979-80	33	1
7	Jason Robinson	Wing	2001-07	51	140	Theo Robinson	Striker	2011-13	96	25
8	Julian White	Prop	2000-09	51	0	Jason White	Striker	1990-91	0	0
9	Dean Richards	No. 8	1986-96	48	24	George Richards	Midfielder	1902-14	308	37
10	Dave Wilson	Prop	2009-	44	5	Kevin Wilson	Striker	1980-85	141	41

Table 2: England Rugby Union internationals by matching full name

#	England Rugby*	Position	Years	App	Pts	Derby Footballer*	Position	Years	App	Gls
1	Chris Martin	Wing	1985-85	4	0	Chris Martin	Striker	2013-	186	64
2	John Middleton	Fly-half	1922-22	1	0	John Middleton	Goalkeeper	1977-79	80	0
3	John Smith	Fullback	1950-50	4	12	John Smith	Goalkeeper	1904-07	10	0
4	Mike Smith	Centre	1956-56	1	0	Mike Smith	Defender	1957-61	23	0
5	James Ward	Wing	1881-82	2	0	Jamie Ward	Striker	2011-15	149	34
6	Peter Williams	Wing	1987-87	4	0	Peter Williams	Midfielder	1952-52	2	0
7	Alf Wood	Fly-half	1908-08	3	8	Alf Wood	Defender	1905-07	66	4
8	John Wright	Fullback	1934-34	1	0	John Wright	Midfielder	1934-35	0	0

Quirk Alert: Swordplay

So Marc Bridge-Wilkinson's Rams stats do look a little sparse when compared to national legend, Jonny Wilkinson. However, left-sided midfielder B-W did go on to rack up 386 league appearances elsewhere, scoring 71 goals. His one game for Derby was actually a Premier League fixture against Liverpool on 7 Nov 1998. It was also a rare win for Derby at Anfield (W 1-2), with Kevin Harper and Paulo Wanchope scoring for the Rams.

Quirk Alert: Lock and Key

World Cup winning lock and captain Martin Johnson brings into play key Derby midfielder, Seth Johnson. Seth's first spell at Derby (1999-2001) saw him win an England cap and exit to Leeds as Derby's record transfer out fee (at that time) of £7m. His second spell culminated in helping the club win the Championship Play-Off Final in 2007. Taken off with a knee injury with three minutes to go, that injury forced Seth's premature retirement from football, aged only 28, but said everything about his commitment to the cause.

Eulogy to Brian Clough and Peter Taylor

We live in a world where the words "legend" and "all-time great" are used frequently, and these words have been attributed to Brian Clough by thousands of people over many decades. However, it's not until you get down to the nitty gritty of profiling a football club's history, over 134 years, that you begin to understand the enormity of what Brian Clough achieved as a football manager – and this for a man who had already achieved the status of "legend" in the North East for his on-field brilliance, and stunning goal-scoring record.

Anyway, most professional English football clubs have been around for well over a century, and many of the older clubs, like Derby County, have contested titles and cups, year after year, decade after decade, in THREE different centuries. So what this project truly opened my eyes to, is a perennial struggle of a great football club (one of England's top 20, for sure) to actually *achieve* something. Derby County came so close to winning the FA Cup 7 times in 9 seasons at the turn of the 20th century, and failed every time. Similarly, between 1927 and 1939, Derby County topped Division One on many occasions, almost every season at various stages, and sometimes as late as March. They were almost always a Top Six side, something which continued for several years after the war as well, and they constantly rolled out a conveyor belt of brilliant strikers. But they didn't win the title. They never won it.

So to achieve top success in football is an extraordinarily rare thing – and by "top success", I mean winning Tier 1 Championships and European Cups. That takes outstanding ability, in-depth experience and a certain *je ne sais quoi*. But to achieve it with "unfashionable clubs" – that takes brilliance and genius.

Brian Clough is, without doubt, the greatest football manager of all time.

Now for impact's sake, it would be stylish to leave this eulogy there – but I can't do so without mentioning Peter Taylor as well. Clough and Taylor were the perfect pairing, and every great manager needs outstanding people around him. It has been commonly stated that Taylor was the talent-spotter while Clough was the motivator. But as Peter Taylor once said himself, this type of generalisation "did an injustice to both of us". And so it did.

Their like will certainly never be seen again, and football is much-the-worse for that fact.

Bibliography

Books:

Barry J Hugman, *Rothmans Football League Players Records: The Complete A-Z 1946-1981* (Rothmans Publications Limited, 1981)

Andrew Ward, Anton Rippon, Gerald Mortimer, *The Derby County Story 1884-1991* (Breedon Books, 1991)

Breedon Books, *The Book of Derby County* (Breedon Books, 1994)

Anton Rippon, *Images of Derby County* (Breedon Books, 1995)

Ian Hall, *The Legends of Derby County* (Breedon Books, 2001)

Gerald Mortimer, *Derby County: The Complete Record* (Breedon Books, 2006)

Andy Ellis, *Derby County Football Club 1888-1996* (The History Press, 2008)

Michael Joyce, *Football League Players' Records 1888 to 1939* (Tony Brown, 2012)

Barry J Hugman, *The PFA Premier & Football League Players' Records 1946-2015* (Jules Gammond and Edward Adams, 2016)

Andy Ellis, *Brian Clough and Derby County – From Glory to Disaster* (DB Publishing, 2017)

Websites:
https://en.wikipedia.org/
http://www.11v11.com/
http://www.statto.com/
http://www.worldfootball.net/